WALKING WITH JESUS,

ONE STEP AT A TIME

Written by

Helen Haidle

Jeannie Taylor

Barbara Martin

Illustrated by

David Haidle

Walking with Jesus, One Step at a Time
Copyright © 2000 by Helen Haidle
Illustrations © 2000 by David Haidle

Requests for information should be addressed to:
Zonderkidz ™
The Children's Group of Zondervan Publishing House
Grand Rapids, Michigan 49530
www.zonderkidz.com

Library of Congress Cataloging-in-Publication Data

Haidle, Helen.
   Walking with Jesus, one step at a time: kid's real-life stories/ by Helen
Haidle, Jeannie Taylor, Barbara Martin; illustrated by David Haidle.
      p. cm.
   Summary: A one-year book of devotions based on true stories, encouraging readers to
trust God and live as a Christian as they encounter peer pressure and temptations. Includes
discussion questions, Scripture verses, and interactive family activities.
   ISBN: 1-57673-568-0
   1. Children Prayer-books and devotions - English. 2. Christian life Anecdotes Juvenile
literature. 3. Devotional calendars Juvenile literature. [1. Prayer books and devotions. 2.
Devotional calendars.] I. Taylor, Jeannie, 1946- . II. Martin, Barbara (Barbara Spencer),
1951- . III. Haidle, David, ill. IV. Title.
BV4571.2.H337 1999
242'.62-dc21

                                                                    99-15764
                                                                    CIP
This edition printed on acid-free paper and meets the American National Standards Institute Z39.48 standard.

Edited by Don Goodman
Interior design by David Haidle
Printed in the United States of America

00 01 02 03 04 05 / ❖ DC/ 10 9 8 7 6 5 4 3 2 1

Foreword

Dear Readers,

We three writers pray that you will be touched by these stories based on true events from the lives of children around the world. Names and personal details were often changed to protect privacy.

Each book we write is our gift to the Lord, and also our gift to you. We pray for God's blessings on the seeds of faith, hope, and love that will be planted in your minds and hearts by this book. May you draw closer to Jesus and closer to your family through these special stories and interactive weekend activities.

Will you join us in praying for the seeds planted by this book? Pray that God will bless other children who read the stories. Pray for all families—that God would fill every home and heart with His love, peace, and forgiveness in Jesus.

Most of all, we pray that God will richly bless each one of you. May you walk with Jesus each day of your life, one step at a time.

Authors: Helen Haidle, Jeannie Taylor, and Barbara Martin

Credit to Other Contributing Authors:

Geneva Iijima - *The Cat Door (week 3)*

Dot Mahoney - *Twos and Fives (week 26)*

Kristi Stringer - *Ashley's Prayer (week 5), Angels for Grandma (week 28)*

Sarah Artman - *Falsely Accused (week 12), Jesus Never Leaves (week 26), Asleep at the Wheel! (week 51)*

Barbara Lighthizer - *Don't Die Yet (week 3), A Shy Girl's Surprise (week 18), Dad, Don't Leave (week 36)*

Beth Sharpton - *Crumbs in the Corners (week 29), Careless Catsup Caper (week 32), Toothpaste Lies (week 34), Movie Blues (week 37), The Christmas Card (week 50)*

Mary Hake - *Mom's Wallet (week 12), Camp Question (week 18), Backwards! (week 23), Rattler! (week 36), Throwing Rocks (week 46), Bee Sting (week 47), Hunchback (week 48), Summer Softball (week 49), Backyard Bonfire (week 51)*

DEDICATED TO

The People Who Shared Their Stories for

Walking with Jesus, One Step at a Time:

Jacob Adderly, Beth Aebischer, Karen Akers, Linda Alexander, Melissa Alexander, Sarah Artman, Judith Baker, Mary Beeman, Kristina Boulter, Scott Brown, Brian Burdon, Cari Carnahan, Christi Carnahan, Mary Jo Carnahan, Vera Collins, Lauren Crebs, Nick Crebs, Mike Dahl, Denny Denman, Nikki DeKorte, Kara Ericksen, Kyle Gilham, William Gillespie, Mary Hake, Tiffany Hickman, Susan Higdon, Carolyn Hopkins, Rebeccah Hopkins, Lindsey Horne, Geneva Iijima and family, Rebecca Jellum, Carrie Johnson, Matthew Jones, Ed Kasser, Adam Kinzinger, Chelise Kinzinger, Jodi Kinzinger, Rus Kinzinger, Amy Kuban, Dale Lance, Karen Law, Christine Lehnen, Samantha Rose Mahoney, Linda Marshall, Barbara Martin, Brianna Martin, Rebekah Martin, Sam Martin Jr., Sam Martin Sr., Sara Martin, Nancy McAvoy, Kathleen McMullen, Annie Mockford, Cynthia Murata, Barbara Neal, Cherie Norman, Beth Sharpton, Lauren Sharpton, Tara Sharpton, Kathy Southworth, Carole Spencer, Don Spencer, Martha Spencer, Nate Spencer, Clare St. John, Ernest St. John, Gladys St. John, Nick Staropoli, Melody Stockwell, Carolyn Taylor, Clifford Taylor, Elsie Taylor, Harold Taylor, Jeannie St. John Taylor, Matt Taylor, Nancy Taylor, Raymond Taylor, Tevin Taylor, Tori Taylor, Ty Taylor, Shirley Thiessen, Judy Thwing, Nina Turner, Amy Watt, Don Westerberg, Alex Whitten, Kathy Winniford.
Also:
Atong Madut from Sudan, Ramian from India, Ibaragi Kun from Japan, N. Ramana from India, and Maria from Spain.

HOW TO RECEIVE JESUS and WALK WITH HIM

God made you. And God loves you!
"God loved the world so much that he gave his one and only Son.
Anyone who believes in him will not die but will have eternal life."
(John 3:16)

No one lives a perfect life nor does everything they should.
Everyone needs God's forgiveness.
"Everyone has sinned. No one measures up to God's glory."
(Romans 3:23)

God sent Jesus to suffer our punishment and die for us.
"But here is how God has shown his love for us.
While we were still sinners, Christ died for us.
The blood of Christ has made us right with God."
(Romans 5:8–9)

Jesus came alive. He rose from the grave.
He comes to you today.
Jesus said, "Here I am! I stand at the door and knock.
If any of you hears my voice and opens the door,
I will come in and eat with you."
(Revelation 3:20)

Open the door of your heart to Jesus.
You can pray a prayer like this one:
Thank You, Jesus, for loving me and dying on the cross for me.
Please forgive all I've done wrong.
Come into my life and be my Savior.
Thank You for giving me the gift of eternal life.
Fill me with Your Holy Spirit. Help me live for You. Amen.
"Say with your mouth, 'Jesus is Lord.'
Believe in your heart that God raised him from the dead.
Then you will be saved."
(Romans 10:9)

When you trust Jesus as your Savior,
you can be sure He will never leave you.
He will help you walk with Him, one step at a time.
Jesus said, "You can be sure that I am always with you, to the very end."
(Matthew 28:20)

WWJ

Weekly Themes

Weekly Themes

WWJ

TRUST JESUS

Walking with Jesus
One Step at a Time

What You Need:

A Bible, 8½-by-11-inch paper, pencil, scissors

What To Do:

1. Trace each participant's foot, with or without a shoe, onto a piece of paper. Then cut it out.

2. Choose a Bible verse to challenge each individual to do one specific thing the way Jesus would do. Write down that specific action or behavior on the footprint, with the verse reference.

3. Tape *footsteps* to the kitchen floor as reminders.

Examples: Ephesians 4:25   Tell the truth
              Matthew 6:25   Don't worry
              Colossians 2:6–7   Give thanks
              Colossians 3:23   Work for Jesus
              Matthew 5:44   Pray for enemies

Variation: Footsteps can be placed in any room of the house, taped to a wall, or hung horizontally on a string or cord. Continue this activity by adding a new footstep each week.

AMY'S BIBLE

"What's wrong?" Amy asked her mom, who stood in the bedroom doorway.

"Grandpa's sick," Mom replied. "Daddy and I are going to take him to the hospital."

Amy ran to her grandparents' room. She sat on the bed and took Grandma's hand. "Is Grandpa going to die?"

"I don't know, sweetheart," Grandma said. "But if he does, I know he'll go to Heaven. I'm thankful God loves us and has made a wonderful place for us to live forever."

"Grandma," asked Amy, "will *I* go to Heaven when I die?"

Amy's grandma gave her a hug. "You will if you ask Jesus to be your Savior. Look in my Bible with me. I've used it to tell many children how to go to Heaven. I'll show you, too." She turned the pages of her Bible as she spoke.

"This verse says that God always does what is best. And here's a verse that explains that we have all done wrong things called sins. We deserve to be punished. But this verse says that Jesus died to wash away our sins so we can live with Him forever."

Amy bowed her head and prayed, "Dear God, please forgive me for the wrong things I've done. Thank You, Jesus, for coming to save me. I accept You as my Savior. Amen."

"Here, sweetheart." Grandma handed her Bible to Amy. "I want you to have this."

From that day on, Amy read it every morning and prayed, *Dear Jesus, I want to tell other children how much You love them, just like Grandma told me.*

"God loved the world so much that he gave his one and only Son. Anyone who believes in him will not die but will have eternal life." John 3:16

Have you accepted Jesus as your Savior?
How would you help someone else accept Jesus as their Savior?
Also read 2 Corinthians 5:15, 17.

COMPUTER GENIUS

"It's finished!" Eric and Roger smiled with satisfaction. "Just in time! Let's print it out."

Eric clicked the print icon on his computer. The monitor screen went dark and the computer fan stopped running.

"What happened? We'd better reboot." Eric pressed the reset button, but the computer stayed quiet.

"Oh no! It's dead," said Eric. "And our final report is due tomorrow! Mrs. Peterson will drop us a grade for every day it's late."

"Maybe your dad can fix the computer," said Roger.

Eric's dad walked through the door. He listened while the boys described the problem, then he flipped the computer's power switch. Nothing happened. Dad opened the computer case and looked inside.

Eric stared at the tangle of cables and circuitry boards. "Wow! It sure is complicated in there. The guy who invented computers must have been a genius."

Dad laughed. "That's nowhere near as complex as your brain. God is the real genius." He glanced at his watch. "The computer store is still open. Let's have a technician take a look at this."

A few hours later, Dad flipped the power switch on Eric's computer. The fan hummed and the monitor lit up.

"Thanks, Dad. Now we can print out our report." Eric smiled. "You know, I'm glad my brain works better than that computer. And I'm glad God can be trusted to keep this universe running!"

WWJ

"How you made me is amazing and wonderful. I praise you for that."
Psalm 139:14

Have you ever taken time to thank God for your brain?
Why don't you do it right now?
Also read Psalm 139:13–16.

NIGHT AT THE BEACH

"We'll be okay by ourselves, Mom." Jayda said, trying to ignore her fear. Outside, the wind howled around the vacation beach house. "Go downstairs. You don't have to stay in our bedroom."

"Sometimes strange places can seem scary," said Mom. "If you want, I'll stay here with you until you fall asleep."

"It's okay," Jayda said. She thought to herself, *I'm not a baby. I prayed not to be afraid of the dark anymore. I know Jesus will help me.*

Mom tucked Jayda and her little brother into bed, kissed them and turned out the light. "I'll be down in the kitchen with Dad."

Jayda pulled the quilt up to her chin and stared into the darkness. Through the wailing wind, she could barely hear her parents' voices downstairs.

"Jayda, can I get in bed with you?" whispered Dominic.

"Sure," Jayda said. Her little brother climbed in and snuggled close beside her.

"I'm still scared," said Jayda. "Maybe there's a Bible in the dresser." She took a deep breath and switched on the light. Then she climbed out of bed and opened the dresser drawer. "There *is!*"

Under her quilt again, she read aloud from the Bible. Dominic soon fell asleep.

Finally Jayda switched off the light and smiled into the darkness.

"Thank You, Jesus. Your words helped me not to be afraid."

"You won't have to be afraid of the terrors that come during the night."
Psalm 91:5

When has reading the Bible comforted you?
What part of the Bible do you read when you feel afraid?
Also read Psalm 91:3–6.

RUNAWAY VAN

"Hurry! We've got to push the van off the road," said Mason.

He and his mom climbed out of their stalled car. He gripped the rear bumper. She grasped the frame of the open door on the driver's side. Six-month-old Lisa sat inside in her safety seat.

Mother and son pushed with all their strength. The van rocked but didn't move forward. Cars and trucks sped past.

"Jesus, please send someone to help us," Mason prayed. He pushed, straining until every muscle in his body burned. Finally, he felt the van move. It rolled slowly, then gathered speed.

Mason tightened his grip on the bumper and dug his heels into the dirt. But the van, which carried his baby sister, kept rolling.

"I'll get in and steer!" shouted Mom. But when she tried, she slipped and fell in the gravel. The van rolled away and headed toward the busy intersection ahead. Mason ran after the van.

"Help!" he shouted. As the van approached the busy cross street, a woman standing by the side of the road leaped inside the open driver's door and slammed on the brakes. The van stopped short of the intersection.

"You saved my baby!" said Mom when she reached the van.

"Jesus sent you to help us," Mason told the young woman.

"Yes," she said, trembling. "He did!"

"Lord, I call out to you. Come quickly to help me. Listen to me when I call out to you." Psalm 141:1

What do you do when you are in trouble?

Did God promise to answer all your prayers right away?

Also read Psalm 86:1–3.

KOYOTO, JAPAN - February 5, 1597

Pain shot through Ibaragi Kun's arm. The guard struck him again with a club. "Keep moving. Let's get this over with."

Twelve-year-old Ibaragi climbed unsteadily up the rocky hillside. He was hungry, and his legs were weak.

It was more than two months since he walked anywhere outside the cramped jail. He had shared that cell with twenty-five other Christians. They had been fed only one small meal a day.

Ahead, Ibaragi saw the long row of crosses silhouetted against the morning sunrise lighting up the hill.

Oh, Jesus. I understand a little how You must have felt. Help us all be faithful to You today.

Arriving at the place of execution, Ibaragi and his Christian friends stood silently in front of the city official. Angrily, the official shouted, "Are any of you finally ready to give up your belief in Jesus?"

Ibaragi spoke up. "Sir, it would be better if you yourself became a Christian and could go to Heaven where we are all going."

Looking at the row of crosses, Ibaragi asked, "Sir, which one is mine?"

The surprised official pointed to the smallest cross on the hill. Young Ibaragi ran to the cross, knelt, and hugged it.

"Thank You, Jesus," he prayed. "You gave Your life for me. I am ready to die for You. Bless the people of Japan. Help them to know You, just as my friends and I know and love You."

WWJ

Jesus said, "If anyone loses his life because of me, he will find it."
Matthew 10:39

When have you suffered for being a Christian?
Would you be willing to die rather than to deny Jesus?
Also read Matthew 10:28–39.

DON'T BE AFRAID

Tokens of Remembrance

What You Need:

> A Bible, table or shelf
> Optional: A picture of a statue or monument

What To Do:

1. Read Joshua 4:1–7. Why did God instruct the Israelites to pile up stones as a memorial after crossing the Jordan River?

2. Talk about a statue or monument in your area that commemorates an important event or person. (Use a picture from a book or encyclopedia.) Ask each person to share a time when God did something special in his or her life. Emphasize living in FAITH.

3. Let everyone choose an object to remind them of God's care. Stack them on a shelf or table. During the week, let the tokens of remembrance be reminders to thank God.

Examples:
> Check stub—reminder of God's provision.
> Favorite toy—reminder of shared fun.
> Baby rattle—reminder of the blessing of a baby.
> Camp award—reminder of a decision to
>   follow Jesus.

STORM AT LOOKOUT TOWER, 1943

"Don't look down!" Mom warned.

Buddy looked anyway. He saw the tops of the fir trees sway in the wind far below. He gripped the ladder's handrail. "Oh, man. It's…a lot higher…than I expected."

"Forty feet to be exact," said Dad, as they climbed up through a trapdoor in the forest ranger station floor. "Look! You can see for miles in every direction."

Buddy eased over to the window. "Is that what we're gonna do for the next two weeks? Just stare off in every direction?" He looked down the slope. "Dad, what are those wires coming up from the ground?"

"They're cables. They keep the tower from falling over in a storm."

"They—they don't look very strong."

The next two days passed quickly. Buddy tried not to think about being so high up. During the day, he helped Dad check the mountains for smoke. At night, he and the family played games.

On the third day, a rainstorm raged across the mountainside. The ranger tower shuddered and swayed. Lightning blazed. Mom shrieked and pointed. Snakes of fire sizzled up one of the cables toward the tower.

"Jesus—save us!" Buddy screamed.

Then, inside his head, Buddy heard a calming voice: "Don't be afraid, My child. You're Mine. And the lightning is Mine."

Buddy's fear suddenly drained away. The fiery snakes crackled and died in a shower of sparks.

Later, Buddy told his parents, "God used the storm to teach me to trust Him."

WWJ

"My brothers and sisters, you will face all kinds of trouble. When you do, think of it as pure joy." James 1:2

When has trouble helped you trust God more?
Why can trouble be an opportunity for joy?
Also read Mark 4:38–41.

BUS TO NOWHERE

I don't know this part of town. Did I miss my stop? Fear twisted Bekka's stomach as she stared out the bus window at strange streets and buildings.

Streetlights blinked on in the late October twilight. Bekka looked at her watch. *Mom said the bus ride would take twenty minutes. But I've been on the bus nearly forty-five minutes.*

The bus slowed. *Should I get off at this stop? Am I getting closer to home or farther away?* Bekka slid to the edge of her seat.

I can't get out in a strange place! Shrinking back in her seat, she prayed, *Dear Jesus, show me how to get home. I'm scared.*

She remembered a Bible verse: *"I will never leave you or forsake you."* Bekka sighed and relaxed.

After a few more stops the bus driver called out, "End of the line. Everybody out."

Bekka walked to the front of the bus. "I missed my stop," she told the driver. "What should I do?"

The driver checked his watch. "Stay on this bus," he said. "The return trip starts in five minutes. Tell the new driver where you live. He'll show you which stop is yours."

"Thank you!" Relief flooding through her, Bekka took the seat directly behind the driver. *Thank You, Jesus,* she prayed silently, *for taking away my fear and showing me how to get home.*

"So do not be afraid. I am with you. Do not be terrified. I am your God. I will make you strong and help you." Isaiah 41:10

When have you gotten lost? What happened?
What Bible verses help you when you feel afraid?
Also read Psalm 139:7–12.

DIRTY HIDING PLACE

Even though Ramon wanted to cry, he didn't. He stayed behind when all the other kids hurried off to swim in the lake. Then he walked down the cabin's concrete steps and opened the door to Aunt Marie's dirt basement. He wedged himself into the narrow place between the furnace and the wall. All the while he thought about what Jack said. And then he cried.

A few minutes later, he heard the door open.

"I know you're down here, Ramon," said his sister. "You came down here last year when you were scared."

"I'm not scared."

"Then why are you hiding?" she asked as she came closer.

"Because Jack glared at me and yelled, 'Why did you come?'" Ramon wiped his nose. "Jack's mean. I know he doesn't like me."

"That's what I said. You're scared Jack won't like you."

"Well, he doesn't." Tears stung Ramon's eyes again.

"So why do you care? Jack's mean to all the little kids. Do you know what the Bible says about this?"

"The Bible doesn't say anything about Jack."

"Yes it does. The Bible tells us to be brave and strong. Don't be afraid that some bully won't like you. God loves you. And God gave you a big sister who loves you." Camellia peeked around the furnace at Ramon. "Want to go swimming in the lake with me?"

"What if Jack yells at me and says, 'Why are *you* here?'" Ramon asked, crawling out from behind the furnace.

Camellia smiled and took his hand. "Then you can say, 'Because my sister wants me here.'"

"If you are afraid of people, it will trap you. But if you trust in the Lord, he will keep you safe." Proverbs 29:25

When have you been afraid that someone wouldn't like you? Why should you care more about what Jesus says and thinks? Also read 2 Timothy 1:7.

NEW GUINEA TIDAL WAVE

An urgent knock startled Bouka and her mother as they prepared dinner. Mother hurried to the door. Their pastor stood outside.

"What's the matter?" Bouka's mother asked.

"I feel that God wants us to have a prayer meeting tonight at our church," said the pastor.

"But our regular prayer meeting is *tomorrow* night," said Mother. "We cannot come two nights in a row."

"I feel strongly we must do this, even though I do not know why God wants it," Pastor said. "Please come. I'm letting all the church members know before evening."

After he hurried away, Mother told Bouka, "I think we will go to church *tomorrow* night as usual, not tonight."

"But, Mama, if God spoke to Pastor, we should do as he says."

After supper, Bouka and her family climbed the hill to the church, which was built on stilts. For two hours they lifted their voices and their hands in worship and prayer to the Lord.

"I am glad we came," Bouka whispered to her mother. "I feel closer to Jesus than ever in my life."

Soon they felt something else. It was wet and cold around their bare feet. They looked down to see water quickly rising to their ankles.

"Stay calm," said the pastor. He shoved open the door.

By the light of his lantern, everyone could see the floodwater that completely surrounded the church. While they had prayed and worshiped, a tidal wave had washed all the houses and the people of their village out to sea. Only the people in Bouka's little church that stood on stilts on the hill were alive and safe.

"God is our place of safety. He gives us strength....The mountains may fall into the middle of the sea. But we will not be afraid." Psalm 46:1–2

What trouble has your family been through?
How has God helped you in the times of trouble?
Also read Psalm 46:1–11.

AFTERNOON BURGLARY

Denny unlocked his back door and stepped inside the kitchen. Broken glass covered the floor. He could hear drawers opening and closing upstairs and the contents crashing to the floor.

"It's a burglar!" Denny whispered.

His friend, Alfredo, yanked on Denny's arm. "Let's leave!"

"Shhh," said Denny. "Let me think."

"You think," said Alfredo. "I'm gettin' outa here."

Alone, Denny prayed, Show me what to do, Jesus. He tiptoed across the kitchen and lifted the cordless phone. Give me courage.

Mom's bedroom door slammed. Denny jumped. He dropped the phone onto the counter. Jesus, don't let that burglar catch me. He quickly snatched up the phone and bolted out the door.

"What were you doing in there?" asked Alfredo.

"Praying," said Denny. The boys ducked behind the bushes while Denny called 911 and gave a hurried report.

The back door of the house burst open. Out ran the burglar carrying a bulging pillowcase. Denny whispered into the phone, "The burglar is wearing a green plaid shirt...and he's heading toward Euclid Street."

A short while later, the boys heard sirens. When the police drove up with the hand-cuffed burglar, the boys high-fived.

"We did okay!" Alfredo said.

"Yeah," said Denny.

"With Jesus' help."

"They saw Jesus coming toward the boat. He was walking on the water.... he said to them, 'It is I. Don't be afraid.'" John 6:19–20

How has Jesus helped you when you were afraid?
Are you willing to trust God, even in times of trouble?
Also read John 6:16–21.

GOD KEEPS EVERY PROMISE

Bread of Life

What You Need:

A Bible, one cup thick whipping cream, a glass jar with a tight lid, and a loaf of warm bread

What To Do:

1. Read John 6:35–40.

2. Talk about how Jesus compared Himself to bread. People of Bible times ate bread at every meal. They made butter by shaking, squeezing, and pounding cream inside an animal skin bag.

3. Let one cup whipping cream sit in a jar with a tight lid at room temperature until it curdles. Then shake it for about ten minutes. It will form a big lump. Mix in a little salt. Spread it on bread and eat. (Store leftovers in the refrigerator.)

4. Thank Jesus for being the Bread of Life. Give thanks for the ways He "feeds" you—with food to eat and with the food of His Word, the Bible.

FIFTY-MILE WALK, 1922

All we have left now are these potatoes and a few beans, thought Harold as he sat down to eat with his family at the kitchen table.

Pa said, "You noticed that we've had nothin' but potatoes for supper lately." Ma touched his hand. "And you know I've been praying for work. Well, today I got a letter from Gilbert Mitchell in Spokane. He must've heard from God 'cause he has a job for me and some food for us. That is, if we can get there."

"How far is it?" Harold asked. He knew he'd be walking.

"Almost fifty miles," said Pa. "It will be a tough trip, too, especially if it snows."

Everything they owned fit in the big flat wagon. Pa drove the horses. Ma rode beside him. Harold and Art walked behind the wagon with the cow and her calf.

At the end of the long day, a farmer let the family sleep in his barn. They ate the beans Ma had cooked up before they left home.

Snow fell heavily. By the next morning it covered the ground twelve inches deep. Every step Harold took was hard work.

The calf grew tired by late afternoon and it laid down in the road. Harold pulled and pushed to get her moving. He wanted to quit, too. *Give us strength to make it, Lord. Please…*

Harold's legs could hardly walk another step when they finally reached the Mitchell's house just before midnight.

He helped Pa settle the animals in the barn, then went in the house to eat a bowl of Mrs. Mitchell's hot beef stew.

Thank You, Lord, he prayed, *for helping me walk fifty miles in two days*….And in the warmth of the fireplace, he fell asleep.

"Are any of you in trouble? Then you should pray."
James 5:13

Why should people who have troubles keep on praying?
How has God taken care of your family?
Also read Philippians 4:18–20.

DON'T DIE YET

"We've been praying such a long time," Penny told her mom. "Do you think Dad will ever become a Christian?"

"I don't know," Mom replied. "But we're not giving up. The doctor doesn't know how long your dad has to live. So the pastor's coming to talk to your dad today."

"Dad grew up in a Christian home, didn't he?" asked Penny.

"Yes. And his parents took him to church every Sunday. When he became an adult, he refused to go to church. He told people he thought it was too late for him to become a Christian. We all explained to him that God loved him. But for some reason, he never understood. Now, he's dying."

At school, Penny could not keep her mind on her classwork. All she could think of was her father. *Dear God, please give Pastor the right words to say. Help Dad hear with his heart. He needs to understand how much You love him. Please don't let him die yet.*

After school, Penny rushed home. She found Dad lying on the sofa with tears in his eyes.

"Honey, I finally became a Christian," he said. "Pastor Blair helped me understand that it wasn't too late for me and that God still loves me. I asked Jesus to be my Savior."

Dad smiled. "And now I'm ready to die. I'm not afraid any-more."

"We know how much God loves us, and we have put our trust in him."
1 John 4:16 (NLT)

Are there people in your family or neighborhood who have not accepted Jesus as their Savior? Are you praying for them? Also read 1 John 4:15–17.

THINKING BIG

Mike looked up from digging weeds in the front yard. His little brother sat down on the porch step and hugged a quart-sized pickle jar full of pennies.

"What are you going to do with all those pennies?" asked Mike.

Timmy grinned. "I'm waiting for the ice cream truck."

"What are you doing with all that money?" asked Mike. "One ice cream bar doesn't cost much."

"Here it comes!" Timmy squealed. "Here it comes!"

The ice cream truck turned the corner and headed down the street with its tinkly tune blaring.

Timmy lurched to his feet but plopped down again. Mike chuckled. He lifted his brother's jar and put it in the red wagon.

"I'll have an ice cream sandwich, please," said Mike, handing the driver the exact change.

"I'll have the truck, please," said Timmy, pulling his wagon. "And I'll take all the ice cream you have."

The driver laughed. "I'm sorry. My truck's not for sale."

"It's not?" asked Timmy, his mouth and chin puckering.

"No. And neither is this. Here. It's free." He handed Timmy an ice cream bar, then drove away.

Timmy looked at his jar of pennies, his eyes wet with tears.

"Why did you want to buy the truck?" Mike asked.

"I was afraid we'd run out of ice cream."

"You can't blow all your savings on ice cream," Mike said. "We can trust God. He gives us everything we need."

Timmy smiled. "Oh, good," he said. "Now I can use my jar full of pennies to buy the zoo!"

WWJ

"My God will meet all your needs. He will meet them...with his wonderful riches that come to you because you belong to Christ Jesus." Philippians 4:19

When have you worried about something silly?
Is there ever a time when it's good to worry?
Also read Luke 12:22–26.

THE CAT DOOR

"Come on, Timmy, c'mon—get into the car!" Stephen said.

As his little brother climbed into the backseat, Mom approached with a picnic basket.

"Hurry up, Mom, please," said Stephen. "We'll be late."

Instead of hurrying, Mom suddenly froze.

"I don't believe it," she said. "I locked my purse and the car keys in the house."

Stephen groaned. "Mom, we can't miss the picnic."

He closed his eyes and prayed out loud. "Oh, dear Jesus, we're in a fix. Please help us get those keys out of the house."

He and his little brother ran to the back door. It was locked. They tried the garage side door. Also locked.

With his fists Stephen pounded the door, then pressed his head against it and shut his eyes.

When Stephen opened his eyes, he saw the solution to their problem—the cat door.

"Timmy! See if you can get through that little door."

His small brother went down on his hands and knees and squeezed through the swinging cat door into the garage.

Stephen cheered, "Yes!" He ran around to the front door.

Moments later, Timmy opened it and held Mom's purse high over his head.

The threesome piled into the car.

Stephen said, "Wait—Thank You, Lord, for hearing our prayers and helping me see the cat door, so we could get into the house."

"Don't worry about anything. Instead, tell God about everything. Ask and pray. Give thanks to him." Philippians 4:6

When has God answered your prayers in surprising ways? Why should you still pray when things seem impossible? Also read Philippians 4:4-7.

LIFT A CAR?

"A man is trapped under his car!" a voice shouted outside the kitchen window. "Somebody help! Hurry!"

Twelve-year-old Ramon rose from his chair at the table and headed for the door.

"Let's go!" he told his sister and his three friends.

They raced across the alley and jumped over the neighbor's picket fence and found Mr. Lewis pinned under his car.

Ramon ran to the front of the car, where it had slipped off the jack. Mr. Lewis could not speak. His face was turning blue.

"Help me lift," he shouted to the other kids. "And pray. God will help us. One, two, three—lift!"

The five of them tried to lift the car, but it was too heavy.

Ramon took a deep breath. *I'm not giving up, Lord. I know You'll help us.* "Keep praying. And keep trying," he told the others.

It took three more tries, but the youngsters finally lifted the car high enough for Mr. Lewis to crawl out.

By now a crowd gathered, and the paramedics arrived.

"These kids saved my life," said Mr. Lewis.

"God put us in the right place at the right time," said Ramon.

"I knew that if we prayed, God would help us."

WWJ

"I can do everything by the power of Christ. He gives me strength."
Philippians 4:13

Have you ever quit praying about something difficult?
How does trusting God's promises help you not to give up?
Also read 2 Corinthians 12:7–10.

SERVE ONE ANOTHER

I Spy

What You Need:

A Bible, construction paper, scissors, string, pencil,
a small plate

What To Do:

1.   Read Colossians 3:12–17.

2.   Draw ten or more *magnifying glasses* on paper
     (trace around a small plate). Draw a *handle* on one
     side of each magnifying glass. Cut them out.

3.   Ask each family member to be a detective or spy.
     Search for instances of encouraging words or good
     deeds. Each time a family member notices positive
     words or behaviors, he or she should write it down
     (or draw it) on one of the paper magnifying glasses.

4.   Ask for a detective report each night at dinner. At the
     end of the week, read the good deeds discovered.

Variation #1: Make a mobile by tying the magnifying glasses to
               a metal clothes hanger with string. Or tape the   magni-
               fying glasses to a clothesline strung across a room, or
               attach with ribbon on a door or door frame.

Variation #2: Look for clues in nature that point to God's   exis-
               tence. (Or search for clues on any subject you   want to
               focus on.)

WWJ

GOOD SAM

"Hold your feet still!" Sam shortened the stirrups on his younger brother's saddle. After weeks of planning, they were actually taking off on their forest camping trip with Dad!

Sam swung into his saddle and waved to ol' Silas, the horse wrangler. "See you in a couple of days!"

He turned his horse onto the trail and looked back to be sure Micky and Dad followed.

Half a day down the trail, Sam spotted a teenage boy hobbling toward them, leaning on a crutch made from a tree limb. Sam reined in his horse and asked, "What's the problem?"

"I fell while rock climbing yesterday," the boy said. "I think my ankle's broken."

Sam's dad dismounted and felt the boy's ankle. "A doctor needs to set this before it heals crooked. Are you all alone?"

The boy nodded. "My parents know I went hiking, but they don't expect me back until tomorrow."

Sam's dad frowned. "Sorry to ruin our camping trip, boys, but we need to take this young man to a doctor."

Sam quickly dismounted. "Dad, we don't *all* have to go back. Lift him onto my horse. I'll take him back to the ranger station. Ol' Silas will let me stay and help at the ranch until you return."

Micky's face brightened. "Then can *we* still go camping, Dad?"

Dad sighed. "I know how much you looked forward to this, Sam. I hate to go on without you."

Sam shrugged. "It's okay. You and Micky go ahead. If I were hurt, I'd want someone to help me."

Jesus said, *"Love your neighbor as you love yourself."*
Matthew 19:19

Have you ever given up your plans in order to help others? What sacrifices have you made lately for your family?
Also read Luke 10:30–37.

SECRET LOVE PATROL

"The coast is clear!" Tim raced into the kitchen, adjusted the chinstrap on his helmet, and saluted his sister, Molly. "Sergeant Riley of the Love Patrol reporting for duty."

Molly giggled. "Take off the helmet, silly. Mom might wonder what we're doing."

"Not a chance," he said. "She's out in the garden. I'll stand guard while you unload the dishwasher."

Later, Mom opened the dishwasher to unload the dishes. She found only empty racks and a paper badge that read, Love Patrol.

"What a wonderful surprise!" she said. Tim glanced at Molly and held back a grin.

On Tuesday, Tim picked wildflowers. Molly arranged them in a vase on the table. They placed a Love Patrol badge beside it.

When Mom saw the bouquet, she smiled and asked, "Did you two do this?" Tim just grinned.

Wednesday morning, Tim woke early and took out the trash. At breakfast, Dad held up a Love Patrol badge. "Look what I found in the bottom of the empty trash can!"

On Thursday, Tim and Molly folded the clothes from the dryer. Mom discovered a Love Patrol badge on top of the neat piles of laundry. She gave her two kids a big hug and said, "God is so good to give me the blessings of His special Love Patrol!"

WWJ

"Lead a life of love, just as Christ did. He loved us. He gave himself up for us." Ephesians 5:2

Think of a loving deed you could do for a family member. How could you show love to a neighbor this week? Also read John 15:9–17.

BROKEN-DOWN VAN

"Look, Dad. That old man up ahead needs help," Justin said. "I think we should stop and see what we can do."

A white-haired man leaned against an old van on the side of the highway. A black dog lay at his feet.

Dad frowned. "I don't like to stop and help strangers. Some people are just lazy. They want others to pay their bills."

But he slowed down, pulled his Jeep off the road, and parked behind the van.

"Do you have any water we could drink?" asked the old man.

Justin reached out the window and handed him a sport bottle.

"Thank you." He poured water into a dish for his dog. Then he opened the van door and handed the bottle to an elderly woman.

"My wife's not feeling very well. I stopped here to help her into the backseat. Now our van won't start. I think it's the battery."

Dad got a towing chain out of the Jeep. He hitched up the van and towed it to the next gas station.

When the old man went into the nearby grocery store, Dad paid for the new battery.

The old man came out with two hot dogs. He handed one to his wife and the other to his dog.

He must not have enough money to buy food for himself, thought Justin.

"I can't thank you enough for everything you've done," the old man said, smiling.

"We'd like to give you some money," Dad said.

"Thanks, but I couldn't accept it. You've done enough already. I know God sent you to help us. God always provides everything we need."

WWJ

Jesus said, "But put God's kingdom first. Then those other things will also be given to you." Luke 12:31

When have you helped someone in need?
How does God provide everything *you* need?
Also read Psalm 23:1–4.

29

MARATHON

"Look! She's still in the marathon." Brendon rolled down the car window, waved his arms, and shouted, "Way to go, Aunt Judy!"

Aunt Judy moved slowly down the empty street on her crutches, swinging her one leg. She gave Brendon a tired smile.

"Maybe she wants something cold to drink," he said. His mom passed him a towel and a sport bottle filled with apple juice. He ran across the street and handed them to his aunt.

She stopped to lean on her crutches as she sipped from the bottle. "I'm heartbroken. I can't finish the Boston Marathon. Look at my hands. They're all blistered. And my arms are sore and weak."

"But Aunt Judy, you're almost there."

She laughed feebly. "Two miles is not exactly 'almost there.'"

"I'll walk with you. And God will help us. Okay?"

As they walked, Brendon told his aunt jokes and Bible stories, and he sang Sunday School songs. After a mile, his mouth grew dry and his legs ached. *Two miles is longer than I thought! Dear God, please help us finish the race.*

Two hours later, Mom snapped photos of her young son and his one-legged aunt staggering across the finish line.

Brendon hugged his Aunt Judy. "You did it!"

She smiled through her tears of joy. "We did it together. Thank you for helping me fulfill my dream."

WWJ

"Cheer up those who are shy. Help those who are weak. Put up with everyone." 1 Thessalonians 5:14

How would you encourage someone who is discouraged?
How might you help someone today?
Also read 1 Thessalonians 5:11–22.

WHOM DO YOU WORK FOR?

"I can't play till later," Karl said. "I promised Mrs. Tysen that I would mow her lawn this morning."

Jesse balanced on his skateboard. "She asked me to help her, too, but I said no. She's cheap. It would be a miracle to pry five bucks out of her for the whole morning."

"But she can't afford to pay much," said Karl. "She's old and poor. Helping her is a good way to serve Jesus."

Jesse rolled his eyes. "You're a sucker for punishment," he said. "See you after lunch."

Karl wheeled his mower over to his elderly neighbor's house. When he finished her lawn, he edged the grass along the sidewalk and pulled the weeds in her garden.

Four hours later, Mrs. Tysen brought him a glass of lemonade and three dollar bills.

Karl smiled. "Thank you, Mrs. Tysen. Let me know when you need me again."

Just after Karl returned home, Jesse rode up on his bike.

"Are you finished?" Jesse asked. "How much did she pay you?"

Karl smiled. "Three dollars," he said quietly.

Jesse laughed until he coughed. "Did you really work all morning for three lousy bucks?"

"No," said Karl. "I worked all morning for Mrs. Tysen...and for Jesus."

WWJ

"Work as if you were not serving people but the Lord. You know that the Lord will give you a reward." Ephesians 6:7–8

Who do you serve willingly?
Who do you find hardest to serve?
Also read 2 Corinthians 9:7–9.

PRAYER TIME

Prayer around the World

What You Need:

A Bible, a pencil, and paper

What To Do:

1.　　Read Colossians 1:3–6.

2.　　Write down seven names of people from other countries that you hear on the news, read in a newspaper, or read in a book at school. For the next week pray for one name each day.

3.　　Remember that each name is a real person. God knows that person, even though you don't. Ask God to save the ones who don't know Him. Ask God to protect them, send them food, or help them. Pray whatever God puts on your heart.

4.　　Remind each other that God is already answering your prayers. You will find out what your prayers accomplished when you get to Heaven.

Variation:　Pray for a different country each day. Ask God to increase the number of Christians in that country. Ask Him to bless and strengthen the people who love Him in that country.

ASHLEY'S PRAYER

"Mom, I think you need to pray," said Ashley.

Her mom slowly raised her head and looked up. Ashley could see in her mother's eyes that she was too upset to pray. She was still grieving the loss of her foster son.

Benny had come to them as a newborn, right out of the hospital. He lived with them for the first two years of his life. But yesterday a state children's services worker had taken Benny back to live with his biological family.

Mom sobbed silently as she rocked back and forth. She clutched Benny's teddy bear to her neck. In a faint voice, she said, "I'm sorry, honey. I can't pray right now. You'll have to do it for us…"

Ashley remembered a lesson she had heard in Sunday School about the Holy Spirit helping people pray. *Dear Holy Spirit, please help me. I need to know how to pray for Mom.*

When Ashley began praying, her words of prayer surprised both her and her mom.

"Ashley," Mom asked, "how did you know to pray all those things? How would any seven-year-old know how I was thinking and feeling? You prayed as if you had a list of all my concerns right in front of you."

Ashley smiled. "The Holy Spirit knows everything, Mom. I asked the Holy Spirit to help me pray for you. That must be why I knew what to pray."

Mom drew Ashley close. "Getting over the loss of the child I loved so much is hard," Mom said. "But I feel better now. I'm thankful that you could pray when I couldn't."

Jesus said, "The Father will send the Friend in my name to help you. The Friend is the Holy Spirit. He will teach you all things." John 14:26

What do you need the Holy Spirit to teach you today?
Who needs your prayers? Ask the Holy Spirit to help you pray.
Also read Isaiah 61:1–3.

SLIDE PRAYER

"Today I'm going down the big corkscrew slide!" Jenny ran into the playground at the park. "But first the merry-go-round!"

While Jenny rode around and around, she eyed the high, triple corkscrew slide. She felt her stomach flutter. *I'm not a baby anymore,* she thought. *I can go down that slide.*

On the teeter-totter with her dad, she felt a little more sure of herself. *I'm brave. I'm not afraid!*

Finally, swinging high on a swing set, she called to her dad, "The corkscrew slide is next!"

Her father climbed the tall ladder of the slide with her. Then they slid down together. Jenny clapped and cheered.

"Now I want to go all by myself," she said.

Dad nodded and gave her the thumbs-up sign. "When you climb the ladder," he warned her, "look up. Don't look down."

Jenny climbed the ladder slowly, placing each hand and foot in the center of the rungs. Higher and higher she climbed.

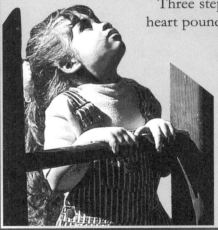

Three steps from the top, she stopped. Her heart pounded. "Help me, God. Help me," she prayed. Taking a deep breath, she climbed the last rungs to the top. Then she slid down the slide. At the bottom her father caught her. "You did it all by yourself! I'm proud of you." She hugged him and whispered, "I got scared at the top, but I asked God to help me. And He did!"

WWJ

"Call out to me when trouble comes. I will save you. And you will honor me."
Psalm 50:15

How do you solve any feelings of fear?
Are all prayers important to God? Why or why not?
Also read Psalm 86:1–7.

KIDNAPPED

Less than a block from her home, three teenage boys walked towards Victoria. She froze with terror as they quickly surrounded her.

"Get in the van," ordered the boy with a spider tattoo on his cheek. He yanked her toward the van. She shrieked and broke loose. But before she could run, the other two boys grabbed her. They shoved her into the van.

They're going to kill me! she thought, sobbing and shaking.

The van jerked forward, tires squealing. The young kidnappers whooped and laughed.

Victoria prayed. *Dear Jesus, save me! And help me calm down.*

"Our Father which art in Heaven," she whispered. She took a deep breath and continued, louder. "Hallowed be Thy name."

The driver looked at her in the rearview mirror. "Hey, back there. Shut up!"

"Thy kingdom come," Victoria shouted, tears drenching her face. She could feel Jesus with her. "Thy will be done, on earth—"

The tattooed boy gripped her arm and squeezed it hard.

"Stop it!" he yelled.

"—as it is in Heaven. Give us this day our daily bread."

The van wrenched to a stop.

"I can't stand it!" the driver yelled. "Shove her out!"

The van door opened and Victoria jumped to the curb. Rubber burning, the van roared off down the street.

Victoria ran to a nearby house. After the people who lived there called the police, she told them, "God saved my life!"

WWJ

"Lord, please save me. Lord, come quickly to help me."
Psalm 40:13

When has God rescued you or someone you know from danger? When have you prayed during a tense time?
Also read Psalm 40:11–14.

PRAYING FOR SERGEI

What's it like when people don't have enough to eat? wondered Shannon as she soared high on her swing in the old oak tree.

On the television news that morning, she had seen pictures of many children starving in Korea. Her mom told her about another orphanage in Russia where children were also starving.

I want to pray for them, Jesus. But how can I since I don't know anyone who lives in those countries? Will You help me pray for them?

As she swung upward, the young Korean girl's face that was shown during the TV news came to her mind.

Dear Jesus, she prayed, *please send her Korean orphanage plenty of food. And help those kids learn to know You.*

The name Sergei sounded in her head. Shannon smiled.

There must be at least one boy named Sergei among all the millions of people in Russia. Dear Lord, help him receive You as his Savior. Give him enough food so he will grow up to be strong and faithful to You.

In her head Shannon heard another name, Ti Ling.

Save her, too, Lord. Please make sure she has food and everything else she needs.

Up and back Shannon swung. Whenever she thought of a country, she prayed for the people who lived there.

Shannon had no idea what they needed besides salvation and food. But she kept praying.

For a long time she swung and prayed, swung and prayed.

In Heaven I'll probably get to meet all the people I've prayed for. It will be like opening a special present. Thank You, Jesus.

"At all times, pray by the power of the Spirit....Always keep on praying for all of God's people." Ephesians 6:18

Look in the phone book or newspaper for names of people. Are you willing to pray for them during the week? Also read Ephesians 6:18–19.

UNANSWERED PRAYER

"I'm crossing all my fingers that Shonna won't be in my class this year." Kelby set her notebook on the school steps and crossed her fingers. "Shonna always fights with me."

"Crossing your fingers is a superstition. It won't help," Paige said.

Kelby uncrossed her fingers. "You're right." On her way to her new classroom she prayed, *Dear Jesus, please make Shonna be in a different room from me.*

Walking into her new classroom, Kelby stopped short—there sat Shonna. *Why didn't Jesus answer my prayer? I'll be miserable all year.*

At recess, Kelby hurried out to the playground. She and Shonna grabbed the same swing at the same time.

"It's mine," said Shonna.

"I got here first," said Kelby.

Their eyes locked. *Here we go again,* thought Kelby.

Then Kelby let go of the swing. "I don't want to fight with you, Shonna. You can have the swing."

Kelby skipped to the parallel bars.

A few minutes later, Shonna walked over to her. "I don't want to fight, either," she said. "Maybe we could be friends this year."

"Okay!" said Kelby. Now she understood why Jesus had not answered her prayer. He had something better in mind—a new friendship with Shonna!

WWJ

"He will listen to us whenever we ask him for anything in line with his will." 1 John 5:14 (NLT)

How can you be sure your prayers are in line with God's will? When has Jesus answered no to one of your prayers? Also read 1 John 5:14–15.

SHOW THE LOVE OF JESUS

Prayer Cards

What You Need:

A Bible, two colors of three-by-five cards, and a file box

What To Do:

1.   Read 1 Thessalonians 5:16–18.

2.   On one color of cards, jot names of people to pray for
      every day. Write down briefly how you want to pray for
      them. *(Save Cindy.)* On the other color of cards, write
      temporary and urgent requests. *(Give Dad a safe trip.)*

3.   Pray through all the cards every day. Pray through the
      urgent request cards as often as possible.

4.   When God answers a prayer, write it on the back of the
      card. File it in your file box. Make a new card for that
      person if needed.

Variation #1: Punch a hole in each card. String on yarn and
      hang in kitchen.

Variation #2: Put the urgent prayer request cards in your lunch
      box. Keep with you all day at school so you can pray
      over them.

WWJ

A LOW BLOW

"It's my turn. You've jumped long enough." Greta's patience with her young cousin was running on empty.

"It's my house," said Ivan, jumping higher on the trampoline.

"Your dad said to take turns!"

Ivan grinned and kept jumping.

"Come on, Ivan! You're supposed to share!"

He stuck his tongue out. Greta tensed with anger. *Jump again, you little brat, and I'll*—He jumped again, and she reached out and clipped him behind the knees with her hand.

He dropped to the trampoline, wailing in pain.

"Oh, be quiet," said Greta. "You're not hurt. I barely touched you!"

Their moms rushed out of the back door. "What happened?" asked Greta's mom.

"She hit me!" Ivan cried.

"*Did* you?" asked Greta's mom.

"I kept waiting, but Ivan wouldn't share. I just wanted to stop him so I could take my turn."

Her mom frowned. "Then you *did* hit him. No jumping for you, young lady. You'll spend the rest of the afternoon in the kitchen with Aunt Marjorie and me."

"Why am *I* in trouble?" asked Greta. "Ivan's the one who was selfish, not me!"

"If someone does something wrong, does that mean you should do something wrong, too?"

"No," admitted Greta. "I know that Jesus wants me to do the right thing, no matter *how* anyone else acts. I'm sorry, Ivan. Please forgive me."

WWJ

"Don't pay back evil with evil. Be careful to do what everyone thinks is right."
Romans 12:17

What do you do when others don't play fair?
When have you ever paid back good for evil?
Also read Matthew 5:43–48.

SCARED SICK

"I hate hospitals," Doug complained. He and his friend, Robert, followed their parents through the children's ward.

"Hospitals smell gross," said Doug. "Germs are everywhere. Do you know why Chad had back surgery?"

"No," said Robert.

Doug frowned. "I hope Chad doesn't show us his stitches."

"Why did you come if you hate hospitals?" asked Robert.

"I'd want someone to visit me if I had an operation," Doug said. They stopped in front of Chad's room and looked inside. They saw Chad lying in bed, his face pale against the blue sheets.

"He looks bad," Doug whispered. "I hope I don't see any blood. I can't stand the sight of blood."

Robert rolled his eyes. While the parents talked in the hall, the boys went in and stood beside Chad's bed. Doug glanced at his friend's sickly white face. *Jesus, I'm going to need Your help here.*

Chad slowly opened his eyes. He held out his hand. "I don't want to hold his hand!" Robert whispered. Doug took Chad's hand and whispered back,

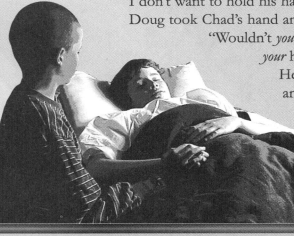

"Wouldn't *you* want someone to hold *your* hand if *you* were sick?"

He watched Chad smile and close his eyes.

"This isn't so bad," Doug whispered. "Actually, it feels good to help someone who needs it." *Thanks for Your help, Jesus.*

Jesus said, "In everything, do to others what you would want them to do to you." Matthew 7:12

How does Jesus feel about sick people?
When have you comforted a sick friend?
Also read Matthew 8:14–16.

LITTLE SQUIRT

"I don't want to play your silly little board game," said Julianne. "Not now, not *ever*."

"Why not?" asked Cassie, her younger cousin.

"Because board games are for little squirts like you. I'm more grown-up. Besides, I'm going swimming with Josh."

"What's happening?" asked Josh as he joined the girls.

Julianne twirled her hair and smiled up at her older cousin. Cassie stared at the ground, feeling ashamed.

"Little Cassie wants to play a board game," Julianne said, rolling her eyes.

Josh tousled Cassie's hair and grinned. "I like playing board games at family reunions. I'll play with my little cousin."

Julianne frowned. "You won't like her game," she told Josh. "It's called Prom Queen."

"Oh, hey, let's play!" Josh laughed. "It will be fun. Set it up."

Cassie eagerly spread out the game. Josh let her spin first. She landed on a square that read, "Twenty dollars toward a prom dress."

Josh took his turn. "Whoa! I got a red convertible!"

I hope Julianne goes away and doesn't want to play, thought Cassie. *I want Josh all to myself.*

Moments later, Julianne came closer and sat down next to Josh. "Can I play, too?" she asked him.

Josh shrugged. "It's up to Cassie."

"Okay. You can play," Cassie said. Then she whispered in Josh's ear, "I'm trying to be nice to her, like you were to me."

Josh whispered, "I'm trying to be nice, too…like Jesus."

WWJ

"Live like children of the light…Find out what pleases the Lord."
Ephesians 5:8–9

When have you played a game with younger children?
Are you willing to do what pleases others?
Also read Ephesians 5:15–17.

WELCOME TO THE NEIGHBORHOOD

"This is a stupid idea!" Stephanie tripped on the bottom step of the neighbor's porch and almost dropped her plate of cookies. Her brother slipped past her and reached for the doorbell.

"Wait, Jon!" Stephanie called, "I'm not ready yet."

She glanced nervously at the front door. "What if a grumpy old man answers the door and yells at us for trespassing?"

Jon grinned. "He won't yell until *after* he tastes your cookies." He reached for the doorbell again.

"Wait! I'm scared." Stephanie shoved the plate of cookies at her brother. "You do this. I'm going home."

"Hey, this was your idea!" He shoved the plate back at her. "You're the one who remembered feeling lonely when we moved here. You decided to welcome these new neighbors."

Stephanie bit her lip. "You're right. I prayed for a chance to show love to our neighbors. I just didn't think I would be this nervous." She took a deep breath and rang the doorbell.

A young woman with a baby on her hip opened the door.

"Hi. We're your neighbors from across the street." Stephanie held out the cookies. "Welcome to our neighborhood."

The young mother smiled. "You're the only neighbors who've welcomed us! Thank you."

"The whole law can be found in a single command. 'Love your neighbor as you love yourself.'" Galatians 5:14

How can you make a new child in your neighborhood or in your school feel welcome? Who can you befriend today?
Also read Romans 13:8–10.

TESS'S TRESSES

"Hey, baldy," said a student who walked past Della in the hall. "Did cooties chew off all your hair?"

Traci tucked her arm under Della's. "Ignore him," said Traci.

Heads held high, the girls marched down the hall as other students called out insults at Della.

Tears glistened in Della's eyes. "I wish I could afford a wig— one that looks like real hair."

"I'd give you my hair if I could," said Traci.

Later that week, Traci came across a magazine ad. It read, "Help kids who experience hair loss from medical conditions. Donate your hair to Tess's Tresses. We make natural hair wigs for children who can't afford them."

Traci fingered her waist-length, silky blond hair. *I can give Della some of my hair!*

She took the magazine to her mom. "Could I get my hair cut...and give it to Della?"

"Are you sure you want to do that?" asked Mom. "You've never had your hair cut. You've always wanted to let it grow."

"How can I keep my hair when Della doesn't have any?"

"If Tess's Tresses is a reliable organization, you may donate your hair," said Mom.

After they gathered information about Tess's Tresses, Traci got her hair cut. She smiled as she tucked her cut hair into a large manila envelope and mailed it.

At school six weeks later, girls crowded around Della to see her new wig. "Wow! You look great, Della!"

In her heart Traci felt thankful as she prayed, *Thank You, Lord, for letting me bless my friend.*

WWJ

"May the Lord make your love grow....May your love for one another increase."
1 Thessalonians 3:12

What do you have that you could share with others?
What do you find hardest to share?
Also read Romans 12:9–17.

CHOOSE WHAT JESUS WANTS

Bible Time Machine

What You Need:

A Bible, pencil, paper

What To Do:

Note: This is a variation of the memory game where objects are listed in alphabetical order: "I'm going on a trip, and on this trip I'll take…"

1. The first person says, "I'm visiting the Bible lands in a time machine, and I might see…" Then he must finish the sentence with a Bible object, place, or person starting with the letter *a*.

2. The second person repeats the sentence and adds something starting with the letter *b*.

3. Play continues to the end of the alphabet.

Variation #1: Simplify for younger children by writing down the key words instead of repeating from memory. Have everyone chant them. Add a new object each time.

Variation #2: Play as a search-for-the-answer game without repeating each object from memory. Simply search through the Bible for the words.

GARAGE DOOR

"Don't open the garage door! Dad might see me," said Casey as he rummaged in his dad's tool chest. "Dad wants me to go to a Bible study. But I want to fix my bike."

Robby jerked up on the garage door handle. "We need more light!" The door rolled up and let in the sunlight.

From the house, Casey's dad called, "Time for Bible study."

Casey frowned. "Let's crawl up above the garage door and hide. It'll be a tight squeeze, but we can lie flat."

He climbed a step stool, grabbed the edge, and pulled his body over the flat door. Robby followed.

Sandwiched between the garage door and the ceiling, the boys heard Casey's dad looking for them in the garage below.

After he left, Robby said, "I'm going home." He jumped down to the step stool.

Without his weight, the garage door started to close. It took Casey with it, head down. But his foot caught in the springs.

Suddenly the door stopped closing. Casey dangled upside down above the cement garage floor.

"Help!" he hollered. *"Help me!"*

Dad heard and ran out. He took Casey down. "You pinched your leg badly, son. What were you doing up there?"

"Hiding from you. I—I wanted to fix my bike instead of go to Bible study."

Casey pulled himself to his feet and limped toward the car. "Please get my Bible for me. I'm ready to go now. If I'd obeyed you, I wouldn't have hurt my leg."

WWJ

"Obey your leaders. Put yourselves under their authority. They keep watch over you....Obey them so that their work will be a joy." Hebrews 13:17

Who has authority over you?
Why is it important to obey your leaders?
Also read Hebrews 13:17–21.

BLIND TO THE PROBLEM (Part One)

"It's snowing!" Jordy tossed a handful of sand in the air.

"No, it's a blizzard!" Alec flung a fistful of sand at him. The boys chased each other around the sand pile, hurling sand.

Mrs. Knight blew her whistle. "Alec! Jordy!" She summoned the boys. "Why shouldn't we throw sand?"

"Because it could get in someone's eyes," Jordy mumbled, "and that person might get hurt."

After recess, Mrs. Knight called Jordy to her desk. "Jordy, to help you remember the playground rule about throwing sand, you are going to be *blind* for a day." She pulled out a large white handkerchief and tied it around his eyes.

At first, Jordy liked being blind. He grinned when he didn't have to take the spelling test. But he also missed art, his favorite subject. He turned red with embarrassment when he stumbled into desks and when he spilled milk in his lap at lunch.

At recess, he sat by himself, listening to shouts and laughter. No one offered to play with him.

At the end of the day, Mrs. Knight removed Jordy's blindfold. "What did you learn today?" she asked.

"I discovered that teachers have reasons for making rules. Sometimes breaking a little rule can give people big problems."

"Oh, why didn't I listen to my teachers? Why didn't I pay attention to those who gave me instruction?" Proverbs 5:13 (NLT)

What rules do you sometimes wish you could disobey?
Why do you think those rules could be important?
Also read Proverbs 3:1–7.

BLIND TO THE PROBLEM (Part Two)

Derek stopped rolling a spit wad as he watched his fifth grade teacher place a blindfold over his friend's eyes.

Mrs. Knight turned to the class. "This is to help Jordy—and the rest of you—remember our playground rule: Never throw sand! It can seriously damage your eyes."

She tied the blindfold tightly. "Remember that safety rules must be obeyed. Now Jordy's going to experience what it's like to be blind."

What a break! thought Derek. *He doesn't have to do any work.* But it didn't look as if Jordy was having any fun, either. He just sat, doing nothing. *Bor-ing!*

When the noon bell rang, Derek grabbed his lunch sack and hurried out. Glancing back, he saw Jordy groping his way between the desks, trying to find the door.

Boy, am I glad I can see, Derek thought.

At recess, Derek lined up to play tetherball. He noticed Jordy at the edge of the playground, just sitting by himself.

I ought to go find out how he's doing. No, I'd better not. I'll lose my place in line if I leave. Besides, Jordy can't see, so it won't make any difference.

At the end of the day, Mrs. Knight took off Jordy's blindfold. "Blind people need friends like the rest of us," she said. "How many of you befriended Jordy today?"

Derek squirmed. He had never once helped his friend. And at recess Derek had purposely avoided Jordy.

He realized, *Jordy wasn't the only one who was blind today. I was blind to what it really means to be a friend. I need to go and ask Jordy's forgiveness...and God's.*

WWJ

"There is a friend who sticks closer than a brother."
Proverbs 18:24

How could you be a friend to someone who is ill or disabled? Who are some other people that need your friendship?
Also read Proverbs 27:10.

WWJD BRACELET

Wow! Jordan's a Christian! Blake thought happily as he noticed his classmate's WWJD bracelet for the first time at recess.

"Hey, Jordan," Blake said, holding up his own What Would Jesus Do bracelet. "I didn't know you had one, too."

Jordan glanced at Blake's bracelet. "Yeah," he said, slamming the ball. "Everybody wears them. Mine really works good, does yours?"

"Yes," said Blake. He thought about once when he couldn't figure out a math problem on a test. When he had looked over at Sara's paper, his bracelet reminded him that Jesus didn't want him to cheat. So he didn't.

"It's the best good luck charm I ever owned," said Jordan proudly. "Better than my lucky rabbit's foot."

"Good *luck?*" said Blake. "I think Jesus wants us to pray and ask for His help rather than trust in *luck.*"

"What?" Jordan frowned. He missed the ball and swore. "Come on WWJD," he said, rubbing his bracelet. "Do your stuff." He swung again and connected with the ball. "Yes!"

Blake finally understood. Even though Jordan wore the WWJD bracelet, he wasn't thinking about Jesus at all.

Jordan lunged at the ball and missed. "Come on bracelet!"

Blake glanced at his own bracelet as he prayed, *Dear Lord, please forgive Jordan for treating You like a good luck charm. Help him to know the truth about You. Help him learn to know You as his Savior. Amen.*

"*The time will come when...people will turn their ears away from the truth.*"
2 Timothy 4:3–4

Do you know any non-Christians who wear WWJD bracelets?
How would you explain what a WWJD bracelet means?
Also read 2 Timothy 4:2–5.

DON'T CROSS THIS LINE!

"Leave me and my friends alone, Andrew." Kyle stepped onto the pile of dirt and waved his digging stick. "If you mess up our roads again, you'll be sorry."

Andrew sneered and stuck out his tongue.

Kyle drew a line in the dirt with his stick. "You stay on that side of the line. We'll stay on this side."

That night at bedtime, Kyle told his mom about Andrew.

To his surprise, she asked, "How would you feel if you were the new kid at school? Some children think they have to act tough in new situations." She bent over, kissed him good night, and asked, "What would Jesus do about Andrew?"

The next day at recess, Kyle looked across the playground dirt pile at Andrew. The Bible words, "Be at peace with all men," popped into Kyle's mind.

But Jesus, it isn't easy to make peace with Andrew. If I'm nice to him, I could lose all of my friends.

His conscience responded, *Who drew the line in the dirt?*

Kyle climbed the dirt pile and with the toe of his shoe rubbed out the line he'd drawn the previous day. "We'll have more fun if we all play together," he told his friends.

After that, all the boys dug in the dirt, played wallball, and shot hoops together. Andrew invited Kyle to go fishing and camping with his family. Kyle taught Andrew to play chess, and they started an after-school chess club.

Wow! thought Kyle at the end of the school year. *There are lots of good reasons why Jesus tells us to be peacemakers.*

WWJ

How do you act when you're new to a group?
How do you treat newcomers to your neighborhood or school?
Also read Matthew 5:44–47.

HEAVEN IS YOUR HOME

Heavenly Bodies

What You Need:

A Bible and one seed from your yard or from a store packet. Buy a small flowering plant like a marigold or a petunia. (Preferably buy the same kind of plant as your seed.)

What To Do:

1. Read 1 Corinthians 15:35–44.

2. Compare the ugly brown seed to the plant it produces. Talk about how the Bible compares your earthly body to the seed and your heavenly body to the beautiful plant. We can recognize a marigold seed, and we know what it will look like when it blooms. Don't worry about whether people will recognize you in your new body. Read how Jesus' disciples knew Elijah and Moses even though they had never seen them before (Matthew 17:1–8).

3. Thank God for the heavenly body you will have someday. Thank God for eternal life and Heaven.

Variation: Start seeds indoors to demonstrate how they change into something far more beautiful. Use tulip or daffodil bulbs planted outside to illustrate how different our heavenly bodies will be. Use a flowering plant as a reminder of Jesus' resurrection. What was different about Jesus after His resurrection?

A FRIEND IN HEAVEN

"Can I pull your oxygen tank for you, Jenny?" Karen slowed her pace to match her friend's slow shuffle.

Jenny smiled and shook her head no. "I want to…," she paused to catch a breath, "do all I can…for as long…as I can."

Karen's eyes filled with tears. She remembered when Jenny played dodgeball every day with her at recess. Now she couldn't walk across the playground without stopping to rest.

Karen clenched her hands. "I hate your cystic fibrosis!"

"I hate…" Jenny paused for breath, "your cancer!…But some day…the medicine you're taking…will make you well." Jenny gently laid her hand on Karen's arm and said, "I'll be well, too,… in Heaven."

Karen spent her summer taking chemotherapy and resting. In September, the doctor pronounced her cured.

On Karen's first day back at school, Shawna told her, "Did you hear? Jenny died last Friday. The funeral was yesterday."

Karen burst into tears. "Why didn't somebody tell me? I didn't get to say good-bye…." She felt so alone. Jenny was the only friend who understood what it was like to be sick a lot.

That night Karen skipped supper and shut herself in her room. *Oh God, why did You take Jenny? Why?* Karen pounded the bedspread and sobbed.

Finally she lay quietly, thinking of Jenny's words: *Some day, the medicine you're taking will make you well. I'll be well, too,…in Heaven.*

Karen stared out the window at the night sky. *Oh, Jenny, because of your example, I'm going to live my life in a way that will make God happy. And someday, when I see you in Heaven, we'll both be well forever!*

WWJ

"We will be taken up in the clouds. We will meet the Lord in the air. And we will be with him forever." 1 Thessalonians 4:17

Do you have any friends or family in Heaven?
Are you certain that Jesus will take *you* to Heaven?
Also read 1 Thessalonians 4:13–18.

FORGET-ME-NOT

The house feels so empty! Erin stepped into her little sister's room. Melissa's teddy bear sat stiffly in an empty crib.

Erin brushed the bear's soft fur against her cheek. *I won't ever feel my sister's sticky kisses or hear her say, "I uv oo, Win."* The ache inside of Erin grew stronger.

Clutching the bear to her chest, she ran into the backyard. Under the broadleaf maple tree, she fell to her knees in the grass.

Crying, she prayed, "Oh, Jesus, I miss Melissa so much. Mom says she's in Heaven with You. If I knew for sure, I could handle not seeing her, not hugging her. Please God, somehow help me know she's with You."

Erin buried her head in her hands and cried until she had no more tears left.

The next day, she returned to the backyard with a book. Reading helped her forget the pain of losing Melissa. As she neared her favorite place under the maple tree, Erin stopped and stared. On the very spot where she had knelt the day before, a small, blue forget-me-not was blooming!

Erin dropped to her knees again. "Thank You, Jesus. I trust that Melissa is with You. I'll never forget her. Take good care of her until I get to Heaven. Then we'll all be happy together!"

Jesus said, "I am the resurrection and the life. Anyone who believes in me will live, even if he dies." John 11:25

Is there someone you love very much in Heaven?
Are you confident that you will see them again? Why?
Also read John 11:1–44.

JUST LIKE HEAVEN

"Leave the curtains closed," called Mom. "No peeking."

Jennifer smiled to herself. She stood in the family room, her hand stopped in midair, near the curtains.

How did Mom know I was going to peek out the curtains? Mom is upstairs with Johnny.

Just then Mom and Jennifer's little brother came downstairs.

Jennifer said, "Mom, for weeks you haven't let us play in the backyard. And you've kept the curtains closed. What's Dad doing outside?"

"It's a surprise. You'll find out when it's time."

"Now it's time!" said Dad, stepping into the room. "Close your eyes, kids." Jennifer and Johnny closed their eyes.

Dad threw open the curtains. "Okay, you can look outside!"

Jennifer and Johnny opened their eyes and gasped.

In the backyard stood a beautiful playhouse. It was white with blue trim, two stories high! Jennifer stared at it, barely able to breathe.

Mom slipped her arm around her shoulders. "Dad built it for you and Johnny."

"Oh," said Jennifer, "it's just like…like Heaven!"

Mom said, "You know, sweetie, as beautiful as it is, it's not half as beautiful as the house Jesus is building for you in Heaven."

Jennifer grinned. "I can't wait to see *that* house."

She slid open the glass door and took her brother's hand. "Come on, Johnny, let's go get a little taste of Heaven."

WWJ

Jesus said, "There are many rooms in my Father's house….I am going there to prepare a place for you." John 14:2

What do you imagine that Heaven will be like?
How can you be sure that Jesus is preparing a home for *you*?
Also read John 14:1–4.

GOD'S GIFT (Part One)

"Scott, we have bad news," Dad said quietly. "The doctor says baby Hannah won't live more than a few minutes after she's born. He wants Mom to have an abortion."

Scott laid his hand on his mother's belly. He remembered how Mom said that when Hannah kicked, it felt like a butterfly inside her.

"The doctor doesn't want Mom to carry Hannah through the whole pregnancy just to lose her after she is born," said Dad softly. Tears filled his eyes.

"Didn't you always tell me that *I* was a gift from God?" asked Scott. His mom nodded and hugged him tightly.

"Isn't Hannah a gift from God, too?" asked Scott.

"You're right," said Dad. "God has given her to us…even if she doesn't live very long.

"The doctor means well," Dad said. "But I think we've all made the decision—Mom will *not* have an abortion. We're willing to take care of baby Hannah as long as she lives." He brushed a tear from his cheek. "And we'll always love her."

Scott laid his head on Mom's belly. He whispered, "I love you, Hannah." And he felt his baby sister kick inside, gently moving like a butterfly.

WWJ

"Children are a gift from the Lord. They are a reward from him."
Psalm 127:3

Who do you value as a gift from God?
How are gifts that don't last long, especially precious?
Also read Psalm 127:3–5.

GOD'S GIFT (Part Two)

"Can I touch Hannah?" Scott whispered. Mom nodded.

Scott climbed up on the hospital bed with Mom while Dad stood beside them. Baby Hannah slept in Mom's arms.

Scott stroked Hannah's fingers and nose. "She's beautiful. How can she be sick when she looks so perfect?"

"Hannah looks perfect on the outside," Mom said, "but she is very sick on the inside."

"Let's pray with Hannah while we can." Dad said softly.

"Do I have to close my eyes?" asked Scott.

"No," his dad said. "We'll all keep our eyes open so we won't miss a second of Hannah's life."

Dad and Scott put their arms around Mom and Hannah.

"Dear Jesus," Dad said, "thank You for our sweet baby girl. We don't understand why she has to leave us, but we know You will take good care of her."

Three days later Scott stood beside a tiny white casket with his parents. "Why did Jesus let Hannah die?" Scott asked.

"There are some things only God knows," Dad said. "We just have to trust that God always does what is best."

"Is it okay for me to be sad?" Scott asked. "Does Jesus care if I miss Hannah?"

"We all miss her," said Mom. "Jesus knows how we hurt."

Scott closed his eyes. "Dear Jesus, I'll always love baby Hannah. I miss her. But I know that someday we will be a family again in Heaven."

"Amen," said Dad and Mom quietly.

WWJ

"The godly often die before their time....God is protecting them from the evil to come." Isaiah 57:1 (NLT)

What makes you sad? Do you pray about it?
What are some ways Jesus has comforted you and your family?
Also read Isaiah 57:1–2.

GOD'S REWARDS

Secrets

What You Need:

A Bible and a loving attitude

What To Do:

1. Read Matthew 6:1–6.

2. Choose a secret friend—a neighbor or someone at school. Or choose a person who has treated you badly.

3. For one week, without letting your secret friend know, do one thoughtful thing for him or her each day. Maybe you could:
    Say nice things about him to others.
    Write down a compliment about him, then mail it or hide it where he'll find it.
    Select a Bible verse or promise for him. Pray that verse for your secret friend.

4. Decide to never reveal what you've done to anyone outside your family. Be willing to treat your secret friend kindly as you bless him. Be encouraged that God sees all you do. And God will reward you.

5. Pray that God will give you a loving heart and a giving spirit.

WWJ

GOD USED IT FOR GOOD

Jason watched his parents sort through a stack of unpaid bills. "How can you keep praying for Mr. Clement? You did what was right, and he fired you! Now we're out of money!"

"Jason, God wants us to pray for those who persecute us. Besides, everything we have comes from God, not Mr. Clement. We'll wait and see how God works this together for our good."

"I'll help all I can," Jason said with a frown. "But it's hard to trust that God will bring something good out of this."

During the next few months, the whole family worked to pay the bills while Dad searched for a permanent job. Jason's older brothers mowed lawns and washed windows.

Jason answered the phone when people called to hire Dad for handyman jobs. He searched the newspaper ads for sales and clipped coupons. He earned extra money by walking the neighbors' dogs. And he gathered every morning with the family to pray that God would take care of them.

Ten weeks later, Dad sat down to dinner with a big smile. "I start work for AA Electronics on Monday. It will pay twice my previous salary!" The family cheered.

"You know the man who hired me today to fix his faucet? He's a Christian businessman. And he knows about Mr. Clement's bad business practices. He offered me this job in sales with his company."

"Wow! We haven't missed one meal. And God gave you a better job with a nicer boss! You were right, Dad." Jason said. "God DID work it all out for good!"

WWJ

Joseph told his brothers, "You planned to harm me. But God planned it for good....He wanted to save many lives." Genesis 50:20

When has it been hard for you to trust God?
When has God turned something bad into a blessing for you?
Also read Matthew 5:10–12.

BIBLES FOR CHINA

With her finger, Serena traced characters on a Chinese Bible. "I'd love to live in China and have a Bible like this!"

"If you lived in China, you could be thrown in jail just for being a Christian," Serena's Sunday School teacher told her. "And your family probably wouldn't have a Bible at all."

"We have lots of Bibles at home," Serena said. "Maybe we could send some of them to China."

"Chinese Christians need Bibles in their own language," said the teacher. "To buy and send one Chinese Bible costs four dollars."

Serena frowned. "I only have two dollars. But this week I can work and earn extra money to buy a Bible...or maybe two Bibles."

Every day during the next week, Serena asked the Lord to help her and her classmates earn money for Chinese Bibles.

On Sunday, Serena brought to class a large glass jar labeled, *Bibles for China.* She dropped five dollars in the jar.

During the week, her Sunday School classmates also did extra chores and gave up their candy, sodas, and allowances.

Over the next Sundays, they slipped the coins and the bills they had saved into the jar. A month later, the class counted the money.

"Sixty-nine dollars!" Serena clapped her hands. "Enough for seventeen Chinese Bibles! God answered our prayer."

WWJ

"There is one thing we can be sure of when we come to God in prayer. If we ask anything in keeping with what he wants, he hears us." 1 John 5:14

Do you pray about what God wants? Or about what *you* want? What could you pray about this week?
Also read Ephesians 3:16–21.

WARM FUZZIES

"Goodbye, Bun Bun." Cissy kissed her stuffed bunny on the nose and packed him into a box.

She also tucked in the teddy bear from her bed. "I'll miss you, Cuddles. Don't be scared. You'll love your new home."

The door opened and Nicole, her older sister, peeked in. "What are you doing with your stuffed animals?"

"The Mercy Ship is coming." Cissy said. She whispered in her stuffed raccoon's ear, then tucked him into the box, too.

"What's the Mercy Ship?"

"It's a big hospital boat that takes doctors and nurses all over the world. They help sick kids who are poor. And they tell the kids about Jesus."

"What does that have to do with your stuffed animals?"

"I'm giving them to the doctors on the ship. I want the kids from Africa to have little animals to hug while they get well."

Nicole snatched up one of the empty boxes and dashed out.

Cissy ran after her down the hall and into Nicole's bedroom. "Hey, where are you taking that?" Nicole gathered up an armful of her stuffed animals and packed them into the box.

During the next few days, Cissy and her big sister invited their friends to give, too. Several weeks later, the girls delivered more than one thousand stuffed animals to the Mercy Ship that docked in their hometown of Amsterdam, Holland.

One of the nurses on board told the girls, "God will reward you for giving so unselfishly."

"God doesn't have to reward us," said Cissy. "Just *giving* made us happy."

WWJ

"[Jesus] said, 'It is more blessed to give than to receive.'"
Acts 20:35

When have you given something to help someone?
Why is it more blessed to give than to receive?
Also read Acts 2:44–45.

CAMI'S TEARS

"First I flunked the math test," Cami said. "And then my soccer coach cut me from the team." Amanda put an arm around Cami's shoulder as Cami burst into tears.

The two girls sat together on the bleachers of the empty baseball field. They had been friends since the first grade.

"I feel like I have nothing," said Cami, "not even hope."

Amanda nodded. "I used to feel like that after my dad left and we lost our house. Then I learned to count my blessings. Why don't we do it together? I'll go first." She looked up at the blue sky. "I thank God that we're alive and that we can run and laugh."

Cami added, "I thank God for my mother and my father. And I'm thankful they love each other."

Suddenly, Cami realized how her words could make Amanda feel sad. "I'm sorry...," she said.

Amanda smiled. "It's okay. I always thank God for Mom. And I pray that God will help my dad."

"I thank God for my brother," continued Cami. "I'm thankful he treats me good and that he loves the Lord." The instant she said that, she remembered that Amanda's brother was mean to her. "I'm—I'm sorry, Amanda. I keep forgetting your troubles."

"It's okay. Really."

Cami gave her precious friend a hug. "Oh, Amanda, you've been through so much. And yet you've helped me remember the things that matter the most. I thank God for *you!* You're one of God's greatest blessings to me."

WWJ

"Give thanks no matter what happens. God wants you to thank him because you believe in Christ Jesus." 1 Thessalonians 5:18

What blessings are you thankful for?
Take time to count your blessings and thank God.
Also read Deuteronomy 28:1–6.

DANIEL'S NEW BIKE

My birthday present looks like a shoebox, thought Daniel. *It's not going to be the bicycle I wanted.* He smiled, trying to hide his disappointment as he opened the box. Then, inside the box, he found a check!

"We thought you'd like to choose your own bike," said Dad.

"Great Idea! Let's look at bikes on Monday after school."

The next morning, after Sunday School class, Daniel told his teacher about his birthday present.

"Why not let your new bike remind you to pray for bicycles for native missionaries in India," she said. "They walk miles between villages. If they had bicycles, they could travel farther and tell more people about Jesus."

At home, Daniel took a quick ride on his old bike. *It really works fine. I don't actually need a new one. I just don't like the way it looks.*

A few minutes later, he laid his birthday check on the kitchen table. "Dad, would you mind if I sent this money to the native missionaries in India? They are the ones who need a bicycle."

"Didn't you want a new bike for your birthday?" asked Dad.

"Yes, but my old bike will last for a while. I want the missionaries to have a bike now. I'm going to do yard work this summer and earn money for a second bike for them. When I get to Heaven, I'll see how many people came to the Lord because of the bikes I helped buy."

WWJ

"Give generously, for your gifts will return to you later."
Ecclesiastes 11:1 (NLT)

For which acts of generosity will God reward you in Heaven? How do you feel when you sacrifice for God? How does God feel? Also read Ecclesiastes 12:1.

GOD LOVES YOU

Birth Certificate

What You Need:

A copy of a family member's birth certificate
Optional: Pens and 8½-by-11 sheets of paper

What To Do:

1. Show birth certificates. Discuss what it means to be related by birth to a family (members love and help each other, no matter what happens).

2. Talk about being part of God's big family. How does our Heavenly Father want us to treat our brothers and sisters in Christ?

3. Discuss adoption, another way of entering a family. The Bible uses both images of birth and adoption to describe our entrance into God's family (John 3:3–8 and Ephesians 1:4–5).

Variation #1: Make your own birth certificate. Include full name, date of birth, hour of birth, parents' names, and place of birth (county, city, state, hospital). Design a seal to make the certificate look official.

Variation #2: Have everyone who trusts Jesus as their Savior create their own *spiritual birth* certificate.

WWJ

BETH'S BOLDNESS

Why does Beth wear brightly-colored jewelry on her artificial arm? Natalie wondered.

All hands were raised in the fifth grade classroom. Mr. Steele was giving a candy bar that day to every student who correctly answered one of his questions.

Natalie eyed the fingernail polish on Beth's fake fingers.

And why does she use bright red polish on that artifical hand? Isn't she embarrassed?

Beth leaned toward Natalie and rolled her eyes. "Mr. Steele never calls on me," she whispered. "Do you like my new bracelets?" she asked, keeping her eyes on the teacher.

Mr. Steele called on another student. Beth slumped in her seat with a groan.

Then Beth surprised Natalie. She quickly detached her artificial arm, pulled it out of her blouse short sleeve, and waved it high overhead. The whole class burst into laughter.

Natalie was glad everyone appreciated Beth's humor.

"Yeah, Beth!" someone said.

Mr. Steele smiled broadly. "Okay, Beth, it's your turn. You're hard to ignore." Beth answered his question, and he tossed her a candy bar.

At the end of class, Natalie leaned toward Beth. "I would hide it if I had an artificial arm. But you don't. Why not?"

Beth shrugged. "I was born this way, so to me it's normal. Besides, I figure Jesus made me the way I am and...Jesus doesn't make mistakes."

WWJ

"Lord, you are our Father. We are the clay. You are the potter. Your hands made all of us." Isaiah 64:8

How would you feel if you had a physical disability?
How would you want people to treat you?
Also read Genesis 1:26–27, 31.

WAKE UP, SAM!

James listened to his little brother Sam crying in the bunk above him. *That's the fourth time this week,* James thought. *I wish I could help.*

He climbed the ladder. "What's wrong?" he asked softly. "Are you afraid you're going to wet your bed again?"

Sam stared at the wall, sucking his thumb and hugging his stuffed elephant.

"Lots of little kids have that problem," James said. "Do you want me to wake you during the night so you can go to the bathroom?"

Sam turned to his brother. "You can try," he whimpered.

James nodded, but he felt worried. He knew his brother was a sound sleeper. *Dear Jesus, please show me what to do.*

At eleven o'clock that night, James woke up. He soaked a washcloth with cold water, climbed up the ladder, and dabbed it on Sam's forehead.

Sam's eyes popped open. At first, he scowled. Then, feeling his dry sheets, he grinned. "Hey! How did you know that would wake me up?"

"I asked God what to do," James said. "He reminded me that when I wash my face with cold water in the morning, it always wakes *me* up. God's great, isn't He?"

"Yeah! And you're a great brother."

"No one has ever seen God. But if we love one another, God lives in us."
1 John 4:12

When have you asked Jesus to help you be a blessing?
How do you show God's love to your family.
Also read 1 John 4:7–12.

BURNED CLASSROOMS

"I changed my mind about the money," Robyn told her older brother as she scattered corn to the chickens.

"You can't do that!" Burt said. "We agreed to buy a video game with the money we made from selling these chickens."

"No," Robyn insisted. "I'm sending my half to Indonesia."

Burt frowned. "Then I won't have enough to buy a game."

"Keep saving and buy it later. Right now Christians in Indonesia need our help. They have no way to rebuild their churches that have been burned."

"Who cares about a bunch of foreigners?"

Robyn stared at him. "How can you say that? You read the same article I did. They're our brothers and sisters. And they are being persecuted simply because they love Jesus! They have to hold Sunday School in burned-out church classrooms."

Later that evening, Burt told Robyn, "I've decided to give my money for Christians in Indonesia, too. I want to help them."

Robyn added, "The mission newsletter said that more than three hundred Indonesian churches have been attacked since 1991. There's just got to be more ways we could raise money."

"We could do yard work for our neighbors," said Burt.

"Yes," agreed Robyn. "And we could sell cookies."

"Good idea! And we could do even more projects."

"Giving is more fun than playing a video game," said Robyn.

"Almost," said Burt. "Anyway, I know that *giving* is what Jesus wants me to do."

WWJ

"Those who are godly give freely to others."
Psalm 37:21

How can you help Christians in other countries?
What will you pray for the persecuted Christians of Indonesia?
Also read Acts 2:44–46.

SING TO YOUR SISTER

"Sing to your sister, Ben, so she'll know your voice."

Ben sang, "Jesus loves me, this I know." Then he gently pressed his palms against Mom's belly and brought his face close as he kept singing, "For the Bible tells me so."

During the next few months, Ben sang every morning to Anna, his unborn sister.

Shortly before Anna was born, Ben was singing with his cheek against Mom's huge belly, and he felt his tiny sister move. "Mom! Anna tried to touch me!"

Mom smiled. "Anna knows your voice."

When Mom packed for the hospital, Ben sang once again to his sister. "I love you, Anna. I'll see you soon."

Two days after Anna was born, Dad told Ben, "Your sister is very sick. The doctors can't help her."

In the hospital nursery, Ben and his parents gazed at their newborn baby in her incubator. Ben slipped his fingers through a gloved opening and touched her tiny arm.

Mom whispered, "Sing to her, Ben…."

"Jesus loves me, this I know."

The instruments attached to Anna's incubator suddenly started moving.

The nurse got excited. "Something's happening! The baby's beginning to breathe on her own! It's a miracle!"

"Keep singing, Ben, keep singing," said Mom. "Your sister loves to hear your voice."

To the doctor's surprise, fourteen days later, Ben and his parents brought a healthy baby Anna home from the hospital.

WWJ

"My sheep listen to my voice. I know them, and they follow me. I give them eternal life, and they will never die." John 10:27–28

How can you hear Jesus' voice?
How does Jesus speak to those He loves?
Also read John 10:2–5, 27–29.

WHO GETS AIDS?

"Get away!" Marissa shrieked at Katie. "You have AIDS!"

Katie stood beside the table, holding her lunch bag. The chair at the table was the only empty place in the grade school cafeteria.

The room grew silent. All eyes turned to Katie. She lowered her head, her face burning with embarrassment.

"I don't have AIDS," she said quietly. "Just HIV."

Marissa jumped to her feet and snatched up her lunch. "It's the same thing. My mom says I'll catch it if you get close." She stepped backwards. "Keep away. Only bad people get AIDS. God hates you."

Katie turned and hurried out the door.

Outside, Miss Hill laid an arm around Katie's shoulders.

"Does God hate people with HIV?" asked Katie.

"Absolutely not," Miss Hill said. "God loves you."

"I didn't do anything wrong to get this disease."

Miss Hill nodded. "I know. Sometimes sickness comes from people doing bad things. But often there are other things that cause the sickness."

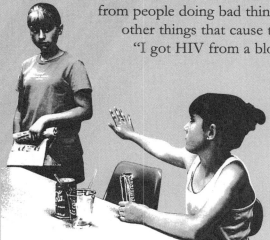

"I got HIV from a blood transfusion," Katie said.

"I'm so sorry," said Miss Hill. "I'll talk with Marissa later. She doesn't understand."

"Thanks," said Katie. "God gives me strength. And I pray that God will help the other kids not to be afraid of me."

WWJ

"Let the Lord make you strong. Depend on his mighty power."
Ephesians 6:10

Have you ever befriended someone when others were mean? How quickly do you judge others without understanding them? Also read Ephesians 6:10–18.

LOVE ONE ANOTHER

Trash or Treasure?

What You Need:

> Each person brings one possession he or she no longer wants.

What To Do:

1. Have everyone place their unwanted possession on a table. Allow family members to choose someone else's discarded item and explain why they chose it.

2. Discuss what things in life that you value (family, friends, a house, a car, good looks, nice clothes and toys, money to spend, popularity, being first). Why are these things important to you? (Make us feel good, others value them, TV advertisements say they're important.)

3. Talk about the type of people we value or don't value. Why do we consider some people more important than others? Talk about how God values people and how He wants us to value them. (Romans 5:6–8, Matthew 10:30–31, Psalm 139:17–18.)

Variation #1: Visit a flea market, garage sale, or resale shop. Look at the items some people don't want, but others value and will pay for. Purchase a "treasure" that someone else discarded.

BECAUSE WE LOVE ZITA

"Oh, no! Is that Zita's village?" Betsy asked her mom.

"Yes, honey. I'm afraid so."

The TV screen showed Zita's village in ruins, destroyed by a hurricane. Homeless children roamed the wreckage, looking for their families. Rescuers shoveled through the rubble.

Betsy hurried into the kitchen and removed a photo of Zita from the refrigerator. Zita was the child in Honduras that Betsy's family supported every month.

"Will Zita be okay?" asked Betsy, returning with the photo.

"I don't know, but God does. Let's pray for her right now." Together they held Zita's photo. "Jesus, please keep Zita safe."

Betsy looked around her warm, cozy living room. What if a hurricane destroyed our house? Would anybody help me?

"Mom, could we send food and clothes to Zita?"

"Honey, there's no way for us to contact her. But we could try sending things through a Christian relief agency."

At the store, Mom filled several grocery bags with powdered milk, rice, beans, and canned fruit. Betsy filled more bags with toothbrushes, toothpaste, shampoo, and soap. They added Band-Aids, vitamins, and small booklets about Jesus written in Spanish.

That weekend, Betsy's family brought their bags to a large warehouse. Volunteers packed them into boxes with thousands of other items donated by people from churches and all over the community.

Betsy said, "Even if our packages never reach Zita, I'm praying that someone else's package will."

WWJ

"Anything you did for one of the least important of these brothers of mine, you did for me." Matthew 25:40

Why is it important to help other people in need?
What will you do to help someone this week?
Also read Matthew 25:31–40.

THE LIE

"I heard that you copied somebody's homework," said Cheryl, as she and Audra walked home from school.

"Who told you that?" asked Audra.

Cheryl looked sideways at her. "I'm not allowed to tell. But I know you got an A on your math test. Is it true? Did you copy?"

"How can you ask me that?" Audra stopped walking. "Of course I didn't. Who told you that I did? Come on, tell me."

Cheryl looked away, then said quietly, "Emily did."

Audra felt sick. Emily was her best friend.

That evening, Emily phone and chatted, but Audra said little. After they hung up, Audra couldn't stop wondering why her best friend would say that she had copied somebody's homework. *Cheryl might lie about me, but Emily would never do that.*

Audra phoned Emily back and asked her, "Did you say that I copied somebody's homework?"

"No," said Emily. "It was Cheryl who started that rumor. I told everyone that you never cheat. Did you really think I would say something like that about you?"

"I'm sorry," said Audra. "I should have asked you about it right away because we both know that Cheryl doesn't always tell the truth. Forgive me for believing one of her lies."

Emily said, "I forgive you. Now let's pray for Cheryl."

"We will speak the truth in love. We will grow up into Christ in every way. He is the Head." Ephesians 4:15

What do you do when you hear a rumor?

What do you think it means to speak the truth in love?

Also read Ephesians 4:13–16.

BLOOD AT BROKE LEG FALLS

"Hey! Slow down, wild boy," Brian called to his little cousin. "You're gonna fall down!" *The little guy better not get hurt,* he thought. *If I see any blood, I'll pass out.*

Four-year-old Tyrone giggled and ran faster, his chubby arms spread like an airplane. Ten minutes later, the two cousins stood at the foot of the waterfall. They looked back to see Tyrone's parents only halfway down the trail.

"Let's swim!" said Tyrone as he dashed toward the water.

Before Brian could yell, "Stop!" Tyrone stumbled and sprawled onto the rocks. He sat up, screaming. Then he showed Brian one of his hands. He had cut it on a broken bottle. Blood ran down his wrist from a gash across his palm. It dripped onto the ground at his feet.

This was a sight Brian had not wanted to see. His legs turned to jelly. His face felt hot and cold at the same time.

Sinking onto a boulder, Brian put his head between his knees. *Jesus, please keep me from passing out. Give me the courage and the strength to help my little cousin.*

Brian knelt down in the pool beneath the falls and got his pant legs wet. Then he went over and knelt beside Tyrone. Blood reddened the boy's arm down to his elbow.

"Give me your hand," said Brian. He pressed the bleeding cut against the cold wet leg of his jeans. "This will stop the bleeding," he told Tyrone as he held him close and prayed until Tyrone's parents finally arrived.

WWJ

"Dear friends, since God loved us that much, we should also love one another." 1 John 4:11

Why is love not just a feeling, but an *action?*
When have you shown love for someone?
Also read 2 John 5–6.

UNINVITED GUEST

Eleven candles lit the faces of Carsten's birthday party guests. "A spaceship! What an awesome cake!"

Carsten smiled. He'd enjoyed planning his party, and everything had gone perfectly—until the doorbell rang. He glanced at his mom. "Who could that be?"

Mom counted heads. "I made eleven treat bags, and all eleven kids are here. Did you invite anyone else?"

"No." Carsten ran and opened the door. Marc, one of his schoolmates, pushed past him without saying a word and headed for the cake.

"Marc bragged he was going to crash your party," Tommy whispered. "But I didn't think he'd do it. Tell him to buzz off."

The party crasher helped himself to a huge slice of cake.

Carsten silently counted to ten to calm his anger. He hated to see his perfect party spoiled, and he wanted to do what was right.

"I'm *not* telling Marc to leave," Carsten said. "That's rude."

"But Marc's the one that's rude," said Tommy. "Treat him the way he's treating you."

Suddenly Carsten knew what he should do. "I need to follow Jesus' example, not Marc's," he said. "This is my chance to show Jesus' love. I'll let Marc stay. And he can have some of my candy and party balloons."

"Love is patient. Love is kind....It is not proud. It is not rude....It does not keep track of other people's wrongs." 1 Corinthians 13:4–5

How do you react when people are rude to you?
How did Jesus react when people treated Him badly?

TOO MUCH TROUBLE

"There's our new brother," said Simon. He held up his five-year-old sister, JoJo, so she could see into the hospital nursery.

"He's beautiful," whispered JoJo.

When it was time to wheel Mom and baby Ray out of the hospital, JoJo climbed onto Mom's lap. Mom smiled and kissed the top of her head, then looked at Dad.

"Sorry, sweetie," Dad said as he lifted JoJo onto the floor. "The baby gets to ride with Mom today."

At home, while Simon and JoJo helped Dad fix hot dogs, Mom sat on the couch and fed the baby. She smiled at him, sang to him, and kissed his cheeks. But the moment they all sat down to dinner, the baby cried.

JoJo dropped her fork and folded her arms. "I'm not hungry."

After dinner, Mom changed a dirty diaper and asked JoJo to throw it into the garbage. JoJo pinched her nose and shook her head. "No! It stinks."

"I'll take it out," said Simon, taking the diaper from Mom.

That night, the baby wailed for hours. Around three o'clock in the morning, JoJo slipped into Simon's bedroom.

"When can we take the baby back?" she asked. "He's noisy. And he gets all the attention. He's too much trouble!"

Simon smiled. "We can't take him back, JoJo. But this gives us a chance to be like Jesus, who loves us and always takes care of us. We need to keep loving our baby brother, no matter what."

JoJo sighed. "But how *long* do we have to love him?"

Simon hugged her. "As long as Jesus loves us—forever!"

WWJ

"The Lord is good. His faithful love continues forever. It will last for all-time to come." Psalm 100:5

Since love is an action, how can you love your brother or sister? When have you loved someone that wasn't lovable?
Also read Psalm 136:1–3.

FORGIVE OTHERS

Hard to Forgive

What You Need:

A Bible, large balloons, markers, a tack or pin to break the balloons

What To Do:

1. Read Matthew 18:21–22.

2. Talk about how it is difficult to forgive others who hurt us. Have everyone think of the worst thing that has been done to them.

3. Give everyone a balloon. Ask them to draw a picture of when someone hurt them on the balloon. (Have everyone work separately so they can't see anyone else's balloon.)

4. Now blow up the balloons. Notice how the more you blow it up, the bigger the offense becomes. When we keep remembering how others wrong us, our pain always grows.

5. Pray and ask God to help you forgive those who hurt you. When you have prayed and forgiven them, pop your balloon and throw it in the trash. Thank God for His forgiveness in Jesus.

FALSELY ACCUSED

It's not fair! Annabelle lost the hammer; I didn't! But I'm the one who got in trouble. Sally pressed her teary face against her teddy bear.

She heard a knock on her door. "May I come in?" asked her dad, peering inside the room.

Sally nodded. Dad walked in and sat beside her on the bed. She stared at the wall.

"I need to explain what happened, honey," Dad said. "I found the hammer in Annabelle's room. But since you were the last one I saw with the hammer, I assumed you were the one who lost it."

He gently pulled a wisp of her hair.

"It was Annabelle, not you," he said. "I know that now. And I'm sorry I punished you for doing something you didn't do. I made a mistake. Will you please forgive me?"

She looked at him, pouted, then faced the wall again.

"Don't I always tell you I love you?" he asked. "Don't I forgive you when you make a mistake or a bad choice? Well, I made a mistake. Now I'm asking you to forgive me."

Sally held up her bear. "What do you think, Teddy?" she asked. She shook the bear's head, as if to make him say he wasn't sure.

Dad tickled Teddy's tummy. "You're going to meet people all through your life that will let you down at one time or another. There's only one Person who will never let you down, and that's Jesus. When I ask Him to forgive me, He does. Always. Will you?"

She held up her bear. "Teddy says he forgives you."

Dad smiled. "What about you?"

She wrapped her arms around his neck and kissed him.

"I forgive you, Daddy," she whispered in his ear.

WWJ

"Put up with each other. Forgive the things you are holding against one another. Forgive, just as the Lord forgave you." Colossians 3:13

When has someone let you down or hurt you?
Is there anyone you haven't forgiven? What should you do?
Also read Matthew 18:21–35.

SPEEDY RED FLYER

Nate watched his sister set up her new dollhouse. *It's not fair,* he thought. *She got more presents than I got for my birthday last month.*

Feeling jealous, he walked past her and bumped against her dollhouse. Its tiny pieces of furniture scattered all across the rug.

"Mom! Nate wrecked my dollhouse!" yelled Cara as she ran to the kitchen and told their mother.

When Mother saw the mess, she sent Nate to his bedroom. "If you can't get along, you'll have to play in your room."

At first Nate didn't mind playing alone in his bedroom. But then he heard the sound of a wagon outside. He ran to the window and saw Cara pulling his Speedy Red Flyer.

"NO!" he shouted. His sister couldn't hear him through the closed window, but he yelled again, "You can't take my wagon! Don't you dare put any dents in it!"

Nate's heart pounded as Cara fastened her helmet, pulled back the wagon handle, and pushed off with one foot.

He groaned as she sped down the sidewalk and disappeared over the hill.

Nate threw himself on his bed. "My wagon is the best thing I own! What if it gets scratched?" For the first time he understood how Cara felt when he messed up her dollhouse. He slid off the edge of his bed and knelt down to pray.

"Dear Jesus," he said, "forgive me for being mean. Help me get along with my sister."

He knew in his heart that he had to tell her he was sorry before he ate supper. Then he asked Jesus, "Please take care of her...*and* my Speedy Red Flyer."

Let the peace that Christ gives rule in your hearts...live in peace."
Colossians 3:15

When have you been mean and deliberately hurt someone?
Is there someone whom you need to tell, "I'm sorry"?
Also read Colossians 3:12–15

MOM'S WALLET

What is Mom's wallet doing here? wondered Michael as he crawled under the dining room table, pretending to be a dog. *I'm going to fetch it for her, just like a real dog.*

The five-year-old clamped it between his teeth and carried it into the kitchen, crawling on all fours.

"Rrrf," said Michael to attract Mom's attention. She turned from the sink and saw her wallet in his mouth.

"Get my wallet out of your mouth! You know that isn't a toy. Why have you done this?"

"But, Mom. I found it under the dining room…"

"I never left my wallet there. Now go to your room. You need to learn to tell the truth."

Michael shuffled into his room, wiping tears from his eyes. *She didn't even let me explain. And she wouldn't believe what happened.*

Ten minutes later, Mom stepped into his room. "Your brother just told me what happened," she said. "I need to apologize to you." She sat on the bed and he climbed up on her lap.

"Jonathan told me that he took my wallet out of my purse to look at the photos. I'm sorry I got angry and didn't believe you. I was wrong. I should have let you explain. Will you forgive me?" She touched her head to his.

"Of course, Mom," said Michael as he hugged her. "I do forgive you. I love you."

WWJ

"When [Jesus] suffered, He did not threaten to get even. He left his case in the hands of God, who always judges fairly." 1 Peter 2:23 (NLT)

Would Jesus want you to argue with a parent? Why or why not? How should you react when you are misjudged by others? Also read 1 Peter 2:18–24.

MODEL PLANE CRASH

"This is my best model yet!" Jay told his four-year-old brother. He turned his new airplane upside down and glued a wheel in place. Soon the Piper Cherokee would join the fleet of planes hanging from the ceiling, out of his little brother's reach.

"Sammy, please remember what Mom said." Jay set the plane on his bookcase to dry. Then he nudged Sammy out the door and into the hallway. "You're supposed to stay out of my stuff!"

Later that day, when Jay returned to his room, he stared in disbelief. The bookcase had fallen onto its side. His new model lay broken and half buried under a pile of books.

"You tried to climb up my bookcase!" Jay whirled on Sammy, who came up the stairs with Mom. "You broke my new plane!"

"I'm sorry," Sammy whimpered. "I just wanted to look at it." Jay's eyes blazed. "I'll never forgive you!"

"Sammy said he was sorry," Mom quietly reminded Jay. "I will discipline him for disobeying. But Jay, don't you need to think about what you just said?"

When Mom and Sammy left the room, Jay sat down by the window. *What if God said He would never forgive me? I've disobeyed many times. But when I am sorry and ask God to forgive me, He always does.*

Jay prayed aloud, "Lord, I'm mad at Sammy. Please help me forgive and love him like You forgive and love me."

WWJ

"Lord, suppose you kept a record of sins. Lord, who then wouldn't be found guilty? But you forgive." Psalm 130:3–4

What do you do when you find it hard to forgive?
Who do you need to forgive today?
Also read Matthew 6:14–15.

WOOLLY WILLIE

"It's Friday! The sun is shining, and there's no school for three whole days." Trisha's heart sang as she skipped home after school with her friend, Kinsey.

"Oh, look!" Kinsey gasped, pointing to the sidewalk.

A brown and black striped caterpillar crept across their path. The sun lit a halo around the edges of its fuzzy body.

Kinsey held out her hand. The caterpillar wiggled onto it, making her giggle. "Hey, little guy," she said. "I'm going to name you Woolly Willie. I'll fix you a good home in a jar with leaves."

Trisha stood with her knuckles pressed into her hips. "I saw the caterpillar *first.* He's mine!"

"He's *mine!*" said Kinsey as she cupped Willie in both hands. She turned around and stomped off toward home.

Trisha screamed after her, "I won't be your friend anymore!"

"So who cares?" Kinsey yelled back. "I've got Willie!" But she felt miserable. Trisha had been her best friend since kindergarten.

Kinsey poked holes in a jar lid to give Willie air. She asked him, "Do you think I hurt Trisha's feelings when I said I didn't want to be friends?"

Willie didn't say anything, of course, but Kinsey knew the right answer.

"You're not much fun to talk to, Willie, but Trisha is."

She lifted the jar off her bed and walked to Trisha's house.

When Trisha answered the door, Kinsey held out the jar.

"I want you to have Willie," she said. "You're a lot more important than a caterpillar. Can we be friends again?"

Trisha smiled. "Sure, and we can take care of Willie *together.*"

WWJ

Jesus said, "Suppose you are offering your gift at the altar....First go and make peace with your brother. Then come back and offer your gift." Matthew 5:23–24

Have you argued with others lately? Did you make peace with them? When have you given up something in order to make peace? Also read Matthew 5:21–24.

YOU ARE SPECIAL

God's Snowflakes

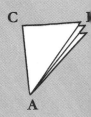

What You Need:

A Bible, paper, and scissors

What To Do:

1. Read Psalm 139:13–16.

2. Make snowflakes: Fold a square of paper in half to form a triangle. Repeat two more times. With point *A* down, cut away parts *B* and *C* from each side near the top.

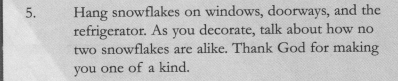

3. Cut away the folded point *A*. Make a variety of delicate cuts on all the edges.

4. Unfold the snowflake.

5. Hang snowflakes on windows, doorways, and the refrigerator. As you decorate, talk about how no two snowflakes are alike. Thank God for making you one of a kind.

UNLOVABLE

"Helen, why is your lip so crooked?" asked Pearl in the school hallway. "What happened to it?"

Instead of trying to explain that she was born with a cleft palate, Helen covered her lip with her hand. Then she hurried into the classroom. Kids always teased her about her lip. That made her feel ugly. She hated looking at herself in the mirror.

Miss Goodman came into the classroom. "Today I'm giving a hearing test." She turned to Jason. "Please walk to the back of the room and cover your right ear."

When he had done so, Miss Goodman whispered at the front of the classroom, "My father owns ten cows. Repeat what I said."

"My father owns ten cows. Repeat what I said."

"Your turn, Pearl."

When Pearl took her place, Miss Goodman whispered, "Your dress has pink ruffles."

"Your dress has pink ruffles."

"Helen, you're next."

Walking to the back of the room, Helen felt self-conscious. She held her hand over her mouth.

Everybody's looking at my crooked mouth. Her face burned with shame. *What will Miss Goodman say? Will she make fun of me?*

Miss Goodman whispered, "I wish you were my daughter."

Everyone gasped. Pearl's mouth dropped open.

Helen took her hand from her mouth and smiled. Then she repeated the words and thought, *If Miss Goodman wants me, I must be worth a lot.* And Helen returned to her seat, feeling loved.

WWJ

"We know what love is because Jesus Christ gave his life for us."
1 John 3:16

When have you felt unlovable? How does God feel about you? What could you say to someone who feels lonely and rejected? Also read 1 John 4:7–11.

SURPRISE AWARD

Cameras flashed as students received ribbons and plaques during the awards assembly at Good Shepherd School. Lily bit her lip.

I didn't win anything, she thought, trying not to cry.

"Wait a minute!" announced the principal. "There is one award left to give. Our teachers made a banner for the student who has been the best example of Jesus during this school year. We'd like to present our special 'Sunbeam for Jesus' award to...Lily Stillwell!"

Applause broke out while Lily stood stunned and unable to move. Another girl pushed her toward the stage. "Go up and get your award!"

Lily hurried up on stage. Everything looked blurry through the tears in her eyes.

The principal handed her the bright yellow banner full of candles and stars. He shook her hand and said, "Congratulations, Miss Sunbeam! Always shine for Jesus."

On the way home from the assembly, Lily's father asked, "What do you think it means to be a *sunbeam for Jesus?*"

Lily's eight-year-old brother spoke up, "I don't know. I *do* know that my bulb's burned out. I'm ready for vacation."

Lily thought for a minute. "Well, Jesus gives me joy in my heart. And He helps me love others. I would never shine at all if it weren't for Him!"

Jesus said, "You are the light of the world...let your light shine in front of others... they will see the good things you do. And...praise your Father." Matthew 5:14–16

How can you shine for Jesus today?
What kind of an *award* would your family and friends give you?
Also read Matthew 5:13–16.

OLYMPIC CHAMPIONS

"Remember the story about the tortoise and the hare?" Deanna told her partner, Kelsey. "Well, the tortoise won!"

Deanna had cerebral palsy. She walked with the help of metal hand crutches. But that wasn't stopping her from taking part in a race.

The Special Olympic athletes and their partners lined up in the lanes. The starting gun sounded. Down the track went the physically challenged athletes. They ran and walked and rolled their wheelchairs.

Kelsey moved alongside Deanna. After a short distance, Deanna stopped, took a sport bottle from Kelsey, and slowly sipped it.

"The Bible tells us to finish the race," Deanna said. "I may not win, but I *am* going to finish."

Kelsey admired her. Deanna had set a goal to complete the race. And in spite of her disability, she was sweet and cheerful.

My worries now seem so small, thought Kelsey. *Like…which clothes should I buy? Will the popular girls at school choose me for a friend? Funny, I thought I was helping Deanna. But it's the other way around. She's the one who's helping me!*

Deanna finally crossed the finish line. The audience applauded wildly. She and Kelsey hugged each other.

"I'll never forget you, Deanna," said Kelsey. "You've shown me the spirit of an Olympic champion and the heart of a Christian. With God's help, if I stand on the winner's platform at the coming summer Olympics, I'll tell everyone about you. I'll say that my friend, Deanna, showed me how to run."

WWJ

"Let us keep on running the race marked out for us. Let us keep looking to Jesus. He is the author of faith." Hebrews 12:1–2

How are you running your race today?
How do you look to Jesus? Are you reading His Word?
Also read Hebrews 12:1–2, 12–14.

PEPPER PROBLEMS

Annie braced herself for trouble. She saw Pepper talking to their soccer coach and glancing in Annie's direction.

Oh no! Pepper's complaining about me again. She always tries to cause trouble for me! Dear Lord, You know that I don't ever hurt her back, even when she screams at me. Why can't she leave me alone?

The game started. The ball rolled toward Annie, and she passed it over to Pepper. Sliding on the grass, Pepper missed it. The other team kicked it and scored a goal.

"Why can't you get the ball to me?" Pepper yelled at Annie. "You're always messing up!"

Annie blushed and hung her head even though she knew Pepper was the one who had made the error.

Every time the two girls came within earshot of each other, Pepper insulted Annie. Once she even swore at her.

By halftime, Annie was fed up enough to remember her mom's advice: "Annie, it's okay to stand up for yourself as long as you do it with the right attitude instead of getting angry. You are God's child. You deserve to be treated with respect."

The whistle blew. Annie jogged off the field and headed straight to Pepper. She faced her, nose to nose.

Firmly, but calmly, Annie said, "Pepper, get off my back. And don't blame me every time you make an error...*understand?!*"

Pepper's eyes widened as she stepped backward.

Annie surprised Pepper with a smile. Then Annie walked away to listen to the coach's halftime talk. She felt fantastic. *Thank You, Lord, for helping me stand strong and not be angry.*

From then on, Pepper treated Annie with respect.

WWJ

"Stones are heavy. Sand weighs a lot. But letting a foolish person make you angry is a heavier load than both of them. Anger is mean." Proverbs 27:3–4

Why should you treat other people with respect?
When have you been firm with someone instead of being angry?
Also read Proverbs 20:15, 22.

LABOR DAY MELODY

"Tell me again how I was born," said Melody. She snuggled against her mom in their big armchair.

"Well, it was September second," said Mom, "and you were late! I had promised to play the piano for a Labor Day Bible conference at the beach. It was a going-away present to our dear friend, Pastor Brandt. I wasn't sure what I should do."

"Pray!" said Melody.

"Right!" said Mom. "There was a hospital nearby, so my doctor told me that I could go to the Bible conference. But my friends kept telling me to stay home. So Daddy and I prayed…"

"And you decided to go to the Bible conference," said Melody, who had heard this story many times.

"I packed a few baby clothes, just in case, and off to the beach we went. I played the piano on Saturday morning. But then, in the afternoon, you let us know it was time to be born."

Melody grinned as Mom continued. "We rushed to the hospital. Our nurse, Grace, was also a Christian. After you were born, Daddy and Grace stood by my bed, and we all sang, 'O praise the Lord, for He is good.' I was so happy. I had a song in my heart.…"

Melody finished the story with a grin, "…and a special *Melody* in your arms."

WWJ

"Children who are born to people when they are young are like arrows in the hands of a soldier. Blessed are those who have many children." Psalm 127:4–5

Do you know the story of how you joined your family?
Ask someone to tell the story of *your* special birth!
Also read Psalm 128:3–6.

DO WHAT'S RIGHT

Be Like Jesus

What You Need:

A Bible

What To Do:

1. Read John 14:9.

2. Jesus said we can look at Him and know what God is like. What are some of God's character traits seen in Jesus? (merciful, loving, faithful, kind, just, trustworthy, giving, forgiving)

3. One way to be more like Jesus is to practice, just like you practice a sport. Pick one character trait of Jesus and practice it all day. If you chose to be trustworthy, don't break a promise or repeat gossip. If you chose kindness, be kind when someone treats you badly.

4. At the end of the day, discuss your failures and successes. What did you learn about yourself? What did you learn about Jesus? Pray that Jesus will help you become more like Him.

Variation: Practice one trait of Jesus for a week. Write down every time you practice the trait. Put the note in a bowl. At the end of the week, read all the notes.

CONNER, THE CON-MAN

"Hey, Con-man!" called Harold. "I was just telling the guys how you used your brother's old cast to fake a broken leg last year."

Conner, "the Con-man," Cunningham grinned as he strolled over to Harold's lunch table.

"Conner came to school on crutches. He got out of gym class for a whole week. And the girls helped carry his books and lunch trays all week." The guys all laughed.

On Conner's way home from school, one of his brother's junior high friends met him by the bus stop. "Hey, Con-man, do you want a ticket for Friday night's Maze Rats concert?"

"Sure, but that concert's been sold out for months, Mitch."

"A friend of mine needs the money. He wants ten bucks more than the box office price. Get me sixty bucks by Tuesday. I'll meet you here with the ticket Friday afternoon."

Conner paid Mitch on Tuesday. On Friday after school, he waited at the bus stop. Mitch never showed up.

Conner rushed home to his brother and asked, "Do you have Mitch's phone number? I paid him sixty bucks. He owes me a ticket to the concert."

"Mitch Gardner? He and his family just moved to Iowa. They left this morning. You might as well kiss all your money good-bye, sucker."

Conner stared in disbelief. He, Conner the Con-man, had been conned! It felt lousy!

Tricking people isn't clever, it's mean, he thought. *Forgive me, Lord. I'm through being a con-man. From now on, I'm plain ol' Conner.*

WWJ

"*A foolish person finds pleasure in doing evil things. But a man who has understanding takes delight in wisdom.*" Proverbs 10:23

When have you bragged about being mean to someone?
How does Jesus want you to treat other people?
Also read Proverbs 12:20 and 20:17.

E-MAIL CURSE

The bowl slipped from Heather's hands and shattered on the floor, sending potato salad everywhere.

"Just my luck!" cried Heather. "Jeannie warned me about this."

"What are you talking about?" asked Dad, helping clean up.

"Last night, Jeannie e-mailed me a story. She told me to send it to ten friends. Jeannie promised that if I sent it out, I'd have good luck. If I didn't, I'd have bad luck—like this."

"This was an accident. Nothing more," said Dad. "You know, sweetie, when I was in college, a friend once sent me a chain letter, telling me to mail it to twenty people. He said I'd have bad luck if I didn't send it. That was a curse—just like Jeannie's e-mail."

"I'm glad I didn't send off the story," said Heather.

Dad smiled. "So am I. You do know where curses come from, don't you?"

"Yes. Curses come from Satan."

"And you know who is greater than Satan, don't you?" said Dad.

"Yes. Jesus is the greatest!" Heather smiled.

"So why fear?" asked Dad. "You believe in Jesus and His power, right?"

"Right. Thanks, Dad, for your good reminder. Jesus is greater than any curse or so-called bad luck."

WWJ

"The One who is in you is more powerful than the one who is in the world." 1 John 4:4

What could you say to people instead of "good luck"?
Why isn't there good nor bad luck when you believe in Jesus?
Also read Isaiah 54:13–17.

THE TERMINATOR (Part One)

Jacob lunged for the soccer ball but missed. It slammed into the net. The referee blew his whistle to signal a second goal.

"Sub!" Coach Scott shouted. Jacob jogged off the field.

"Sorry, Coach," he said, out of breath. "I've never played defender before."

"You'll have to do better if you want to stay on the squad."

Jacob paced the sidelines. *Will Coach give me a chance to prove myself?* he wondered.

"How much do you want to stay on the team?" Coach asked.

"A lot," said Jacob.

"Good. You're going to be my Terminator. Number Fourteen made two goals already. Do anything to stop him."

"I'll do my best."

"That's not good enough," said Coach. "You *will* stop him. Understand? Next time he goes down, make sure he doesn't get back up. Kick him in the knee. Make it look like an accident. Sub!" He pushed Jacob onto the field.

It's wrong to deliberately hurt someone, thought Jacob. *But if I don't, I'll be off the team.*

The next play, a midfielder tackled Fourteen. Jacob swung back his foot and slammed Fourteen in the leg. The player grabbed his knee, writhing in pain. No one saw, except his smiling coach.

Jacob acted casual, but he felt miserable.

Never again, he promised himself. *I'll play to win, but I'm not going to hurt somebody to do it.*

"My son, if sinners tempt you, don't give in to them."
Proverbs 1:10

What should you do if an authority figure wants you to do something wrong? Who sees *everything* that happens?
Also read Proverbs 1:10–19.

THE TERMINATOR (Part Two)

Number Fourteen's coach rushed onto the field and knelt beside him. "What happened, Troy?" he asked.

"Someone kicked me in the knee," Troy sobbed in pain.

"Who?" asked Coach. "Did he do it on purpose? He'll be thrown out of the league."

Jacob stood nearby. Fear lumped in his throat.

Coach Scott sauntered over. "How's your kid doing?"

Troy's coach faced Coach Scott with clenched fists. "I know you sent one of your 'terminators' after Troy."

"What?" Coach Scott tried to look innocent.

"Everyone in the league knows that Troy has knee problems. You told one of your 'terminators' to take him out."

Coach helped Troy stand up, then looked back at Coach Scott. "You wait. I'll prove it this time."

"Forget it, Coach," Troy said. Pain twisted his face.

Jacob glanced at Troy, and their eyes locked.

After the game, Jacob forced himself to apologize to Troy. "Why didn't you tell your coach what I did?"

"I'm a Christian. Every day my family and I pick one of God's traits and try to imitate it. We picked mercy this morning." Troy smiled. "So I *had* to forgive you."

Jacob dropped his eyes. "Thank you. I'm a Christian, too, even though I didn't act like one. I've already told Coach Scott that I won't play for him anymore. I'd rather play at a lower level than to hurt anyone again."

"Yeah," said Troy. "It's better to please God than a coach."

WWJ

Do not want what evil men have. Don't long to be with them. In their hearts they plan to hurt others." Proverbs 24:1–2

When have you tried to please people instead of God?
When have you done what was right in order to please God?
Also read Proverbs 24:1–2.

GETTING AWAY WITH IT

"Look what I bought," Jennie told her friend, Kim. She emptied her shopping bag on the bed. Out tumbled a fashion doll, two doll outfits, and a plush cat.

"How could you afford all that?" Kim asked.

"I've been saving my allowance," said Jennie.

Kim picked up the store receipt. "Look at this! You only paid for *three* things. The store forgot to charge you for the kitty."

"What?" Jennie looked at the receipt. "How did that happen?"

"Hey," said Kim with a grin. "You made out like a bandit."

"A bandit is right," said Jennie, loading her toys back into the shopping bag. "I need to go back and pay for it."

"You've got to be kidding!" said Kim. "It was *their* mistake."

Jennie shook her head. "If *they* charged *you* too much, wouldn't you want them to make it right and give you the money back?"

"Well, yeah," Kim said. "But they're a big company. They'll never miss it. Besides, everybody knows they charge too much."

Jennie started for the door with the bag of toys in her hand.

"I can't believe you're doing this!" said Kim, following her friend to the door. "They'll never know."

"But you know and I know and God knows," said Jennie. "I want to please God. Five dollars isn't much to pay for a clear conscience."

"Those who do what is right are guided by their honest lives."
Proverbs 11:3

Why is it important to be honest in all you do?
When have you been tempted to get away with something?
Also read Ephesians 4:24–30.

GOD'S LOVE & PROTECTION

How Did Noah Feel?

What You Need:

A Bible, a flashlight, and a large calendar

What To Do:

1. Take the Bible, flashlight, and calendar into a darkened room. Read Genesis 7:12–13 and Genesis 8:13–18.

2. Turn on the flashlight and talk about Noah. The window (light source) on the ark was shut for the first forty days. Did God tell Noah when the rain would stop? Did God tell Noah how long he would be on the ark?

3. How long did it rain? Count off forty days one by one on the calendar. Then keep turning pages on the calendar until you finish the entire year. Do you think Noah and his family ever wondered if God had forsaken them during that long year on the ark?

4. Thank God for His faithfulness and protection. Thank God for all the times He protected you when you didn't even know it.

WATER, WATER EVERYWHERE
(Part One)

Ben shivered and stretched his hands toward the fireplace of the campground's clubhouse. "Some reward *this* is—rafting in the rain! Next year I won't bother to memorize all those verses for the Sunday School contest."

Haley spread her sweatshirt on the hearth of the stone fireplace. "I hope this dries out by the time we're finished with lunch."

She and Ben lined up with twenty other campers for hot dogs and beans.

Mr. Stark, their Sunday School teacher, raised a large metal spoon to gain the kids' attention. "The river is rising. Mrs. Stark and I need to move the church vans to higher ground. Everyone stay here until we return."

After lunch, Haley and Ben played a couple of rounds of table tennis. Haley walked to the window, cupped her hands around her eyes, and peered out. "I thought Mr. Stark would be back by now."

The camp's floodlights lit the surrounding area.

"Hey, look!" Ben pointed outside. "Our tents are floating!"

"Forget that. Water's seeping into the clubhouse floor!"

The water rose quickly. Campers sloshed through ankle-deep water, stacking games and equipment on the tables and high cupboards. Fear crept into Haley's heart.

White-faced with worry, Ben grabbed Haley's arm. "Let's get out of here!"

She shook her head. "Where can we go? Let's stop and pray."

In knee-deep water, the campers formed a close circle and joined hands. "Dear Jesus, keep us all safe...help us...show us what to do."

"When I'm afraid, I will trust in you....I trust in God. I will not be afraid."
Psalm 56:3–4

How often do you pray together with others?
What do you do when you feel afraid?
Also read Psalm 34:4–7.

WATER, WATER EVERYWHERE
(Part Two)

Mr. Stark burst through the clubhouse door. "We must move to higher ground quickly," he told the campers.

Haley sighed with relief. The water in the clubhouse had already risen to her knees. She grabbed Ben's hand. The line of campers headed out the door into the cold, rainy darkness. Only the beam of Mr. Stark's flashlight showed the way.

Haley's sandaled feet felt numb as she struggled to walk in the waist-high water. Her foot slipped. She grasped Ben's hand even tighter. *What if I go under? I can't swim!*

"Hold your hands together above the water to keep your grip," Mr. Stark called to the shivering campers.

Fear gripped Haley's heart. "Help me, Jesus," she whispered. Then she started to sing softly, "Jesus loves me…" Soon the others joined in. The waist-high water receded to Haley's knees, and then to her ankles.

She saw a welcoming light from a barn up ahead where the church vans were parked.

Hurrah! Dry clothes and food. We're going to make it! Thank You, Jesus!

Everyone changed clothes, set out their sleeping bags in the barn, and fell asleep.

The next morning, Mr. Stark roused them. "We've found a road out of here that's not under water. Let's pack up and head home. But first, let's thank God for taking care of us."

When their prayers ended, Haley led them in one last song: "God is so good…God answers prayer, He's so good to me…"

WWJ

"Save me from the deep water I'm in. Don't let the floods cover me."
Psalm 69:14–15

When have you experienced trouble and hard times?
Why do you think God allows trouble to come into our lives?
Also read Isaiah 43:1–2.

SURPRISE STORM

"Help!" Caleb shouted into the wind. He hugged a thick limb high in his backyard tree. He had been reading a book when the breeze brushed his ears and fluffed his hair. It wasn't quite strong enough to stop him from reading. At least not yet.

Then a sudden wind ripped at the pages of his book. Small branches lashed against his back and his head.

Lightning flashed and thunder clapped.

Dust stung Caleb's eyes. The sky grew darker. A few small drops of cold rain began to fall. Then larger and larger drops, until the downpour drenched his clothes and his book.

"Help!" *Can anybody hear me? Dad, where are you?*

The howling wind swallowed his shout. Leaves whipped around him. The tree swayed. Caleb dropped his book to cling to the limb.

Just then, the front door opened and Dad ran out to the base of the tree. "Let go, son!" he called.

"I can't! It's too far down!" Caleb tightened his grip on the limb.

"I'll catch you," Dad shouted. He held up his arms.

Jesus, help me! Caleb prayed as he let go and dropped into Dad's arms. He clung to Dad all the way into the house.

"Dad, you know what? You're like Jesus. He's always there when I pray for Him to come."

WWJ

"God has said, 'I will never leave you. I will never desert you.'"
Hebrews 13:5

What are the "storms" in your life today?
Will you pray to the Lord and trust His care for you?
Also read Isaiah 43:3–7.

AUSTIN'S HEDGE

"Time to go shopping. Where's Austin?" Mom called to Heather through the screen door.

Heather leaned over from the branch of the backyard apple tree where she was reading a book. "He's inside helping Grandma," she told her mother.

"Grandma said he's with you." Mom stepped outside, and Heather jumped down from the tree.

"But I haven't seen him in over an hour," said Heather.

"Austin!" They took turns calling for Austin while they searched the house and the basement.

As Heather searched, she prayed, "Dear Jesus, surround Austin with a hedge of protection as You did for Job."

When she entered the kitchen, she heard Mom call 911.

"He's only two and a half years old," Mom told the operator.

"Grandma should stay here in case the police find Austin," said Heather. "Let's you and I drive around and look for him."

Heather and her mom drove for two hours. They kept praying aloud, "Dear Lord, please put a hedge of protection around Austin."

"Mom, look!" Heather pointed to a small group of teenagers walking on the sidewalk. Holding hands, they moved slowly with someone inside their circle.

It was Austin!

"He couldn't tell us where he lived," said one of the teenagers a few minutes later, "so we formed a hedge around him to protect him. We wanted to keep him safe until someone found him."

WWJ

"Have you not put a hedge around him and his household and everything he has?" Job 1:10 (NIV)

Who could you ask God to protect?
When has God answered a prayer you've prayed?
Also read Psalm 91:1–2.

ALONE ON THE BUS

Curtis rested his head against the backseat of the school bus. The rocking of the bus relaxed him. After a while, he stretched out in the seat. Using his backpack for a pillow, he fell asleep.

A sudden loud clang made him jerk upright. He opened his eyes and glanced around. For a moment, nothing looked familiar. Then he recognized the school bus.

But why is it empty? he wondered as he walked to the front and stepped outside. *Am I dreaming?*

On either side loomed rows of school buses—but no people.

"Hello?" No one answered, except his echo. Curtis ran to the steel garage door and pushed. It was locked. "Hey! Anybody here? Hel-lo?" Only his echo rang through the building.

Curtis panicked. He ran along the walls. He pounded on the windows and doors as he hollered for help. Through a window, he saw more parked buses and a chain-link fence—but no people.

"I'm trapped," he realized. "What am I going to do?"

Shaking with fear, he climbed into his bus and knelt in the aisle. "Jesus," he prayed. "I'm scared. Please, help me. And let me know You're here with me."

He calmed down, remembering Jesus' promise, "I am with you always." And long before the police unlocked the bus garage and found him, Curtis felt safe.

WWJ

"Don't worry about anything....Ask and pray....Then God's peace will watch over your hearts and your minds." Philippians 4:6–7

When have you felt worried? Did you remember to pray?
When have you experienced Jesus' peace?
Also read Philippians 4:4–7.

WHAT'S YOUR ATTITUDE?

Fruit of the Spirit Tree

What You Need:

A Bible, an old tree branch, a pencil, scissors, construction paper, string, and tape

What To Do:

1. Secure your "tree" in a large plastic food carton with dirt and rocks or florist's clay.

2. Read Galatians 5:22–23. Discuss how the fruit of the Spirit affects our lives and attitudes each day.

3. Cut out seven different fruit shapes from construction paper. Label each with the name of a fruit of the Spirit: love, joy, peace, etc. Use these as patterns. Make several copies of each fruit.

4. Set the stack of fruit beside your tree. Pray that God will grow His fruit of the Spirit in your lives. Every night this week have the family share times when they've seen the fruit of the Spirit demonstrated that day.

5. Write your findings on the back of the appropriate fruit. Hang it on the tree. See how full of fruit the tree is by the end of the week!

PEACE TALK

Logan edged around the rows of empty desks, making his way to his assigned seat. He kept his back to his teacher, Mrs. Krimm.

"Good morning, Logan," she said. "I asked you to come in early today so we could talk."

He opened his desk and pretended to search for a book.

Mrs. Krimm laid down her book and stood up. "Is there a problem between us, Logan?" she asked, walking toward him.

Three weeks ago, when Chad threw an eraser and hit Melanie, Mrs. Krimm blamed Logan. Even though Logan had insisted he didn't do it, she didn't believe him. She had held him in for recess to do an extra assignment.

Chad and Melanie told jokes about him after school.

Ever since then, Logan had avoided his teacher.

"I hope we can be friends." She stood beside his desk. "Tell me. Have I done something to offend you?"

Logan glanced up at her. Her eyes looked sad. He thought about how bad he felt when someone held a grudge against him or didn't understand him.

"You blamed me when Chad hit Melanie with an eraser," he told her. "You treated me…unfairly. And I felt hurt."

Mrs. Krimm studied him for a moment. "Sometimes it's hard for a teacher to see what really happens in the classroom. I did the best I could, but I see that I made a mistake. Now I understand why you're angry. Please forgive me."

Logan's bitterness drained away. "I forgive you."

Mrs. Krimm smiled and hugged Logan. "Thank you."

WWJ

"You must make allowance for each other's faults and forgive the person who offends you." Colossians 3:13 (NLT)

When have you been falsely accused or misunderstood?
How do you react when you are falsely accused?
Also read Colossians 3:12–17.

ALANNA'S RECORD

"That's the girl who beat all the boys last year!" Tommy told Alanna as they stretched on the grass beside the track. They were warming up for the annual mile race between the area grade schools. "And I hear she can beat anybody."

Alanna tightened one of her shoelaces. *How would I feel if that new girl beat me?* She thought for a moment, then shook her head, even though Tommy wasn't watching. *That probably wouldn't make me feel bad. I just want to do my best and glorify God.*

"On your mark," the official called. Alanna took her position on the starting blocks beside the new girl.

"Get set!" Alanna licked her lips and took a deep breath.

"Go!" The gun went off. Alanna's feet pounded the track.

She soon pulled ahead of everyone—except the new girl. Side by side they ran. Chins up. Arms swinging. Near the finish, Alanna strained every muscle and ran just a little faster.

But the new girl won by inches.

Dad hurried over with his stop watch. "Alanna, you beat your record by twenty seconds!"

"I did? Wow!" She smiled and gave Dad a hug. "Let's go meet the winner. She's great! Without her, I don't think I would have broken my record."

"Most people are motivated to success by their envy of their neighbors."
Ecclesiastes 4:4 (NLT)

When have you been motivated by envy of someone else?
What (or who) makes you want to do your best?
Also read Hebrews 12:1–2.

TEACHER TROUBLE

"My math teacher is a real pain!" Brandon told his mom.

"Mrs. Clark? Why? What did she do?"

Brandon peeled a banana. "We only started fractions two days ago, right? Mrs. Clark wrote a problem on the board and asked me a question about it. I said I didn't know the answer. She said to quit daydreaming and pay attention. I told her I didn't understand fractions. But she just asked me the same question again."

"Were you paying attention?"

"Yes! But I don't get fractions. I think Mrs. Clark stinks."

"You can't always run from problem people, honey. Some day you might have a boss like Mrs. Clark." Mom sat down at the table beside him. "Are you willing to try an experiment?"

He shrugged.

"Try changing one thing in this situation—your attitude. You can't change your class or the math assignments. You can ask God to change you. What about going to Mrs. Clark and respectfully asking for her help?"

"I hate asking for help," said Brandon.

"Don't you think it's worth a try?" asked Mom.

The next day, before class, Brandon took his math worksheet to the teacher's desk. "Would you please help me, Mrs. Clark? I try to do these fractions, but I keep getting stuck."

Mrs. Clark smiled. "Of course I'll help you. Show me where you need help."

Before the opening bell rang, Brandon returned to his desk and finished his assignment. *Asking for help isn't so bad. And Mrs. Clark isn't so bad, either. This attitude experiment really paid off!*

WWJ

"Get rid of your old way of life...be made new in your thinking."
Ephesians 4:22–23

What situation in your life needs to be changed?
What attitudes would God want to help you change?
Read Psalm 119:65–66.

WHY DOESN'T DAD LOVE ME?

Frank felt left out. He stood in the doorway while his dad and little Jonah shared popcorn and watched football on TV.

"May I have some popcorn, too?" asked Frank.

"It's in the kitchen," Dad said without taking his eyes off the football game.

"Who's winning?" asked Frank. Dad ignored him.

A wide receiver caught a long, high pass at the two-yard line. Dad whooped and tousled little Jonah's hair.

"Touchdown next play, huh?" said Frank, his last try for his dad's attention—and affection.

Dad didn't answer. He leaned forward as the quarterback kept the ball and dived into the end zone.

"Touchdown!" Dad leaped to his feet, lifting little Jonah with him—both of them laughing.

Frank shuffled to his room. He stared out the window at the rain. Soon, little Jonah brought in a bowl heaped with popcorn.

"Thanks," said Frank. His little brother gave him a big hug and hurried out.

At least my brother loves me, thought Frank. And then, through his pain, he remembered that God loves him, too. He still missed his dad's touch. But remembering God's love

"The Lord loves us very much....His great love is new every morning. Lord, how faithful you are!" Lamentations 3:22–23

When have you felt like you weren't loved by other people? What helps you remember that God loves you? Also read Lamentations 3:22–26.

TOUGH GUY

"I'll be gone for a couple of minutes," Mrs. Kelner told her class. "Stay in your seats and read quietly till I get back."

When the door closed behind her, Ethan climbed onto his chair. He stood tall and puffed out his chest. "Last night I caught a cobra just before it bit my sister. I grabbed it right behind the eyes so its fangs couldn't get me. Then I cut off its head."

Someone called out, "If you're such a tough guy, swallow that goldfish."

Ethan looked over at the fish in the aquarium. Then he looked at his classmates. They all watched him, waiting to see what he would do. He glanced at the clock.

Mrs. Kelner will be back any minute now. I don't really want to do this. But I don't have a choice. Here goes.

Ethan scooped the fish out of the aquarium and dropped it into his mouth. The fish felt slimy on his tongue. He shut his eyes and forced himself to swallow. The fish wriggled in his stomach.

He clapped a hand over his mouth to keep from throwing up.

Just then, the class heard Mrs. Kelner's high heels approaching in the hallway. They flipped open their books and pretended to read.

Ethan's stomach churned. *Yech. There's a fish swimming in there.*

When Mrs. Kelner walked in, Ethan threw up.

"*Eww!* Gross!" Several students jumped onto their seats, others pointed and giggled.

Ethan watched the goldfish flop in the mess on the floor.

His face burned. *I lost more than my breakfast,* he realized. *I lost my classmates' respect. So much for trying to be a tough guy.*

"If a man is proud, he will be made low....But if he isn't proud, he will be honored." Proverbs 29:23

What can you do when you are tempted to brag and be proud? When have you been humbled and "made low"?
Also read James 4:6–8.

SHINE LIKE JESUS

Salt and Light

What You Need:

A Bible, a salt shaker, a flashlight, a deep metal pan (that fits over the flashlight)

What To Do:

1. Read Matthew 5:13–16 and discuss.

2. Use the salt shaker to explain how salt makes food taste better. In Bible times, salt that lost its flavor was thrown out on the roads and trampled.

3. Use a flashlight to show the importance of light. Turn off the lights. Hide the flashlight under the pan. Sit in the dark and talk about why light is important. Next, hold the flashlight high to light a broader circle.

4. How can we be like salt and light to the world? How can we "flavor" the world by doing what Jesus would do? How do each of us make the world a better place to live? Why does Jesus want us to shine with His love? (So others will learn to know Him.)

5. Pray that God will use you as salt and light to your friends and neighbors.

JESUS IN ME

"I don't want to leave!" Melissa set her suitcase down on the front porch of the orphanage.

"I love the kids in this orphanage," she told her father. "This mission trip has taught me to love Africa." Tears filled her eyes as she watched the little children playing in the dirt.

"Missy, Missy! Don't go!" A five-year-old boy ran up and threw his arms around Melissa.

She lifted him up in her arms and hugged him tightly.

He kissed her cheek and whispered, "I love you."

The orphanage director standing nearby said, "Jim, why don't you show Melissa where Jesus is."

The boy pointed to his chest. "Jesus is in my heart."

His smile faded. "I'll miss you," he said, giving her another hug.

Melissa's voice broke. "I'll miss you, too."

"Tell Melissa about your name," urged the director.

Jim grinned and pointed to his heart. "JIM!" he said proudly. He spelled out, "J-I-M." He paused. "It means 'Jesus-in-me!'"

He pulled a small yellow truck out of his pocket and handed it to Melissa. "It's for you. Don't forget Jim."

Melissa remembered what the orphanage director had told her when she first arrived: "Jim was left at our front door when he was only a year old. He wore a diaper. And he clutched that yellow truck that he plays with all the time."

She wanted to tell Jim, "No! I won't take your precious toy." But she couldn't hurt him by rejecting his gift of love.

"I'll always treasure your gift, Jim," she said. "And I'll pray for you every day."

"Don't forget to do good. Don't forget to share with others. God is pleased with those kinds of offerings." Hebrews 13:16

How can you "do good" so that others will see Jesus in you? When have you given away something that meant a lot to you? Also read 1 Corinthians 13:4–5.

JACK-O'-LANTERN

"I'll get the knife!" Clay ran toward the kitchen drawer.

"No," said Simon, his big brother. "You're not old enough." He placed an oversized pumpkin on the newspaper-covered floor. "Here's a marker. You draw the face and I'll cut it out."

With the marker, Clay drew eyes, a nose, and a large, toothy mouth. Simon sliced off the top to make a lid.

"Now we can scoop out the insides." He handed Clay a spoon. "Here, put the gunk in this bowl."

Clay scowled. "Yuck! I'm not going to touch that slimy stuff!"

"If you don't, I can't carve the face and stick a candle inside."

Reluctantly, Clay helped Simon dig out the gooey pulp. Then Simon cut out the pumpkin's face and pressed a candle inside.

The two boys carried the jack-o'-lantern to the front porch, where Simon lit the candle. "See? By cleaning out the nasty gunk inside, we made room for the light."

Clay stared at the glowing pumpkin. "Last week, our Sunday School teacher said we couldn't shine for Jesus if we had sin in our hearts." He added quietly,  "I want Jesus to clean all the gunky sin out of my heart. Then He can shine through me."

Clay grinned at his older brother. "Hey! This pumpkin just taught me a Sunday School lesson!"

WWJ

Jesus said, "You are the salt of the earth....You are the light of the world." Matthew 5:13–14

How does Jesus take the sin from your life?
How are you a light in your home and in your neighborhood?
Also read Matthew 5:14–16.

NEVER TOO YOUNG

"Why do *I* have to come along?" Andy slouched in the front seat of the van. "I don't speak Chinese."

"You'll enjoy Mount St. Helens visitors' center. And all of our Chinese guests speak English. Maybe you'll get to tell one of them about Jesus."

"But I'm just a kid," said Andy. "No one will listen to *me.*"

"You never know. Sometimes children can talk about Jesus with people who won't listen to adults."

Later, Andy sat next to Miss Han. She talked about her home in China and asked questions about America. She asked Andy, "Tell me about your favorite American holiday."

Andy said, "My favorite holiday is Easter Sunday. On Good Friday, we remember that Jesus died on the cross to take the punishment for our sins. On Sunday, we have a church service at sunrise. We sing songs to celebrate Jesus rising from the dead. We'll give you a Chinese Bible so you can read all about it."

Months later, Andy received this letter from Miss Han: "Dear Andy. Thank you for telling me about Jesus. I am reading the Bible you gave me. I have decided to become a Christian."

Andy gave his mom a high-five. "Who would've thought a Chinese teacher would listen to me…an American kid!"

NOTE: Miss Han continued to write to Andy. She returned to China and led many people to the Lord. She came back to the United States and taught English as a second language, using the Bible for a textbook. Now she teaches in Canada and tells her students about Jesus.

WWJ

"Don't let anyone look down on you because you are young. Set an example… in what you say and in how you live." 1 Timothy 4:12

With whom have you shared the news of Jesus?
What would you tell someone about Jesus?
Also read John 4:35–38.

T-SHIRT DILEMMA

"This one is cool." Aaron held up a gray T-shirt with a cartoon angel blowing a trumpet. "How much is it?"

"Fourteen bucks," Pastor Mike replied. "That's a bargain."

"I'll take it." Aaron dug into his pants pocket and counted a ten-dollar bill and four crumpled ones into Pastor Mike's hand.

"Thanks." Pastor grinned. "Do you think you could talk your friend here into buying a shirt, too? It's for our youth group retreat."

Aaron's friend Brett lowered his eyes. "My family can't afford it."

Pastor Mike laid his hand on Brett's shoulder. "I'm sorry, son. Pick one out for yourself. I'll pay for it."

Brett smirked as he chose a T-shirt with JESUS IS THE TRUTH written across the back.

Aaron's stomach turned. He knew Brett's family owned a house with a three-car garage and a swimming pool. Pastor Mike rented a two-room apartment.

On their way home Aaron told Brett, "You have a choice. Apologize to Pastor Mike and pay for the shirt—or hand the shirt over to me now!"

Brett pulled money out of his pocket.

"I wondered if you'd say something. You're not only dragging me to church—now you're making me honest."

"The path of honest people takes them away from evil. Those who guard their ways guard their lives." Proverbs 16:17

Why is it important to tell your friends when they are doing wrong? In what situations do *you* need the courage to speak out?
Also read Proverbs 16:18–22.

UNCLE GEORGE

Serena sank into Uncle George's maroon leather couch and pulled her little sister Meg onto her lap.

"Thank you for the ferry boat ride, Uncle George," Serena said. She loved spending time with her favorite uncle.

"You're quite welcome." He lit another cigar. "Tomorrow, we'll go to the zoo."

"Go give Uncle a hug," Serena whispered in Meg's ear.

Her little sister shook her head.

"No!" she whispered to Serena. "His cigar smells bad."

Serena was glad that Uncle George hadn't heard what Meg said about him.

Uncle George puffed on his cigar and smiled at the girls from across the room. Circles of smoke swirled around his face.

Serena sneezed. Meg coughed.

Putting his cigar in the ashtray holder, Uncle George laughed at the girls. He held out his arms. "Sit with me, little Meg. I'll read you a book."

"No!" She shook her head and leaned against Serena. "You smell yucky!" she told him.

Serena gasped. Uncle George looked as if someone had tossed ice water on him. "Wh-what? Do you really think I stink?"

"*You* don't stink," explained Serena. "Meg just doesn't like your cigars. I hope she didn't hurt your feelings. We both love you, Uncle George. We wouldn't want to make you sad."

"I like Meg's hugs better than any old cigar!" Uncle George tossed his half-smoked cigar in the garbage.

And he never smoked again.

WWJ

"Wounds from a friend can be trusted."
Proverbs 27:6

How easy is it for you to tell the truth when it hurts?
Who has told you something true that hurt you?
Also read Proverbs 16:23–25.

GOD LOVES YOU

Gift or Payment?

What You Need:

A Bible, several coins of the same denomination (dimes, nickels, quarters), paycheck stub, gift tag

What To Do:

1. Show paycheck stub to family. Ask if anyone knows what it is. Be sure everyone understands it is a record of payment for work that has been done. Then show the gift tag. What is a gift? Why do we give gifts? (Talk about how a gift is freely given out of love.)

2. Instruct one child to do a minor chore and pay him for it with a coin. Hand another child a coin of the same denomination without requesting him to work for it.

3. Hold out the paycheck stub and the gift tag. Let the children choose which child received payment for work and which received a *gift*.

4. Read Ephesians 2:8–9 and Romans 6:23. Discuss how salvation is a free gift of God, not something we earn. Pray and thank God for His free gift.

Variation: One child could perform both activities. Use small toys instead of money as payments and gifts.

A SHY GIRL'S SURPRISE

"I really don't want to go to Vacation Bible School," Dee told her mom. "I don't know anybody at that church. And I don't like going anywhere new by myself."

"Once you're there, sweetie, you'll have fun," said Mom.

Dee walked to the neighborhood church, still feeling shy about meeting strangers. As she neared the little white building, she could hear piano music coming through the open door. Her feet moved in rhythm.

Dee kept her eyes on the stairs as she walked down to the basement. She hoped no one was looking at her.

Downstairs, a dozen kids sat and sang in a half circle around an old piano. At that moment, Dee decided to go home even if that meant risking her mom's disappointment. As Dee turned around, she bumped into a young woman who smiled and said, "Hi. My name's Mrs. Lester. What's yours?"

Dee was trapped. She had no choice but to tell the young woman her name. "Welcome, Dee. Shall we go join the singing?" She took Dee's hand and walked her to the piano, where they sat and sang with the others.

One of the leaders stood up and acted out the exciting Bible story of Samson. Then Mrs. Lester helped Dee learn a Bible verse and make bead jewelry. All too soon, it was time to go home.

"Mom!" Dee shouted as she ran into the house.

"You had fun, didn't you?"

"I can't wait to go back tomorrow. But right now, I want to get out our Bible and read the story of Samson."

WWJ

"We used to enjoy good friendship as we walked with the crowds at the house of God." Psalm 55:14

Why does God want you to get together with other Christians? What can you do to welcome visitors at your church?
Also read Hebrews 10:19–25

CARD FROM MOM

"Why would I want a card from *her?*" Kelli asked. She dropped the postcard onto the table.

"Your mom does the best she can," Dad replied quietly.

"Then where has she been the last six years?" Kelli sniffled. "There must be something wrong with me if my own mom doesn't even want me."

"It's not your fault, honey." Dad took Kelli in his arms. "You need to understand that your mom has problems."

"Then why doesn't Jesus help her?"

"She has to ask Him. She has to let Him."

Kelli wiped her teary eyes and wet cheeks. "She doesn't want to, does she? And I know she doesn't love me."

"I can't answer for your mom. But *I* love you," said Dad.

"I know." She pressed her face against his shirt.

"God loves you, too. You're precious to Him."

"I forget that sometimes," she said, picking up her mom's postcard. "I still love her—even if she isn't much of a mom."

"That's called unconditional love," Dad said. "When you know how very much your Heavenly Father loves you, you can pass that love on to others—even when they've hurt you."

Kelli nodded. "I guess I'll go ahead and write Mom back."

WWJ

"How great is the love the Father has given us so freely!"
1 John 3:1

How does your Heavenly Father's love comfort you?
Who shows you God's love? To whom do you show God's love?
Also read 1 John 3:1–6, 16.

WHERE ARE YOU, DAD?

Did you show up this time, Dad? As Kyle looked over at the risers, the pitcher threw the ball. "Strike one!"

"Eyes on the ball!" shouted Nathan, another teammate.

Kyle turned toward the pitcher too late. "Strike two!"

Concentrate, Kyle told himself. *Make Dad proud.* This time he hit the ball. Kyle ran as it sailed high into left field. The ball tipped the outfielder's glove. Kyle ran across third base just as the outfielder fired the ball. Kyle headed for home, running hard. He dove for home plate.

"Safe!" yelled the referee.

Kyle scanned the risers. *Where are you, Dad?*

With one last surge of hope, Kyle scanned the hillside behind home base. *I made a home run, Dad, and you missed it....*

Returning to the dugout bench, Kyle stared at his sneakers. He didn't watch the rest of the game.

"Way to go!" said Nathan. "We won!—Hey, what's wrong?"

"My dad...he didn't show up...again," said Kyle.

"Neither did mine."

"Don't you care?"

"Sure. I care a lot," said Nathan. "But I know that my dad's not perfect. My Sunday School teacher says there's only one perfect father—and that's God. He never fails us."

Kyle stared at the ground again.

"Why don't you come to Sunday School with me?" Nathan asked. "You'll learn all about your Father in Heaven...the One who never lets you down."

Kyle looked into his teammate's beaming face. "Okay," he said, with just the hint of a smile.

WWJ

"My father and mother may desert me, but the Lord will accept me."
Psalm 27:10

When you are disappointed in people, will you depend on God? Why can you trust that God won't ever fail or forsake you? Also read Isaiah 49:13–16.

DADDY

Nathan pulled his little sister close in their dark hiding place under the stairs. "Don't be afraid, Abby," he whispered. "Jesus will keep us safe."

From the kitchen they heard Dad shout and dishes break. Nathan felt as if his heart broke with every dish.

"I wish Daddy never got drunk," Abby whimpered.

"Me, too."

"We pray for him," said Abby. "Why doesn't he stop drinking?"

"I don't know," said Nathan. "But we need to keep praying."

Silence in the kitchen now. Suddenly, they heard their father's heavy footsteps on the stairs directly overhead. Nathan's heart thumped, even though he knew Dad wouldn't find them.

When the house was quiet, Abby asked, "Is it safe yet?"

"Soon," Nathan whispered.

Then he pulled his little sister close. "You know what, Abby? God is our Heavenly Father who never drinks. He's with us all the time. He loves us. He always takes care of us, even when Dad doesn't. And He watches over us when Dad drinks."

"I'm glad God is here," said Abby. "He's taking care of us. I think I'm ready to go to sleep."

"Lord, you are like a shield that keeps me safe....I lie down and sleep.... because the Lord takes care of me." Psalm 3:3, 5

How do you know God loves you even during times of trouble? Why can you be certain that God cares for you at all times? Also read Psalm 27:1—5.

CAMP QUESTION

"Are you a Christian?" Roddy asked his cabin partner on the way to the campfire sing-along.

"Oh yes," replied Kevin.

Roddy had his doubts. *I don't think he is a Christian. I'd like to help him become one.* "When did you get saved, Kevin?"

"I grew up a Christian. My parents are Christians. So am I."

"Well, that's not exactly the way it works," said Roddy quietly.

"I know a lot about Jesus. And I go to church every Sunday."

"But Kevin, you never pray out loud in our prayer groups."

"I just think good thoughts," said Kevin.

"We've been roommates for five days now," said Roddy. "And I've never seen you read that Bible you carry around."

"Well, I don't read it, but I pretty much know what it says."

"Did you ever ask Jesus to forgive all your sins?"

Kevin thought a moment. "Not really."

"So you've never asked Him to be your Savior?" Kevin shook his head. "Then you're not really saved. Would you like to be?"

Kevin shrugged, then he nodded.

They neared the campfire, where the others were singing.

"Right now, why don't we stop," said Roddy. "If you tell Jesus you're sorry for all the bad things you've done, He'll forgive you. Then ask Him to be your Savior."

Kevin sat down on a log with Roddy.

After he prayed, he looked up with a big smile and asked, "I'm a Christian now, aren't I?"

Roddy nodded, also with a big smile, and shook the hand of his brand new "brother."

WWJ

"[The jailor] asked, 'Sirs, what must I do to be saved?' They replied, 'Believe on the Lord Jesus. Then you and your family will be saved.'" Acts 16:30–31

When did you accept Jesus as your own personal Savior?
How can you be sure you are a Christian?
Also read Romans 10:8–15.

GOD'S PROVISION

Deprivation Dinner

What You Need:

A Bible, a pot of cooked rice, a small bowl and a spoon for each person

What To Do:

1. Gather at the dinner table. Spoon half a cup of rice into each bowl. Talk about children in other countries who eat only one half cup of rice during an entire day. (Show pictures if possible.)

2. Eat your rice while you talk about the many ways God blesses you. Thank Him for food and health.

3. Read Deuteronomy 28:1–6.

4. Take time to pray for starving people. Pray for countries where there is famine, such as Sudan and North Korea. Pray for countries where hurricanes and flooding have ruined crops, such as China, Bangladesh, Honduras, and Guatemala. Pray for protection for all the workers who take food to starving people.

5. Take the money that your regular meal would have cost and give it to missions.

BLUE EYES

"Please, dear Jesus, please make my eyes blue." Amy finished her prayers and fell asleep. The next morning, she looked into the mirror and saw that her eyes were still brown.

"God hasn't answered my prayers," Amy told her mom later. "I asked for blue eyes. But look, they're still brown."

"When you ask Dad for something, does he always say yes?" Amy shook her head. "God is our loving Heavenly Father. He knows what's best for His children. Sometimes He tells us no."

Amy grew up and became a missionary to India.

One day, a girl rushed into Amy's room. "Please let me stay here. My mother sold me to the temple priests, but I ran away because they beat me." On the backs of her hands were burn marks from a hot branding iron.

Amy was determined to help save the temple slave children.

"I'm going there tonight," she told a missionary friend.

The friend grabbed Amy's arm. "No! Foreigners who are caught in the temple are severely beaten. Some are killed!"

"God loves those children!" Amy stained her hands and face with coffee, then pulled her shawl across her face.

"With your dark hair and brown eyes, you look just like an Indian woman!" said Amy's friend.

At that moment, Amy knew why God had not answered her prayer for blue eyes when she was a little girl. *Thank you, God, for answering no. You knew what was best.*

Amy visited the temple that night and rescued another girl. During the following years, Amy Carmichael (1867–1951) rescued many babies and children from lives of temple slavery.

"Lord, you are my God....You have done wonderful things. You had planned them long ago." Isaiah 25:1

Why can you trust God, even when He says no?
What are you trusting God to work for good in your life?
Also read Romans 8:28, 31–39.

A VEGGIE LESSON

"Why are the Linders coming to dinner?" Angie frowned as she counted out five extra dinner plates. "We barely have enough food for ourselves."

"Somehow God always provides," replied her mom, looking through the kitchen cupboard. "We have a couple of cans of tuna. I could make that go further with a white sauce and serve it over homemade biscuits."

Angie wrinkled her nose. "It would taste better with peas and carrots…which we don't have. Plus, there's nothing for dessert."

She set plates on the counter and thought, *The Linders know Dad is out of work. How could they just invite themselves to dinner? It's not fair.*

Twenty minutes later, Angie heard a car door slam. She peered out the kitchen window.

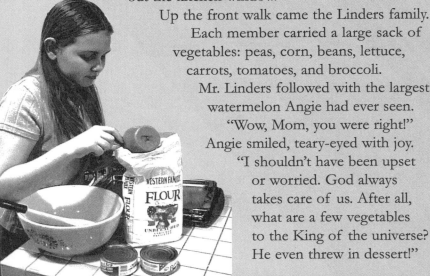

Up the front walk came the Linders family. Each member carried a large sack of vegetables: peas, corn, beans, lettuce, carrots, tomatoes, and broccoli.

Mr. Linders followed with the largest watermelon Angie had ever seen.

"Wow, Mom, you were right!" Angie smiled, teary-eyed with joy. "I shouldn't have been upset or worried. God always takes care of us. After all, what are a few vegetables to the King of the universe? He even threw in dessert!"

"My God will meet all your needs….Give glory to our God and Father for ever and ever. Amen." Philippians 4:19–20

What needs do you have today?
Will you pray and trust God to meet those needs?
Also read Philippians 4:10–14.

GOD'S WATCH DOG

The mantle clock chimed ten. "Mom and Dad should have been home before now," Allison told her dog, Tippy. "They promised to be back at nine-thirty."

The house creaked and moaned. *Why did I tell Mom I was old enough to stay by myself?* Allison checked the front door. It was locked.

"We're being silly, Tippy. God will protect us." Tippy dropped his ball at her feet. She tossed it, and he brought it back.

Allison glanced at her watch. Five minutes after ten. "We don't have to be afraid. God is watching over us, remember?"

Tippy ran to the kitchen cupboard where his dog treats were stored. "Oh, all right," said Allison. "Roll over." He rolled over. "Good boy!" She gave him a treat.

"Play dead." This time, instead of obeying, Tippy scurried to the patio door and barked at the curtain.

Allison laughed. "You won't get a treat for barking."

The little fox terrier looked into Allison's eyes, then turned back to the door and barked furiously. "Tippy, stop it! You'll bother the neighbors." He continued to bark.

"What is the problem, you crazy dog?" She pulled open the curtain and flipped on the backyard light. Her heart nearly burst.

On the lawn stood a man wearing a black mask. Allison screamed. Tippy barked with renewed fury. The man in the mask ran, jumped over the fence, and disappeared into the night.

Allison breathed so hard that she felt dizzy. She sank to the floor and pulled Tippy close.

"Good dog, good dog. God used you to protect me."

WWJ

"The Lord helps me. I will not be afraid. What can a mere man do to me?"
Hebrews 13:6

How do you deal with your fear?
How can you help others to trust God and not be afraid?
Also read Proverbs 3:25–26.

SPECIAL DELIVERY

I hate this place already! Cindy thought as she stared out the car window. Her father stopped the car in front of a small white church. *It's awful here. This town is so small even God couldn't find it!*

Her dad turned off the engine. "Let's thank God for a safe trip and ask Him to bless our new life here."

Cindy clenched her teeth. *I'll pray, all right! God, how could You make me leave my friends and my home? Why did You send us here?*

"...and I thank You, Lord," prayed her dad, "for directing us to the honest mechanic who fixed our car..."

Dad spent our last dollar fixing this car. He only has seventy-six cents left in his pocket! That's not even enough to buy one dinner.

"...and please give us this day our daily bread...." A knock on the car window cut short Dad's prayer. A mailman standing outside the car said, "I have a letter for Reverend Patterson. Is that you?"

Dad nodded and took the envelope. "How did this reach us?" he asked. It read, "Reverend David Patterson, West Fork, Colorado." There was no street address.

When Dad opened it, he found a hundred-dollar bill.

Dad laughed. "God knew we needed money before we did! He had it here waiting for us. Thank You, Lord!"

Okay, God. So You do know where this town is. And You do care for us. I guess I can trust You to help me like it here.

"Put yourselves under God's mighty hand....Turn all your worries over to him. He cares about you." 1 Peter 5:6–7

What have you worried about recently?
What do you do when you worry?
Also read Matthew 6:31–33.

MYSTERY MONEY

"Dad, I'm worried. You haven't worked since you hurt your back. How will we live?" Marty knelt by his dad's recliner chair.

"God runs our lives, son. Whenever I start to worry, I try to remember that God wants to bless us, not hurt us. God gave food and water to the Israelites in the wilderness. God refilled a poor widow's flour barrel during a famine. He can do that for us, too."

After school the next day, Marty found a sack of groceries on their doorstep. He and his mom unpacked flour, sugar, eggs, milk, orange juice, and a loaf of homemade banana bread.

Mom smiled. "See how God provides? He laid it on someone's heart to share with us." Marty ate a slice of banana bread while Mom emptied the small sack of flour into a canister. "Mom, may I use that flour sack?" asked Marty.

With a marking pen he wrote "God Provides" on the sack. He laid it on the living room mantle where everyone could see it.

"This is our widow's flour barrel," Marty said.

In the mailbox the next day, Marty found a fifty-dollar bill. He stashed it in the flour sack. Then a cousin sent a check for an overdue debt. Into the sack it went, along with an unexpected income tax return check from the government.

Three months later, Marty's dad returned to work. The night of his first day on the job, Dad said, "I kept track of the money we received while I was out of work. Praise God! The amount each month came to within ten dollars of my paycheck!"

Marty grinned and patted the flour sack. "Thank You, God, for refilling our widow's flour barrel!"

"I know the plans I have for you," announces the Lord. *"I want you to enjoy success....I will give you hope for the years to come."* Jeremiah 29:11

Have you thanked God for planning good things for your life?
How can you be sure God has good plans for you?
Also read 1 Kings 17:8–16.

FOLLOWING THE CROWD

You Are a Star!

What You Need:

> A Bible, cardboard, scissors, a pattern in the shape of
> a star, a pencil, aluminum foil, glue, and glitter

What To Do:

1. Read Ephesians 2:10.
   Talk about each of us being stars in God's kingdom.
   Why is each one of us a special masterpiece of God?
   Do you see yourself as God's masterpiece?
   Name some people who are called "stars" (movie
   stars, sports stars, rock stars).

2. Have each family member trace around the star-
   shaped pattern. Cut the star out of the cardboard.
   Cover the cardboard stars with aluminum foil.

3. Write family members' names in glue on their stars.
   Sprinkle with glitter. Hang on bedroom door or wall
   or on the refrigerator to remind each person that he
   or she is special.

Variation: Write names with yarn; glue to the star.
Or cut letters of each name out of shiny gift wrap.
Or simply write the name on a piece of paper and
glue it to the star. Decorate!

MAILBOX MADNESS (Part One)

"To join our gang," said Franklin, "you have to knock down five mailboxes." He handed Gordy a baseball bat.

Gordy glanced at the gang of older boys and nodded.

At the first driveway on the block, he grasped the bat with both hands and swung. The mailbox fell with a clang. The boys cheered. Gordy smiled. *All right! These guys like me!*

He smashed three more mailboxes. Gene laid his arm around Gordy's shoulder. "One more mailbox, and you're *in*."

Gordy felt bad about what he was doing. But when the guys cheered, he felt accepted. He felt like part of their gang.

At ol' man Hensen's house, the clang of wood hitting metal echoed in the night. Truck headlights approached from up the street. The truck pulled into the driveway. Ol' man Hensen stepped out. "Who wrecked my mailbox? Tell me…or tell the *police*."

The gang members looked at Gordy. Through a throat as dry as sandpaper, he croaked, "I…I did."

Soon Gordy faced his father's grim questioning. "What? You wrecked *how* many mailboxes? Why?"

"Five." Gordy looked at the floor. "I can't believe it, either, Dad. I was a real jerk. It was wrong to do it."

"You'll have to apologize to the neighbors and replace their mailboxes. You'll be doing major chores for months to cover the expense. I'm disappointed in you, son. Why did you want to hang around with those boys?"

"To feel like I belonged to their gang, I guess. I've learned not to hang out with guys like that. I want to be satisfied with belonging to Jesus…even when others don't accept me."

WWJ

"Do not envy violent people; don't copy their ways."
Proverbs 3:31 (NLT)

Have you ever been urged by others to do the wrong thing? What did you do? What did you learn from that experience? Also read Proverbs 3:29–32.

MAILBOX MADNESS (Part Two)

"Tell my son how it feels to have your mailbox bashed in, Mrs. Lewen."

"It's terrifying," she said. Her eyes brimmed with tears. "I have a young daughter, as you know. And I was afraid that the person who smashed our mailbox might attack *us!*"

Gordy's face burned with shame. "I'm sorry, Mrs. Lewen. I never meant to scare you. Please forgive me."

They visited Mr. Burkett's house next. As they walked up the driveway, Gordy felt sick at the sight of the mangled mailbox hanging from its post.

Mr. Burkett pointed his bony finger in Gordy's face. "Do you know how many times I've replaced that mailbox? Four times! You punks like to destroy things others work hard for."

Three more times Gordy faced his neighbors, apologized, and asked their forgiveness. After visiting all five homes, he felt so ashamed that he cried. "I did more than wreck mailboxes. I scared or hurt those *people!*"

On Saturday, Gordy and his dad drove to the hardware store. They bought five new mailboxes, one wooden post, and a sack of cement. Together, father and son returned to each neighbor's house and replaced the battered mailbox. Mr. Burkett stood on his front porch, his arms folded across his chest, and frowned until his new mailbox was in place.

By the end of the day, Gordy's body ached and his blistered hands stung, but he felt good inside.

Thank You, God, for helping me do what's right. Now I can face my neighbors with a clear conscience.

"Cling tightly to your faith in Christ, and always keep your conscience clear."
1 Timothy 1:19 (NLT)

Have you done something wrong that you need to make right?
Are you putting Jesus or friends first in your life?
Also read Numbers 5:5–7.

TATTOO TROUBLE

"Look what I have!" Lisa pulled up her shirtsleeve.

Jenny stared at the small, fire-breathing dragon inked onto her friend's skin. "I can't believe your parents let you get a tattoo."

"They don't know about it," said Lisa.

"But you're only eleven. Didn't you have to get your parents' permission?"

"Trish's uncle is a tattoo artist. He gave it to me when I spent the night at her house on Friday. Trish has five tattoos!"

"Lisa! You're a Christian." Jenny shook her head. "I don't think that a dragon honors God."

"But it's my body!" Lisa folded her arms and glared at Jenny.

"No, it's not," said Jenny. "The Bible says our bodies belong to God. Didn't you give your life to Jesus?"

Lisa thought a moment. "Yes, I did. I guess I'd better tell my parents and ask their forgiveness. I should have talked to them about it instead of being sneaky." She looked at her shoulder. "Now I'm sorry I got this tattoo. It wasn't such a good idea."

Jenny lifted her bangs to show her forehead. "See this scar? I disobeyed my dad one time and rode my bike without a helmet. I hit a rock, flew over the handlebars, and cut my forehead open. This scar is permanent. But it reminds me to obey my parents. Your tattoo could remind you that your body belongs to God."

"Don't you know that your bodies are the temples of the Holy Sprit?...So use your bodies in a way that honors God." 1 Corinthians 6:19–20

How can you honor God with your body?
What reminds you that your body belongs to God?
Also read Romans 12:1–2; 14:7–8

WWJ

THE PAIN KILLERS

Jerry rubbed gel into his hair to form spikes. Looking in the bathroom mirror at his torn jeans and ripped T-shirt, he grinned.

His brother Mike walked by the door and looked inside.

"Hey! What are you doing? You look awful."

"Who do I remind you of?" asked Jerry. "Don't I look like I could be one of the Pain Killers?"

"The rock band?"

With his comb, Jerry tapped a rhythm on the sink. "Yes! I'm going to be their drummer some day. I've memorized their songs."

Mike met his brother's eyes in the mirror. "Did you listen to the news report this morning? The Pain Killers' lead singer died last night from an overdose of heroin. Is that how you want to end up?"

"It would never happen to me!" said Jerry.

"People don't *plan* to end up in trouble," said Mike. "But that lifestyle can lead to all kinds of it. You'd better rethink your goals, little brother."

Jerry stared at his reflection. A song he once heard on one of his brother's CDs played in his head: "I have decided to live like a believer; I'll turn my back on the old deceiver...."

Jerry spent some time talking to God while he rinsed the gel from his hair and brushed out the spikes.

"And do not bring sorrow to God's Holy Spirit by the way you live."
Ephesians 4:30 (NLT)

Whom do you admire? Who are your heroes?
Are they good or bad influences in your life?
Also read Ephesians 4:17–30.

MIXED MELONS

"Don't scatter the seeds all over, Olivia. Grandpa said to plant the watermelon and pumpkin seeds *separately.*" Rose knelt in the patch of dirt Grandpa had given her for her very own garden.

"I'm your guest," said Olivia. "You're supposed to do what *I* want! I don't want to plant seeds. I want to swing." She dropped the seeds on the ground and ran to the swing. Rose covered the seeds with soil and joined Olivia on the swing set.

During the next few months, Rose spent no time at Grandpa's house. Instead she went with Olivia and her family to the beach, the zoo, and all the latest movies.

At the end of summer, Rose finally visited her garden. It was overgrown with weeds. The watermelons looked weird—they were colored orange instead of green.

Grandpa cut one, and Rose tasted it. "Yuck!" She spit it out.

"How close together did you plant the watermelons and the pumpkins?" asked Grandpa.

"Well…I guess we planted them all in the same patch."

"That's the problem. They grew so close to each other that the bees cross-pollinated them. That can happen with Christians, too. If they spend too much time with the wrong people, they stop acting like Christians."

"Oh, Grandpa, that's me," said Rose. Tears filled her eyes. "I haven't even taken time to visit you. Some of the movies I saw wouldn't please Jesus. And now, when I'm angry, I swear like Olivia. We were so busy this summer that I didn't take time to read my Bible or go to church. I'm sorry. I want to live my life for Jesus. Please pray with me, Grandpa."

"Don't be fooled. You can't outsmart God. A man gathers a crop from what he plants….plant to please the Holy Spirit." Galatians 6:7–8

Do you influence others? Or do others influence you? What choices have *you* made about your activities and friends? Also read Galatians 6:4–8.

GOD KNOWS YOUR HEART

My Very Own Psalm

What You Need:

A Bible, paper, pencils or marking pens

What To Do:

1. Read a short Psalm, such as Psalm 1, Psalm 100, or Psalm 123. Explain that a psalm is a song. Talk through the meaning of the psalm you read.

2. Have each person write out the main idea of the psalm in his or her own words. Then ask everyone to write their personal song to God. (Let younger children draw pictures to express their thoughts.)

3. Let individuals share their psalms, or have the family write a psalm together.

Note: The parent may want to write their own psalm ahead of time as an example. Make your own family psalm book. Other psalms to include are Psalms 8, 19, 27, 34, 90, 91, and 121.

WWJ

LOST DOG (Part One)

"It's Friday!" Macey raced out of school. She stopped short when she saw a skinny, old golden retriever standing outside the school door.

"Why, you old dear. Are you lost?"

She knelt beside the dog and checked for a collar and tags. There were none. The dog looked at her with huge brown eyes.

Macey petted his matted hair. "You need a home. And you need someone to love you." Her heart soared.

I've prayed for a dog for years. Maybe God sent me this one!

"Would you like to be my dog? I'll name you Henny."

The old dog cocked his head at her and wagged his tail. He trotted beside her all the way to her house.

When Macey's dad got home, she told him all about finding the dog. "Please Dad—can we keep him? Please?"

"You must look for the dog's owner," Dad said firmly. "Besides, where would we put a dog?"

"We could keep him at Grandma's until you build a fence."

Dad smiled at Macey's persistence.

"We'll see," he said quietly.

Macey halfheartedly printed up "Dog found" signs to post in the neighborhood. She called the animal shelter. No missing dogs were reported. After a week, she and her parents agreed that Henny was now Macey's dog.

Macey hugged her mom and dad. "Thanks for helping my biggest dream come true! And thank You, dear God, for Henny."

WWJ

"When dreams come true, there is life and joy."
Proverbs 13:12 (NLT)

How does it feel to get something you've always wanted? What dreams and hopes are you waiting to have happen? Also read Psalm 37:3–4.

LOST DOG (Part Two)

"You're mine now, Henny," said Macey as she bathed the dog she'd found last week. She brushed the tangles from his golden coat, then buckled on his new collar.

Macey's dad called on the phone. "A man answered our ads about Henny. I'm pretty sure he's the dog's owner."

"No!" cried Macey. "Henny's mine. I love him!"

"I'm sorry. I'll come pick you and Henny up in an hour."

Macey threw her arms around Henny and sobbed. "How can I give you up? You're an answer to my prayers. I love you!"

An hour later, she stared out the van window, one arm around Henny. *Dear Jesus, please let me keep him. I can't give him up.* Then a thought popped into her mind. *Henny's owners love him too…maybe even more than I do.*

Dad drove to a house several blocks from Macey's school.

A little boy and his father answered the door. The boy held out his arms and cried, "Buffy! You're back! We missed you!"

The dog wagged its tail and strained against the leash Macey held. Her eyes filled with tears as she let go of the leash. With a loud yelp, Buffy rushed into the boy's arms and licked his face.

Mr. Williams explained to Macey, "We were out of town over the holiday weekend and left Buffy in the care of a neighbor. We returned to find Buffy gone. It broke our hearts." He showed them a collar still attached to a chain in front of the doghouse. "We think someone deliberately let Buffy go," he said.

Macey pulled three lollipops from her pocket. "Here," she said, handing them to the boy. "Lollipops cheer me up. Maybe they'll help make up for your sad days without Buffy. I took good care of him."

WWJ

"[God] comforts us in all our troubles. Now we can comfort others when they are in trouble." 2 Corinthians 1:4

When have you comforted someone?
Who needs God's comfort today?
Also read 2 Corinthians 1:3–7.

AN EASY "A"

"I'm Nick's study partner," Jarred told Nick's mom when she opened the front door. "Miss Wilson gave us a history report to work on together."

Nick heard Jarred's voice and came downstairs. "Hi, Jarred. Let's spread out our books and papers on the table over here."

"This report won't be much work," said Jarred, tossing a blue notebook onto the kitchen table. "Here. I 'borrowed' Valerie Brown's history project from last year. She got an A on it. And now so will we. With two hundred kids in Miss Wilson's class, she'll never know that we used Valerie's report."

Nick frowned. "I don't cheat," he said firmly.

Jarred laughed at him. "Don't worry. We won't get caught."

"That's not the point," Nick said. "I *won't* cheat."

Jarred rolled his eyes. "No way. Everybody cheats."

"Cheating's wrong," insisted Nick. "I could never respect myself if I cheated. And God wouldn't be happy with me, either."

"God? Well I see now why the teacher teamed us up," said Jarred. "She hopes you might rub off on me. Sorry to disappoint her. I'm not willing to give up an easy A in history for the sake of *your* conscience."

Nick handed the folder to Jarred. "Take this back. I don't want Valerie's report. I'm sorry you aren't willing to write a report together. I'll do one on my own."

WWJ

"We know that the law is good if it is used properly....It is made for those who break the law." 1 Timothy 1:8–9

Do you need rules to make you do what's right?
When have you been tempted to cheat?
Also read 1 Timothy 1:8–11.

JACOB'S BATTLES

"En garde!" Jacob thrust his rolled-up newspaper sword into Karl's stomach. His mom's words echoed in his brain: "Don't use anything as a weapon when you play. Our family is against violence."

Jacob ignored the twinge of his conscience. *I'm having too much fun to stop now,* he thought. *Besides, Mom will never know.*

At supper that evening, Jacob couldn't look Mom in the eye. Somehow, not even his favorite meal of corn on the cob tasted good.

"Is something wrong, Jacob?" Mom asked.

"No," he said. But inwardly, he cringed.

Oh great! Now I've added a lie to my disobedience. I have to stop this.

The next afternoon at Karl's house, a pinecone battle broke out—with Jacob in the thick of it. *Just one more time,* he told himself as he lobbed another pinecone at Karl's shield.

"What did you do today?" Mom asked when he got home.

"Played a board game," lied Jacob. He tried to watch a new video, but he couldn't concentrate. Finally he got up and went to his mom.

Tears filled Jacob's eyes as he confessed his disobedience and lying. "Once I started disobeying you, it only got worse. You didn't know what I'd done, but I realized God was watching."

Mom put her arms around Jacob. "I'm sad to find out you've been making wrong choices, but I'm proud that you've told me the truth."

"Anyone who hides his sins doesn't succeed. But anyone who admits his sins and gives them up finds mercy." Proverbs 28:13

Is your conscience urging you to confess a sin?
What happens when you try to cover up your disobedience?
Also read John 8:32.

TASTE BUDS (AND HEARTS) CHANGE

"I'm starved!" Trevor opened the refrigerator door.

"I don't want you to spoil your appetite. How about munching on a few carrot sticks?" Mom said.

"You know I hate carrots." He poured a glass of grape juice and sat down at the counter. "John's family got a letter from Shiro, their Japanese exchange student."

"Really?" His mother stirred the rice.

"Yep. Shiro met a girl from Russia who asked him about God. He showed her the Bible John's family gave him and told her about the *Jesus* film. While Shiro talked to her about Jesus, he finally made a decision—right then—to become a Christian! And so did she!"

"That's wonderful!"

"But, Mom, our exchange student stayed with us a whole year. But Gaku never accepted Jesus. We loved him, prayed for him, and took him to church, just like John's family did with Shiro." Trevor paused. "What did we do wrong, Mom?"

"Nothing, Trevor. It's Gaku's choice now."

Fifteen minutes later, the family sat down to eat.

"Mom! You put *carrots* in the stir-fry!"

"Why don't you *try* one?" his mother suggested. "Maybe you'll have a change of heart for carrots."

Trevor watched his older brother wolf down his food, carrots and all. He decided to give it a try. "Hmm, it doesn't taste too bad. In fact, it's pretty good!" Trevor scooped up another forkful.

"You know, Mom, I think Gaku is a lot like me. I'm going to keep praying for him until his heart changes. I hope he decides to give Jesus a try...like I did with the carrots."

"We work together with God....I tell you, now is the time God shows his favor. Now is the day he saves." 2 Corinthians 6:1–2

Is there someone you pray for who has not accepted Jesus? Keep praying! Only God changes hearts.
Also read 2 Corinthians 6:1–10.

GIVING HEARTS

Cup of Blessing

What You Need:

A Bible, a container (mug, cup, tin can, small plastic dairy carton), pens, construction paper, glue or scotch tape, scissors, stickers, and glitter

What To Do:

1. Talk about the meaning of the word *blessing* (Webster defines it as "a means of happiness" or "a gift"). Read Psalm 41:1 or Acts 20:35. Ask family members to list the blessings God gives them. Talk about how you can bless others.

2. Cut construction paper in the proper rectangular shape to cover the outside of the container. Print or write "Cup of Blessing" on the paper. Decorate it, and tape or glue it around the container.

3. Set a time period (a week, a month, etc.) to drop all spare change into your "Cup of Blessing." Choose a missionary or a charitable organization to receive the money. At the end of the time period, count the money together, then send a check for the amount with a handwritten note.

Variation: Count the money each week and keep an ongoing tally. Use the funds to shop for an organization that sends boxes of relief supplies.

CUP OF BLESSING

Harry frowned at the coins he had dumped onto the table from the big mug his family called the "Cup of Blessing."

"Couldn't we collect any more than $12.85? How many gloves will that buy for the homeless?"

His older brother Jess scooped the change into his pocket. "Money is tight around here right now. Come on. Mom is waiting in the car. Let's pray we can buy at least *one* pair of gloves."

Their mom dropped them off in front of the department store. "See if you can find a sale, boys. Then take the gloves over to the rescue mission. I'll meet you there in an hour."

One pair of gloves took all the money the boys had. On the way out of the store, they watched a little boy drop a quarter in the Salvation Army donation bucket. He smiled at the bell ringer. "It's my whole allowance! Merry Christmas!"

At the mission, the director thanked the boys for the gloves. Harry felt embarrassed. "It's not very much," he said.

The mission director replied, "It will mean a lot to a person on the street. Remember, Jesus praised the widow who could only give two pennies. And He fed thousands of people with one boy's lunch."

"You mean Jesus just wants us to give what we have…even if it isn't very much?" asked Harry.

The director smiled. "God multiplies little gifts into great blessings. He blesses those who receive—and those who give."

Harry grinned. "So *that's* why our mug is called the 'Cup of Blessing.' Giving makes *everyone* happy."

WWJ

"You shouldn't give because you are forced to. God loves a cheerful giver."
2 Corinthians 9:7

What is your attitude when you give? Are you a cheerful giver? How can you give generously this week?
Also read Mark 12:41–44.

UNCLE ERNEST

"Uncle Ernest, I'm here!" Jeannie ran to the back porch, where her great-uncle waited with pink lemonade and oatmeal-raisin cookies. She gave him a hug and sat down beside him with her paper bag on her lap.

Uncle Ernest offered her a plate of cookies.

As always, he said, "Take two, they're small." And as always, they laughed at his joke. She took several, then handed him her bag and said, "I brought something for you."

He looked inside. "More cookies? Oh, my."

"I baked them for you 'cause you always bake for me."

"Let's put them in the kitchen by the fried cakes and the muskmelon," he said. Jeannie giggled at his old-fashioned names for donuts and cantaloupe.

In the kitchen, they opened a can of tuna and fed Uncle Ernest's old calico cat. Then they strolled out into the garden to smell the roses and pick a bouquet of zinnias.

Over the red and yellow flowers, Jeannie gazed into her uncle's eyes.

"Uncle Ernest, you always make me feel special."

"You *are* special," he said and handed her a rose.

"When I grow up, I want to be just like you."

"That's good," said Uncle Ernest with a smile. "Because I want to be just like Jesus."

Jesus said, "I have given you an example. You should do as I have done for you." John 13:15

Whose example do you try to follow?
How can you set a good example for others to follow?
Also read John 13:12–17.

HOSPITAL VISITOR

"Would you give this to Bruce the next time you see him, please?" Isaac handed his teacher a new comic book.

"You and Bruce are good friends," said Mrs. Gimbel. "You should give the book to him yourself."

Isaac shuddered. "I don't like hospitals."

"Do you think Bruce likes them?"

"Oh no! He *hates* being in the hospital."

"It's too bad Bruce doesn't have a choice."

Isaac stared. He hadn't thought of it that way before.

That afternoon, the class made get well cards for Bruce. Isaac drew a spaceship on his card with colored pens. When he wrote "Get Well Soon" on the inside, he felt a stab of guilt.

It's crummy to send a card when I could visit Bruce in person. O Jesus, he prayed, *I need Your help to do this.*

Isaac stopped by the teacher's desk after school. "I'll go to the hospital with you, Mrs. Gimbel, if my mom says it's okay."

The next afternoon, they walked through the big glass entry doors of the hospital. When they stepped into Bruce's room, he grinned at them. "Hello! I'm glad you didn't forget me!"

Mrs. Gimbel handed him an envelope with all the cards.

"I hope this isn't my homework!" said Bruce.

"Your classmates made them for you."

Isaac handed Bruce the comic book.

"Is that Isaac, the hospital wimp? I thought you never wanted to go near a hospital. What are you doing here?"

"Making sure they treat you right," said Isaac. *This place isn't so bad,* he thought. *Anyway, it's great to be a blessing to Bruce.*

WWJ

"*Treat everyone fairly. Show faithful love and tender concern to one another.*"
Zechariah 7:9

Do you have a sick friend or family member who needs your help? How could you encourage him or her?
Also read Hebrews 13:16, 20–21.

WATER SACRIFICE

Oh no! Joe wet his pants! Robyn couldn't help noticing.

He sat across the aisle from her, his face a dull red. He looked close to tears. A dark wide stain striped the inside of his pant leg, ending beside his shoe in a yellow puddle.

I remember how the kids never stopped teasing me when I wet my pants in first grade. Dear Jesus, please show me how to help Joe.

Robyn glanced around the room. Her teacher and classmates were all absorbed in their work. She hurried to the back table, picked up the fishbowl, and carried it down the aisle.

When Robyn neared Joe's desk, she pretended to trip. She dumped the water across his lap and his shoes.

"All right, class, settle down!" said the teacher. "Somebody put that fish in water! Joe, go dry off! Penny, bring a mop! Hurry now!"

During recess, schoolmates giggled and told other students, "Robyn dumped the fishbowl water on a kid in our class!"

At lunch, no one ate with Robyn. After school, she stood alone, waiting for the bus.

Now they all think I'm dumb, but I'm not sorry I did it. Thank You, Jesus, that I could do something to help Joe.

WWJ

"Live a life of love, just as Christ did. He loved us. He gave himself up for us. He was a...scarifice to God." Ephesians 5:2

When have you sacrificed time or money for someone else?
What did Jesus sacrifice for you?
Also read Ephesians 5:1–2, 8–10.

MORE THAN ENOUGH

"Why are you throwing out unopened cartons of milk?" eleven-year-old Nevin asked the cafeteria lady. "Are they spoiled?"

"No. But at the end of lunchtime, we have to throw away any food we've set out that hasn't been eaten." She dumped an enormous bowl of fresh salad greens into the garbage.

"How can you waste all that food!" said Nevin. "I know that people here in the United States go hungry every day."

The cafeteria lady shook her head and shrugged. "We have to obey the government regulations."

"It's not right," said Nevin. "I'm going to try and do something about it."

After school Nevin talked to his mother. "Would Jesus want us to waste all that good food? I want to go to a school board meeting and get permission to collect cafeteria leftovers for our city food bank."

A week later, the school board approved Nevin's plan with a standing ovation. Then Nevin convinced a local manufacturing company to donate the plastic containers required by the health department.

Over the next five years, the school district sent nearly 400,000 pounds of cafeteria leftovers to local shelters and food banks.

When the President invited Nevin to the White House to reward him for his work, Nevin asked him, "What do you do with all the White House leftovers?"

WWJ

"Each of you has received a gift in order to serve others....use it faithfully. If you serve, you should do it with the strength God provides." 1 Peter 4:10–11

Do you think Jesus cares if you waste food and water?
How do you show wisdom in caring for the gifts God gives you?
Also read Acts 6:1–7.

GETTING ALONG

Name Acrostics

What You Need:

A Bible, a name book, pen, paper, colored markers

What To Do:

1. Read Isaiah 43:1.
    God has called us by name. We belong to Him. Share
    the meaning of each person's name. If you don't know
    it, look it up in a book of names and their meanings.

2. Take turns printing the letters of each person's name
    in capital letters vertically on the left side of a large
    sheet of paper.

3. As a family or individually, think of words (or phrases)
    beginning with each letter to describe that person.
    Write these after the appropriate capital letter.

4. Children can decorate the capital letters with colored
    markers. Hang the name acrostics on each person's
    bedroom door.

Variation: Try to find a Bible verse that begins with each
letter, or write down ways you can serve Jesus that
begin with each letter.

BACKWARDS!

"Look! Her dress is on backwards!" said Barbie.

Marla looked around. *I wonder who Barbie is talking about. I don't see anyone's dress on backwards.*

The bell rang and Marla grabbed her books and hurried out of the locker room after gym class.

Back in class, Marla sat down at her desk and pulled out her science book to study for the test. She overheard two girls whispering in the next row of desks. *Did they say my name?* Marla wondered. She didn't want to turn around to see if they were looking at her.

Later that morning, Marla left her desk to sharpen her pencil. Several other girls giggled as she walked past.

"It's on backwards! Marla's wearing her dress backwards!" said Barbie. The whole class broke out laughing.

Marla hurried into the restroom and looked in the mirror. *Oh no! It's true! I dressed in such a hurry after gym class that I didn't notice that my jumper was backwards.*

Quickly she turned her jumper around and returned to the classroom. She blinked back the tears that stung her eyes.

All morning the muffled laughs continued. *I'll get back at Barbie,* thought Marla. *I'll tease her. Then it will be my turn to laugh.*

But Marla knew—*I was the one who put my jumper on wrong. They weren't lying about me. It was the truth. Help me, Jesus. I can be mad at them or tease them back...or I can laugh with them.*

At recess Marla told Barbie, "Was I ever blind! I would have walked around all day without noticing my jumper was backwards. Next time I do something stupid, please tell me!"

WWJ

"Be kind and tender....Don't pay back unkind words with unkind words. Instead, pay them back with kind words." 1 Peter 3:8–9

When have you been courteous and kind instead of mean? How should you treat someone who teases you? Also read John 15:9–13.

BLISTERS

"Terry really ticks me off!" Brad sat on the couch, drumming his fingers on his leg. "We drive him to church every Sunday. The least he could do is get here on time."

"He's never been late before," Mom said, looking out the window. "I hope nothing happened to him."

"Let's not wait," said Brad. "I don't want to be late. Let's go."

On their way to church, Brad continued to fume. *Terry ran in a cross country meet yesterday. He probably slept in this morning.*

Later, during dinner, Brad glanced out the window to see Terry walking with a heavy limp. The moment Brad opened the door, Terry said, "I'm sorry for being late this morning."

He eased himself onto the living room floor and slowly slipped off his shoes and socks, flinching with pain. Huge red blisters covered the sides and the heels of both feet. "I got them in the race yesterday. I can barely walk."

Brad gave his mom a sheepish look.

"This morning it took me twice as long to walk here," said Terry, gently slipping into his socks and shoes. "You guys drove off just as I came around the corner." He sighed. "I hate missing church. I should have started walking to your house earlier."

"And I should have come looking for you instead of getting ticked off," said Brad. "It's my fault you missed church. I'm really sorry."

Jesus said, "Do not judge others. Then you will not be judged. You will be judged in the same way you judge others." Matthew 7:1–2

Why doesn't God want you to judge other people?
When have you jumped to a wrong conclusion about someone?
Also read James 4:7–12.

REVENGE (Part One)

Burt cringed as Alyssa made her tenth free throw shot. That was four more than he made. *His record beat by a girl!*

Later, in class, the teacher passed out English papers. Burt glimpsed the A+ on Alyssa's paper, then glared at the F on his own. He ground his teeth. *She beat me. Again.* He wadded his paper and tossed it at the wastebasket. He missed.

The bell rang for recess. Burt waited for his teacher and classmates to leave the room, then he grabbed a large marking pen off Alyssa's desk.

"Hey, Alyssa!" he hollered as she was walking out the door. When she turned around, Burt held her pen in front of his face. He aimed it like a basketball toward the snake aquarium. He knew snakes terrified her.

"Wanna see me make a free throw?" he teased.

"No!" Alyssa shrieked and ran at him, waving her arms. He tossed the pen. She snatched it out of the air. Still running, she slammed into him and knocked him against a bookcase. Burt sprawled on the floor as books crashed down on top of him.

Just then, the teacher marched into the room. His eyes blazed with anger. "Burt! You pick up that mess at once!"

Burt pushed himself to his feet, then set the books back on the shelves. *Three times today she beat me!*

Alyssa folded her arms. "I have a radical idea for you," she said. He ignored her. "Try practicing your free throws with a *ball*."

Burt narrowed his eyes. *You think you beat me again, don't you, Alyssa Morrison? You just wait. I'm not through with you yet.*

"My friends, don't try to get even....It is written, 'I am the One who judges people. I will pay them back,' says the Lord." Romans 12:19

What problems can jealousy cause?
When have you felt jealous? How can Jesus change your feelings?
Also read Proverbs 27:3–4.

REVENGE (Part Two)

Burt slammed the ball into the basket—*Yes! Maybe now the new basketball coach will notice me.*

The coach called everyone together. "Let's scrimmage. I want to check out all of you players. Show me what you can do!"

Alyssa smiled at the coach. He smiled back and winked. Burt ground his teeth.

In the middle of a play, Burt threw his shoulder against Alyssa, then dropped to the floor. "Coach! She rammed me!"

Alyssa stamped her foot. "You rammed *me!*"

With a smirk on his face Burt rose to his feet. *Finally, I'm getting back at you, Alyssa Morrison.*

The coach blew his whistle as the scrimmage began. "Burt, come over here."

"Sure, Coach." Burt jogged to the sidelines.

"I want you to know something, Burt. My name's not Coach. It's Coach *Morrison.*"

Morrison? Is he Alyssa's father? Burt felt faint as he realized. *I've ignored the Bible's warning against taking revenge. Now I'll pay for it.*

"I don't like your attitude, son. I'm taking you off the team."

Alyssa walked over. "Dad, if Burt apologizes and changes his attitude, can he stay on the team? He's really a good player."

Coach Morrison looked at his daughter and thought for a moment. "All right," he said. "But Burt's attitude has to change."

After practice, Burt apologized to Alyssa. "I'm sorry. I was jealous of you. Thanks for helping me stay on the team, even though I acted like a jerk."

"It's called *mercy,*" Alyssa said with a smile. "And you're welcome."

Jesus said, "Love your enemies. Do good to them....have mercy, just as your Father has mercy." Luke 6:35–36

Why does God want us to show mercy to other people?
Who has been merciful to you? To whom have you been merciful?
Also read Luke 6:27–36.

SAY "UNCLE"

Jack sat on Gunther's chest while their classmates watched during recess.

"Give up," Gunther grunted, kicking his legs.

Jack held him down. "I'm on top of *you*. Why should I give up?"

He shifted his weight for a firmer grip on his opponent's flailing arms. *This is the third fight in a week the new kid picked with me*, thought Jack. *I wish he'd leave me alone.*

"Say 'uncle!'" yelled Gunther. He squirmed, red-faced, but he couldn't shake Jack's hold on him.

The spectators jeered. Jack gazed steadily into Gunther's eyes and asked, "If I say 'uncle,' will you stop picking fights with me?"

"I'm going to fight you until I beat you," Gunther said through clenched teeth. "Say 'uncle!'"

With a shrug, Jack stood up, stepped back, and folded his arms across his chest. Slowly and firmly he said, "Uncle!"

"Don't worry, wimp." Gunther jumped to his feet. "I won't mess with you again. I won this fight. Now I'm the toughest kid in school!"

Walking away with his friends, Jack said, "I guess Gunther thinks he's a hero now."

Jack shook his head. "I'm just glad to get back to playing ball at recess instead of fighting."

WWJ

"Avoiding a fight brings honor to a man. But every foolish person is quick to argue." Proverbs 20:3

Does it take more courage to fight or to walk away from a fight? When have you tried to be a peacemaker?

Also read Matthew 5:7–10.

HOW DO YOU VIEW YOURSELF?

Hobo Party Time

What You Need:

A large cardboard box, colored markers, small party favors or small toys or homemade "treasures"; a container for the treasures, soup and crackers or pork and beans, baggy old clothes

What To Do:

Note: Follow activities in Monday's story, "Hobo Party."

1. Create and put on hobo clothes. Use sticks with bundles tied to them. Decorate, play in, and perhaps even eat a picnic in the large box.

2. Conduct a treasure hunt (parents need to hide clues and treasure earlier in the day).

3. Have a hobo parade along your street.
    Invite another family and have double the fun.

4. Afterwards, talk about ways to have fun without spending money (walk, hike, cook together, make up games, attend free museum exhibits, sing together, read with each other). Emphasize the value of relationships over money.
    Talk about how valuable each of you are to one another.

HOBO PARTY

"I hate this T-shirt! And these jeans!" Mia blinked back her tears. "All the kids at my new school wear expensive clothes... except me."

Mom put an arm around Mia. "Money and possessions don't make people happy."

"But, Mom, you don't understand. These kids are rich!"

"Look, I've volunteered to be room mother for your class. God will show us how to plan some fun events without spending money. Maybe we can help your classmates focus on something besides the nifty things they own."

Mia hesitated. "Well...okay."

Soon a "hobo" party was planned for the last Friday of the month. All the students came to school dressed in old clothes.

First they decorated several empty refrigerator boxes to be their "homes." Then they searched the playground for clues to find hidden treasures of gum and candy treats.

Finally, they all paraded through the school halls and showed off their hobo costumes to other classes.

They ended the morning by fixing peanut butter sandwiches and eating lunch inside their cardboard homes.

When the party was over, Mia hugged her mom.

"Thanks, Mom. For the first time, all the kids in class really worked together. We *enjoyed* each other instead of trying to show off the stuff we own. I'm glad God helped us plan a fun party without spending any money."

WWJ

"Command people who are rich in this world not to be proud....Wealth is so uncertain....Be rich in doing good things." 1 Timothy 6:17–18

Why does God warn us not to trust in money or possessions?
What can you do to have fun without spending money?
Also read 1 Timothy 6:17–19.

NEEDING HELP TO FORGIVE

Marie fumed. "I'll never forgive Sally for calling me names!"

"But you have to forgive her," said Jennifer. "The Bible says we should forgive, no matter what anyone says or does to us."

That's not fair, thought Marie. *Jennifer acts as if I did something wrong. But Sally's the one who did something wrong—against me!*

Marie told Jennifer, "Why do you insist that I have to forgive Sally? That makes me feel bad."

"I was only trying to help," said Jennifer. "The Bible shows us what's right and wrong. When you disobey God, you *will* feel guilty. That bad feeling is like a built-in alarm system. But God wants to forgive you. You just need to make sure you forgive others."

Marie frowned. "But I don't think I can forgive Sally."

"Don't worry. God will help you forgive her....just ask Him."

Marie grabbed Jennifer's hand. "Right now I hate Sally. I can't forgive her without God's help. Please pray with me."

"I will. Let's walk around the soccer field. We can pray out loud as we walk. God will answer our prayers. He'll help you forgive."

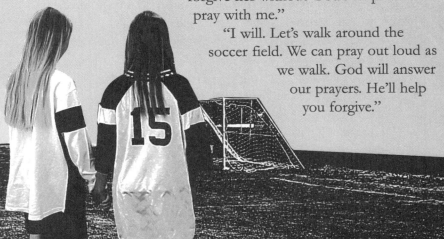

Jesus said, "Forgive people when they sin against you. If you do, your Father who is in heaven will also forgive you." Matthew 6:14

What have you felt guilty about? Does your conscience bother you? How quick are you to forgive those who hurt you?
Also read Proverbs 28:13-14.

GOD IS ABLE

"Want a piece of apple pie?" Darla asked her little brother.

"No," Able replied. "And I don't want to smoke, either."

Darla sliced a piece of apple pie for herself. "What does smoking have to do with eating apple pie?"

"Smoking is bad for you. So is sugar."

Darla studied her little brother. He looked different—cleaner than usual. "Did you wash your face?" she asked.

He sat up straight. "Yes. And I combed my hair, too."

His sister leaned close and sniffed. "You used hair gel! What are you doing? Are you trying to be 'Mr. Perfect' or something?"

He scooted closer to her. "I found out how special I am." He added in a hushed voice, "I'm named after God."

"You're what?"

"You know," he said. "They sing about it at church. 'God is able.' Get it? God is *Able!* That's His name, too. Mom and Dad named me...after God."

"Oh, wow..." Darla wondered how she could explain this without crushing her little brother. "Able isn't God's name," she said slowly. "That's a way of saying that God can do anything."

"Do you mean I'm *not* named after God?" Able wrinkled his face, about to cry. "I'm not...special?"

"You are precious to God," said Darla. "God made you. God loves you and knows your name. God even knows how many hairs grow on your head." She smiled. "Best of all, you belong to Him."

"Yes!" Able grinned. "I *am* special to God!"

The Lord says, "Do not be afraid....I will send for you by name. You belong to me....You are priceless to me. I love you and honor you." Isaiah 43:1, 4

How can you be sure that you are special to God?
Do you have to be perfect in order for God to love you?
Also read Psalm 139:1–3.

VICTORIA'S HATS

Victoria tugged her straw hat down over her ears and gazed at herself in the restroom mirror. She lifted her chin and puckered her lips. Meeting her friend's eyes, she wiggled her eyebrows and winked. "Not bad for a baldy," she said.

Carmen laughed. "How many hats do you own, Victoria?"

"Ten." Victoria yanked her hat off with a flourish. Her head was as soft and bald as a baby's cheek.

Just then, two older girls entered the restroom. "All right, Victoria!" one of them said. Victoria grinned and waved her hat.

When the girls left, Carmen said, "I think you're more popular now than before you got cancer. I admire you. I'd be so insecure without any hair. Don't think I'm saying you're ugly—you look great in hats. But if it were me, I'd have to wear a wig."

"I wanted a wig at first, but they cost too much. And they itch." Victoria adjusted her hat as the girls walked outside.

"You know why I've stopped worrying about how I look?" said Victoria, smiling at everyone who passed by. "Because God uses my bald head for His glory. When people find out I have cancer, it gives me lots of opportunities to tell people about Jesus. Besides," she said, looking up with a grin, "to Jesus I look *gorgeous*."

"Let your way of thinking be completely changed....Don't think of yourself more highly than you should." Romans 12:2–3

How can troubles give you opportunities to share Jesus?
How do you measure your worth?
Also read Romans 12:1–8.

ROTTEN GOALIE!

I'm a rotten goalie! Tad thought as he dived for the soccer ball. It shot past him and landed in the net. The other team cheered.

Not again! Why did Coach make me play goalie? I'm such a loser.

Tad's face burned with shame. *Jesus, please help me,* he prayed, *or I'll be a total flop out here.*

The ball rolled toward him again. He nudged it with his foot and it dribbled to a defender.

What a wimpy kick I made! Worthless goalie! Tad told himself. Then he remembered what his Sunday School teacher said last week in class:

"Anytime you feel like you are worthless, you should know right away that it's Satan, not Jesus, who is talking to you. You are worth a lot to Jesus. He loved you so much that He died for you on the cross. You are *not* worthless."

"But I *feel* worthless," Tad muttered to himself. "It's hard to believe Jesus thinks I'm worth anything."

The ball rolled toward Tad, but a defender kicked it away.

I wish I'd made the save. But somehow, this time I don't feel like such a failure. Thanks Jesus, for reminding me of Your love.

Tad took his place in front of the goal. Moments later, the ball flew at him like a rocket.

Catching it, Tad quickly boomed it nearly halfway up the field. The crowd jumped up and down and cheered!

Wow! Thank You, Jesus, for the double answer to prayer! You helped me remember what You think of me. Then You helped me play better.

WWJ

"God, your thoughts about me are priceless. No one can possibly add them all up." Psalm 139:17

When have you felt like a "loser"?
Why are you valuable to Jesus? How does He feel about you?
Also read Psalm 139:13–18.

CHOOSE RIGHT

Who Am I?

What You Need:

A Bible or Bible story book, paper, pencils

What To Do:

1. Using the Bible or Bible story book as a reference,
    choose a Bible character for the rest of the family to
    guess. Write down at least five facts about that person.
    (From the facts given, listeners must guess which
    Bible character was chosen.)

2. Without mentioning the character's name, read off
    the first fact. Allow participants to guess. If the guess
    is incorrect, proceed to the second fact, and so on.

3. Talk about why the Bible character is important.
    What can we learn from him or her?
    In what ways did that person choose to do right?

Note: This may be played as a team competition or merely as
       a guessing game, with one or more family members
       choosing the characters.

Variation: Play WHERE AM I? Choose places in the Bible
            instead of Bible people. Play as above.

WWJ

CLASS MONITOR

Mrs. Davis, please don't make me class monitor, Lori pleaded in her mind. *Please!*

"I will appoint a different class monitor each day," said Lori's teacher. "The monitor will watch the class when I'm out of the room. The monitor will write on the chalkboard the name of anyone who talks or doesn't do his work." The class groaned. "Today's monitor is Lori Avery."

Lori sighed. *I don't want to tell on anybody.*

"Students, I'm going to the principal's office," said Mrs. Davis. "Work on your spelling words." She handed Lori a piece of chalk. "I hope Lori won't have to write any names on the board."

When Mrs. Davis closed the door behind her, Lori's best friend, Trina, leaned over to talk to the girl behind her.

"Trina, shhh. I don't want to have to write your name on the board," said Lori.

"Then don't. Friends don't snitch on friends."

"I have to obey the teacher."

Trina ignored her and turned back to the other girl.

Reluctantly, Lori chalked her friend's name on the board.

She'll hate me, thought Lori. *I just know it!*

When Mrs. Davis returned, she glanced at the board. "Trina, you will stay in from recess this morning."

Lori stopped by her friend's desk during recess. Trina looked away and told her, "You're not *my* friend anymore."

"Please don't be mad, Trina. Since I've become a Christian, I want to please God. And that includes obeying my teacher."

"You used to be slaves of sin. But thank God that...you obeyed the teachings you were given!...You have become slaves to right living." Romans 6:17–18

When have you felt torn between loyalty to a friend or to God? What did you choose to do?
Also read Romans 6:15–23.

WWJ

DO YOUR OWN JOB!

"Phil, don't leave before you unload the dishwasher!" Chelsea called to her older brother. He sprinted for the back door with a basketball under one arm. "Remember," she said. "It's *your* turn."

"Aw, Chelsea, I'm supposed to shoot hoops with John. I'm already five minutes late. Could you help me out, just this once?"

"I've already helped you out three times this week."

"I'll do all your jobs next week," he promised.

"It's not just that. You know Mom wants us each to do our own chores. She says that it's part of becoming responsible."

Philip grinned at her. "I wasn't going to tell you yet, but I bought you a giant chocolate bar."

Her favorite candy! Chelsea could almost feel the smooth chocolate melting in her mouth. She hesitated.

"Sorry, Phil. I can't keep doing your work when Mom thinks you're doing it. That's like telling a lie. Let's each do our own work." She grinned. "When you're done with the dishes, I'll share some of *my* chocolate bar you bought for me."

Chelsea curled up on the living room couch with a book. She heard the clatter of dishes in the kitchen. It felt good, knowing that she and her brother had done the right thing.

"All hard work pays off. But if all you do is talk, you will be poor."
Proverbs 14:23

When have you tried to avoid chores?
Why does Jesus want you to work and do a good job?
Also read 2 Thessalonians 3:6–13.

PAINTBRUSH CAPER

I don't have enough money for a paintbrush. And I need a fine-tipped brush to paint details on my Mustang model. Bryan selected a bottle of red enamel paint. Then he picked out a small paintbrush and turned to his younger brother.

"Travis, I need this brush. Mom didn't give me enough money to pay for it. Slip it in your sock and cover it with your pant leg."

Travis looked worried. "I don't want to get in trouble."

"Mom will never know." Bryan glanced around, then slid the brush into his brother's right sock.

Bryan paid for the paint. The boys walked into the parking lot and ducked behind a car. Bryan removed the brush from Travis's sock and dropped it into their bag. "See? No sweat!"

At home, Mom met them at the door. "Which color did you buy?" She looked inside the bag and frowned. "Where'd you get the money to buy a brush?" she asked.

"Well…it came with the paint," said Bryan.

"No, it didn't," said Travis. "He put it in my sock."

"Bryan, you didn't…steal it, did you?"

He lowered his eyes. "Well…yes."

"I'm really disappointed," said Mom. "First you stole, and then you lied to me. We're returning the brush and the paint right now. And I'm keeping your model. Go bring it to me."

"But, Mom, I've almost finished building it."

"We need to talk and pray about this, Bryan. Stealing is bad enough, but you made your little brother help you. That's a double sin. Doesn't God expect you to be a good example?"

"You're right, Mom. I'm really sorry. Travis, I won't do this again to you. Please forgive me, both of you."

"Set an example in how you love and in what you believe. Show the believers how to be pure." 1 Timothy 4:12

Why should you be a good example to others?
Why should you try to help younger children do what's right?
Also read Luke 17:1–2.

MATH FRAUD

If I don't finish this worksheet in three minutes, I'll have to stay in during recess. Rory frowned at his half-finished arithmetic paper, then at the clock. *This math is impossible!*

Rory took his paper and pencil and walked to the basket of completed worksheets. He took Joe's paper from the top of the pile. Erasing Joe's name, he printed his own on the worksheet. Then he threw his own worksheet in the wastebasket.

When the bell rang, Mr. Fuller dismissed students by reading out the names on the completed work-sheets. As Rory hurried out to recess, he overheard Joe protest, "But Mr. Fuller, I *did* finish my math!"

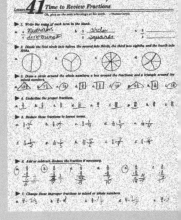

Over the next few weeks, Rory used Joe's math sheets more and more often. He felt sorry for Joe, but not sorry enough to admit he'd cheated.

Then, one day after recess, Mr. Fuller handed a sheet of paper to Rory. "Is this *your* worksheet or is it Joe's?"

"That's my name," said Rory. His heart pounded.

"I can see *two* names on this paper," said Mr. Fuller. "You didn't erase Joe's name very well."

Traces of Joe's name showed faintly through Rory's. He had pulled off this trick so often he had become careless.

Rory clenched his teeth and muttered, "I didn't think I'd get caught. I was wrong! I guess God knew I needed to stop cheating."

WWJ

"You can be sure that your sin will be discovered. It will be brought out into the open." Numbers 32:23

Why is it good for you when your sin is discovered?
What does Jesus want you to do when you've done wrong?
Also read Psalm 25:6–10.

WILL YOU CHOOSE TO PRAY?

Stop! Please stop the killing! Twelve-year-old Atong wept silently while Muslim raiders killed all his family and set fire to their huts. He knew that many Christian villages in southern Sudan had already been destroyed by the Muslims.

The raiders killed everyone in the village except for the strongest eleven- and twelve-year-old boys. They forced the boys to carry food and household goods from the village to their boats at the river.

Atong struggled with his load. Each time he stopped to rest, the men hit him with their sticks. He overheard the raiders say, "After we reach our boats, we'll kill the boys."

During the long four-day march, Atong prayed to escape. On the morning of the fifth day, he woke up early. *Everyone is sleeping. Now's my chance. Help me, Jesus.* On his hands and knees, he crept out of camp and ran back home.

When he finally reached his burned village, Atong found four missionaries standing by his family's hut. They gave him water and food. He cried when he told them what had happened to his family and friends.

"Ever since we heard about the raid, we've been praying for your village," they said. "Are you sorry you and your family became Christians?"

Atong smiled through his tears. "No! If I live or die, my life belongs to Jesus." Atong paused. "Do other Christians in the world know about our troubles? Are they praying for us?"

"We will tell them," said the missionary. "They will pray."

WWJ

"I am absolutely sure that not even death or life can separate us from God's love." Romans 8:38

Will you choose to pray for persecuted Christians in Sudan? Will you pray for the children who live as slaves in Sudan? Also read Romans 8:31–39.

GOD'S DIRECTION

Family Prayer Center

What You Need:

A Bible and a special place in your house
Optional: A small table and tablecloth, cross, pillows,
file cards, and pencils

What To Do:

1. Read 1 Timothy 2:1–3, 8.

2. Set aside a corner in your house for prayer. Set up a
small table or a chair. Place a Bible and a cross on the
table. Gather pillows to sit or kneel on. Do whatever is
necessary to set this place apart as a place of prayer to
God.

3. Have each person write a prayer request on a file card.
Tape cards on mirrors, windows, etc., as reminders to
pray for your family's needs, for missionaries, for other
countries, and for people around the world who are
facing hardships.

4. Once a day, or at least once a week, gather in the family
prayer center to pray.

BIRTHDAY BLESSING

"We've been stuck in traffic for an hour!" fussed Estaban. "The movie is half over by now. My birthday is ruined."

"I'm sorry," said his mom quietly.

A police officer arrived at the scene and told them, "The freeway is closed up ahead. Everyone must get off at this exit."

Angry, Esteban punched the seat cushion. "This really stinks!"

Baby Rosita whimpered from her car seat. Mom backed up the car and turned off the freeway. "Let's go home," she said. "I'll try to think of something to do tomorrow to make up for today."

"Sorry about my attitude, Mom," said Esteban. "The accident wasn't your fault. I'm really happy about the new book you gave me by David Helena!"

Turning a corner, Mom pulled up next to the curb. "This may sound crazy, but would you like to go look around in the city library across the street? I need to stop and feed Rosita her lunch."

"Sure," Esteban said. *Dear Jesus, please forgive my lousy attitude. Help me be satisfied with whatever You bring me for the rest of my birthday.*

In the library, Esteban looked through some magazines, then talked with the woman at the reference desk. He told her it was his birthday and he missed a movie because of traffic. "One good thing," he said, "Mom bought me David Helena's new book."

A man nearby spoke up. "I couldn't help overhearing you. I'm David Helena. Would you like me to sign your book?"

Esteban ran out to the car and brought in the book. The author wrote in it, "To Esteban, God bless you on your birthday."

"Wow! Thank You, Jesus, for one of my best birthdays ever!"

WWJ

"*We can make our plans, but the Lord determines our steps.*"
Proverbs 16:9 (NLT)

How has God brought surprise blessings into your life?
How can you be sure that God cares about the details of your life?
Also read Habakkuk 3:17–19.

PEANUT BUTTER APPENDIX

"That peanut butter sandwich hurt my stomach!" Brandon doubled over in the beanbag chair and moaned.

An hour later the pain increased.

"We'd better get you to the doctor," said Dad. "It could be your appendix."

The doctor pressed on Brandon's abdomen. "I find nothing wrong with his appendix. Go on home. Come back if he feels worse."

During the next two days, Brandon made three more trips to the doctor. His stomach pain increased steadily until he could barely move. Still, the doctor ruled out surgery.

"Dad, what should we do?" Brandon clenched his teeth against the pain. "Even the doctor doesn't seem to know."

"We've prayed for healing," said Dad. "Let's pray for wisdom."

After praying, Dad said, "I feel God wants us to find another doctor who will operate on Brandon as soon as possible."

Later that day, following surgery, the new doctor told Brandon's father, "The boy's appendix had ruptured. If you had waited one more hour, you would have lost him."

When the surgeon left, the family joined hands and thanked God for helping them know how to save Brandon's life.

"If any of you need wisdom, ask God for it. He will give it to you."
James 1:5

Do you pray together every day with your family? Start today. When have you trusted Jesus to help you with your decisions? Also read Proverbs 3:5–7.

JESUS NEVER LEAVES

"Mandy, what's wrong?" A voice asked softly.

Startled, Mandy looked up. She hadn't seen her day care teacher coming. She quickly wiped her tears.

"Hi, Miss Taylor," Mandy said softly.

Mandy looked around the room to see if anyone noticed that she had been crying. But all the other children were busy playing or watching a cartoon.

"May I sit down on the floor beside you?" asked the teacher.

Mandy nodded. Tears rolled down her face.

"Here." Miss Taylor opened her arms. Mandy crawled into her lap and leaned against her shoulder.

"Can you tell me what's wrong?"

"Mama told me last night that she and Daddy are...are getting a divorce. Mama won't even let me talk to him on the phone! I miss my daddy." Tears rolled down Mandy's cheeks.

Miss Taylor rocked her gently. "Mandy, I can't make your mama and daddy not get a divorce. And I can't make your hurt go away. But I know Someone who can help you."

Mandy looked into her teacher's eyes. "Is it Jesus?" she asked softly.

"Yes. Jesus never goes away. He cares for you, remember?"

Mandy nodded. She wiped her tears, leaned into her teacher's arms, and prayed softly, "Thanks for loving me, Jesus. I feel better. I know You will help me through this."

"The Lord himself will go ahead of you. He will be with you. He will never leave you. He'll never desert you....Don't lose hope." Deuteronomy 31:8

When have you felt alone and upset? What did you do?
How would you encourage someone who felt upset?
Also read Psalm 34:4–8, 17–18.

SACRED PLACE

"Take off your shoes! This is my sacred place."

Marjorie stopped in the doorway of her cousin's bedroom. She stared at her cousin and asked, "What do you mean, Alice?"

"This is my sacred place. My teacher told us how to set it up."

Uneasy, Marjorie took off her shoes and stepped into the room. In the corner stood a small table with a crystal, a vase of flowers, and a bottle of perfume.

"Sit with me." Alice sat cross-legged in front of the table. She sprayed perfume into the air. "I should burn incense, but I'm not allowed to have matches."

"Isn't incense sometimes used for worshiping spirits?"

"I'm not worshiping," said Alice. "I'm emptying my mind."

"But Alice, aren't we supposed to fill our minds with thoughts of God and His Word? You could be opening your mind to Satan!"

"I just come here to find peace," Alice said.

Marjorie shook her head. "Isn't Jesus the One who gives us peace? I think your teacher is teaching you w____ ideas."

Alice saw the concern in her cousin's eyes. "What do you think I should do?"

"I suggest you clear all this stuff off the table. Lay your Bible there, instead. Then go ask your mom what she thinks of your teacher's ideas. I'll pray that Jesus will show you what is right."

"Watch out for false prophets. They come to you pretending to be sheep. But on the inside they are hungry wolves." Matthew 7:15

How can you avoid being led away from God by false teachings? How much time do you spend with Jesus and His Word? Also read Psalm 119:97–104.

TWOS AND FIVES

"Tyler, can I do my homework with you?" Samantha climbed onto the kitchen stool next to her brother.

"What homework? You're in preschool. All you do is color." Tyler flipped open his math book, then tapped his pencil on the pages.

"I need to learn to print my numbers. Can I work here?"

"Sure. I'll be here all day doing these stupid math problems."

They worked side by side for a long while. From time to time, Tyler watched her painstakingly print numbers on her wide-ruled paper. "I wish I had simple homework like you," he said.

"Only the *ones* are simple," said Samantha. "The *twos* and *fives* are the hardest."

"Wait till you have to multiply them!" Tyler struggled with several math problems, then slammed his book shut. "These problems are too hard. I need a break."

"Shhh," whispered Samantha, with her eyes shut. "I'm asking Jesus to help me with my *twos* and *fives*."

"*I'll* help you when I get back," Tyler said. He shot baskets in the driveway, then he sat down and flipped through a magazine. Finally he joined his sister at the kitchen counter. She was still practicing her *twos* and *fives*.

"Oh! I promised to help you, didn't I? Sorry about that."

"That's okay," she said with a smile. "Jesus didn't forget. He's been helping me ever since you left."

My little sister is wiser than I am, thought Tyler as he opened his math book. *Now it's my turn to ask for help, Jesus. I need all the help I can get.*

WWJ

"I look up to the hills. Where does my help come from? My help comes from the Lord. He is the Maker of heaven and earth." Psalm 121:1–2

What do you do when you can't solve a problem?
When have you asked Jesus to help you with your homework?
Also read Psalm 121:1–4.

What Is in a Name? Bookmark

What You Need:

> A Bible with concordance, a baby name book, pen, stiff white paper, colored markers

What To Do:

1. Find the meaning of each person's name in the baby name book.

2. Using the Bible concordance, search for a verse to match your name (or choose your favorite Bible verse).

3. Cut the cardboard to bookmark size.
    Write the person's name and verse on it.
    Decorate with colored markers.

Variation: Write the letters of your name in capitals down the left-hand side of the bookmark. Beside each letter, write one way you can show your faith to others.

Example: MARY =
M—merry heart
A—able to serve
R—rich in friendship
Y—youthful energy.

WWJ

BUCKLE UP JESUS

"Lexie, you're silly! You don't have to buckle the middle seat belt. It's *empty*." Hal smiled at his three-year-old sister. He rolled down his window to let cooler air inside the hot car.

"It's not an empty seat," said Lexie. "Jesus is sitting there."

Mom slid into the driver's seat and turned on the air conditioning. They drove to the sports store where Hal tried to find new reflectors for his bicycle.

Lexie kept tugging on Hal's shirt, but he pulled away. "Cut it out, Lexie!"

Tears ran down Lexie's hot cheeks. "I can't find Mommy. And I'm worried. Jesus might die!"

"What?" Hal stared at his sister. "How could Jesus die?"

"The man on the radio said not to leave any pets or children in hot cars. We left Jesus in our hot car. We have to get Him out."

Hal laughed and laughed. "Lexie, you don't understand!"

Mom walked up with several packages of batteries in her hands. "What's so funny?"

"Lexie didn't unbuckle the middle seat belt in the car. Now she's afraid Jesus will suffocate." Hal laughed again.

Mom smiled. "You know, Hal, it's not as far-fetched as you think. Lexie doesn't understand that Jesus doesn't have a physical body. She *does* understand that Jesus is real."

"She's doing a better job of that than I am," Hal admitted.

He turned to his sister. "You love Jesus, Lexie. And you know He is with us all the time. But it's a little different than you think. You'll understand someday. In the meantime, let's go roll down a couple of our car windows. Okay, little sis?"

WWJ

Jesus said, "You can be sure that I am always with you, to the very end."
Matthew 28:20

How often do you remember that Jesus is always with you?
How does that affect the way you live?
Also read Matthew 28:16–20.

WWJ

GIVE ALL YOUR HEART

"Not just a part, but all of my heart, that's what I give You, Jesus," Tina sang along with the cassette tape.

Tina could remember the very moment she had accepted Jesus into her heart as her Savior. That was only a few years ago.

But Tina still quarreled with her brother. And she often griped and grumbled when she took out the trash and did chores.

That doesn't make You very happy, does it, Lord? I want to please You in everything I do. I want to give my whole heart and my whole life to You.

Tina hurried into the kitchen. She dragged a chair to the highest cupboard where her mother stored the flowered china dishes.

Standing on tiptoe, Tina found small china plates, teacups, and saucers. She set them on the counter, then searched the drawers and other cupboards for candlesticks and a tablecloth.

I know I'm not going to change all at once, Jesus. I also know I'm going to need Your help. Tina hummed as she stacked cookies on a plate and poured apple juice into the teacups. When she finished setting the table, her dad walked in and asked, "What are you doing, Tina?"

"Daddy, I listened to a song today that made me want to give my whole heart to Jesus. I'm throwing a 'Give All My Heart to Jesus' party so our whole family can celebrate!"

"Good idea," said Dad. "Maybe it's time for us to give all our hearts to Jesus, too."

"Always remember the God of your father. Serve him with all your heart."
1 Chronicles 28:9

Have you given Jesus all your heart? Would you like to do that? In what ways do you need to change? Ask Jesus for His help. Also read Psalm 119:9–16, 33–35.

DONKEY BOY (Part One)

Please, God, send me a miracle! Ramian inched toward the river on calloused hands and stub feet. The dirt and rocks of the village road, hot from the summer sun, burned his hands.

He knew people called him "Donkey Boy," but he didn't hate them for it. They were right. He did look like a donkey as he moved on all fours when he walked. The disease he contracted as a baby had twisted his legs in the wrong direction at the knees and locked them in place.

Ramian prayed as he crawled. *Dear God, help me walk upright like other people.*

"Are you heading to the river?" asked Manuel.

"Yes. My hands burn."

Manuel walked beside Ramian, slowing his pace to stay with his friend. *I wish I could crawl faster. But someday God will straighten my legs,* he thought. *Then I will* run *with Manuel.*

Swimming in the river, Ramian laughed and splashed with other village children. He spun and turned somersaults in the water. But even as he laughed, his heart ached. *I can't wait to be healed!*

A cloud of dirt came down the road. The van stopped by the river. A tall blond man carrying a black bag climbed out. He walked over to the children playing in the water.

"Are you a doctor?" Ramian asked.

"Yes, I'm a missionary doctor. God has sent me here."

The doctor looked at Ramian, studying his legs. "I think I can help you, but you will have to suffer a lot of pain first."

Ramian grinned. "I *knew* God would help me. Now I will finally walk—I won't mind the pain."

WWJ

"Faith is being sure of what we hope for. It is being certain of what we do not see." Hebrews 11:1

What is faith? What are you trusting God for?
When have you believed God for something you couldn't see?
Also read Hebrews 11:1–3.

DONKEY BOY (Part Two)

"I'll have to cut your legs off at the knees," the missionary doctor explained to the young boy in India.

Ramian gasped. He had thought that the American doctor would straighten his legs, not cut them off!

"Is that how I will be able to walk upright?" Ramian asked Dr. Jackson.

"Yes. It's the only way the new legs will work. Don't worry. The new legs will fit perfectly. Someday soon you will walk as smoothly as I do—on sturdy steel legs covered with plastic." The doctor smiled at the twelve-year-old. "Are you afraid?"

"A little. But I trust that Jesus will help me and protect me."

When Ramian woke up after the surgery, he saw bandages where his lower legs used to be. But he kept trusting Jesus.

Finally, the big day arrived. Dr. Jackson carried Ramian's new legs into the hospital room. Ramian ran his hands over the soft plastic. "It feels and looks like real skin."

"Squeezing into these will hurt," Dr. Jackson warned. "They have to fit tight."

Ramian flinched with pain when the doctor attached the new legs to his stubs. He grabbed the nurses' arms as they eased him into a standing position. The nurses held onto him and steadied him so he wouldn't topple over.

For the first time in his life, Ramian stood on straight legs—just like everybody else.

"Thank you, Dr. Jackson! And thank You, Jesus! You have answered my prayers. Now I will be able to walk like a man."

WWJ

"Jesus…healed every illness and sickness the people had."
Matthew 4:23

Are you willing to trust Jesus while you wait and pray?
How long have you waited for God's answer to one of your prayers?
Also read Hebrews 11:4–6.

TUTOR

"What? Me, a tutor? But I'm only in sixth grade." Anthony stared at his teacher. *How can I teach someone else?* he wondered.

Mrs. Limper nodded. "You're a good student and you are friendly. We have Russian twins in the fifth grade who struggle with their studies. They don't know enough English."

"I guess it's pretty hard to study in another language when you don't know it real well," said Anthony. "What would I do?"

"Talk with them, play games, read books out loud."

"Okay. I can do that," Anthony said. *With Your help, Lord.*

After school the next day, Anthony met Dasha and Misha. He played board games with them. Then he read *Peter Rabbit*. He asked questions about Russia so they could practice speaking English.

Within three weeks, Misha beat Anthony regularly at word games, and Dasha knew *The Cat in the Hat* by heart.

Anthony read them the story of David from a Bible story book.

"I like that story," said Dasha. "Read us some more."

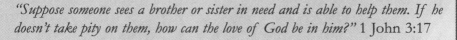

"I will. And you could come to Sunday School with me," said Anthony. "You'll learn lots of Bible stories there."

On Sunday, Anthony shared a church pew with Dasha and Misha and their entire family. Anthony felt warm inside.

I planned to bring just Dasha and Misha to Sunday School. Then God worked it out for the whole family to hear about Him!

WWJ

"Suppose someone sees a brother or sister in need and is able to help them. If he doesn't take pity on them, how can the love of God be in him?" 1 John 3:17

When have you helped someone to learn?
How can you help someone with a need today?
Also read Hebrews 13:20–21.

SHARE THE LOVE OF JESUS

You Are Invited

What You Need:

A Bible, pencils or pens, purchased invitations that say "You Are Invited"
Optional: Tract explaining how to become a Christian

What To Do:

1.   Read John 3:16 and Romans 10:9.

2.   Fill in the blanks on the invitation:
Invitation: <u>To receive Jesus and eternal life.</u>
When: <u>Today.</u>
Time: <u>Anytime. The sooner the better.</u>
Place: <u>Anywhere. Just ask Jesus to forgive</u>
             <u>your sins and come into your heart.</u>

3.   Write out Romans 10:9 at the bottom of your invitation, or slip a tract inside the envelope.

4.   Pray for God to open the hearts of the people who receive your invitation.

5   Hand out the invitations in your neighborhood, outside the mall, or at school.

Variation: Make your invitations from construction paper and markers. Cut out hearts or crosses. Glue onto the invitation. Decorate with stickers, ribbons, or glitter.

ANGELS FOR GRANDMA

"Why did Grandpa have to die now?" Ashley asked. "I was just adopted into your family. I wanted to know him better."

"Grandpa's body was old," said Mother.

"I miss him a lot," said Ashley. "But I don't feel sorry for him. He knew Jesus. And right now he's probably riding in a rodeo with the angels."

Mother smiled. "I don't know about the rodeo. I do know that Jesus promised to make a home in Heaven for each of us."

"Just like your family made a home for me here?"

"That's right, honey. When we adopted you, we made you a part of our family. When God adopts us, He makes us a part of His family all over the world. Everyone, everywhere, whoever accepts Jesus as their Savior is our family."

"I'm glad I'm part of this family…and God's family."

"So am I," said Mother. "We love you. And we're here for you, especially to help you get through the hard times."

Later, Ashley found Grandma crying. "You miss Grandpa, don't you?" Grandma nodded.

I want to help her, thought Ashley. *I'll help her through this hurting time. That's what God wants families to do.*

Ashley drew a picture of angels. She wrote some Bible verses on it. Then she wrapped it up and gave it to Grandma.

"Read these verses when you're feeling sad, Grandma," Ashley said. "The angels will remind you that God loves you and your family loves you. We will always be here to help you,… especially when you're hurting."

WWJ

Jesus said, "There are many rooms in My Father's house….I am going there to prepare a place for you….And I will take you to be with me." John 14:2–3

How can you cheer up someone whose loved one has died?
How is your family growing closer to each other and to the Lord?
Also read John 14:1–6.

BODY WORK

"Looking for anything special?" Aaron asked his new friend Tan, a Vietnamese. They rummaged through toys at a resale store.

"A skating board," Tan said.

"Okay. But it's called a skateboard. If the store has any, they'd be over in the sports corner." Aaron led the way to the table. The boys dug through baseball mitts, hockey sticks, and football helmets.

"I found one! Here." Aaron handed his friend a skateboard. "It looks like it went through a war. But it will still work."

Tan smiled. "Okey-dokey."

An hour later, Aaron sat in Taco John's, watching his friend eat his first taco. Tan chewed slowly. Then he grinned. "Okey-dokey."

I like introducing Tan to new experiences. I want to tell him about Jesus, too. But where do I start?

Aaron's mind went blank. Then he heard himself say, "Will you come to the Easter program at church with me? We'll sing and then watch a play about Jesus."

Tan thought for a moment. Then he smiled. "You good friend. I come. Okey-dokey."

Dear Lord, use the service tonight. Touch his heart—be His Savior, prayed Aaron.

"We are all parts of [Christ's] one body, and each of us has different work to do." Romans 12:5 (NLT)

In what ways can you serve God and others today?
What is your job in the body of Christ?
Also read 1 Corinthians 12:4–7.

ANGEL GIFTS

Who will open the door? wondered Luke as he and his family stood outside of apartment 220. *Do they know we brought Christmas presents from the Angel Tree Project?*

A neatly dressed young woman answered their knock.

"Are you Mrs. Johnson?" asked Luke's father. "I'm Dan Hubble. I phoned you this afternoon about stopping by."

The young woman smiled. "Of course, come in." Luke and his family trooped into a small room with a table and three chairs, a hotplate, and a refrigerator.

"April! Johnny! Come here!"

Two little kids ran in from the other room. Their eyes widened at the sight of the wrapped gifts.

Luke held out his packages. "Your daddy couldn't be here for Christmas, but he wanted you to have these presents."

April beamed as she unwrapped a doll and a teddy bear. Johnny ripped opened a model airplane and a dump truck.

Luke's parents unloaded two large boxes of food.

"I included some of my favorite recipes," said Luke's mom.

Tears glistened in Mrs. Johnson's eyes. "Since my husband went to prison, you're the only people who have visited us."

Luke handed a Bible storybook to the children. "This is my favorite book. It tells you about Jesus. He loves you."

After Luke and his parents climbed back in the car, Dad said, "Life is tough for that family. Sin imprisons everyone."

Luke thought for a moment. "Let's pray that the Johnsons will accept Jesus as their Savior. Then they'll *really* be free."

WWJ

Jesus said, "The Spirit of the Lord is on me. He has anointed me to tell the good news to poor people....to announce freedom for prisoners." Luke 4:18

How could your family help a prisoner or a prisoner's family? What are some ways you can share God's love today? Also read Matthew 25:34–40.

EVANGELIZING MUFFIN

"Have you ever accepted Jesus?" Carolyn asked Muffin.

Hiding in the bushes by the porch, Matt listened to his little sister talk to Muffin, her gray and white striped cat.

Every Sunday, Carolyn dressed Muffin in doll clothes and tucked him into her doll stroller. Then she wheeled him onto the back porch, where they could be alone.

Matt listened to their latest conversation.

"You have to say you're sorry for your sins." Carolyn spoke softly to her cat. His legs dangled through the short sleeves of a knitted doll dress. He flattened his ears and yowled.

"Yes. You're sorry. That's good, Muffin. Now ask Jesus to come into your heart."

Muffin wriggled out of the stroller and ran into the house.

"I heard you trying to teach Muffin about the Lord," said Matt as he stepped out of hiding.

Carolyn blushed. "Cats can't really accept Jesus as their Savior."

"No, but what you're doing is great practice for telling your friends about Jesus."

"I know. I've already told Lisa and Dori and Catherine."

"You're sure a great witness for Jesus," said Matt. "I'm proud of you, sis."

WWJ

Jesus said, "Take this message of repentance to all the nations."
Luke 24:47 (NLT)

When have you told someone else about Jesus?
Practice explaining how to accept Jesus.
Also read Luke 24:46–48.

WHY CAN'T I GO?

Patti pulled on her father's sleeve and asked, "Why can't I go with Sandra's youth group to Mexico? I want to tell Mexican children about Jesus, too."

Patti's dad gave her a hug. "Maybe you can go someday when you're in the youth group. Right now you're too young. Let's think of some ways to help Sandra earn money for her trip."

"I'll give my allowance money."

"That's a good idea. And we can pray for her every day."

Patti ran to her room and returned with her allowance money and one of her school pictures. On the back of the picture, she printed, "Jesus loves you, and so do I."

I'll ask Sandra to give my picture to a Mexican child, thought Patti.

A month later, Sandra left for Mexico. Patti and her father prayed for the youth group and the Mexican children every day.

When Sandra returned home, she shared many stories about Mexico. "A truck nearly hit our van on the way down. We could have been badly hurt. Thank you for praying."

Sandra hugged Patti. "When my guitar string broke, I used your money to buy another one."

"What about my picture?" asked Patti.

"I gave it to a little boy who caused lots of trouble the first day. He carried it around with him all week. The last day, he said, 'If someone far away loves me, then Jesus must love me, too.' Oh, Patti, you helped us in so many special ways!"

Patti smiled. "So I *did* get to tell Mexican children about Jesus."

WWJ

"How can they call on [Jesus] unless they believe in him?...How can they hear about him unless someone preaches to them?" Romans 10:14

Choose a missionary or a foreign country to pray for this week. How else can you help spread the good news about Jesus? Also read Romans 10:13–15.

ATTITUDES

How to Love List

What You Need:

A Bible, paper, and a pencil

What To Do:

1. Read Matthew 5:43–48.

2. Talk about what Jesus says about our attitudes toward our enemies. How does Jesus want us to react to those who are mean? How is this different from the way we usually react?

3. Fold a sheet of notebook paper in half down the middle to make two columns. Write: "Enemy" at the top of one column. At the top of the other column write: "How to Love."

4. In the first column list enemies by action, not by name. Example: "someone who laughs at me," or "someone who stole my ring." In the second column, list ways to treat that person with love rather than revenge. Children might say: "Pray for them," "tell an adult," or "be kind."

5. Pray together. Ask Jesus to help you love your enemies.

WWJ

BLACK HOLES

"Let *me* help!" begged Ryan. "I can hammer."

"You're too little," said Kirk, his older brother. Kirk proudly finished sanding the drywall in his new bedroom in the basement. Three-year-old Ryan watched Dad pound in the last nail.

"How does this wall look, Dad?" said Kirk.

"Great job, son." Dad wiped his forehead with the back of his sleeve. "You've done excellent work on the sanding."

Ryan frowned. "Why can't *I* help?"

"I'll tell you how you can help," said Dad. "You can help by eating Mom's fried chicken. Okay? Now go wash your hands."

After dinner, Kirk sat in the kitchen and worked on his math homework. For once, Ryan was not around. He wasn't messing with Kirk's books and pencils and papers like he usually did.

Kirk finished his math. He walked downstairs to take a last look at their work in the basement. What he saw was the last thing he expected.

Black holes, no higher than his knees, dotted all four walls of his new bedroom. Little Ryan stood near one of the walls, gripping a hammer and smiling.

"I helped," he said proudly. "I can hammer, too."

Kirk took a deep breath. *He's only three years old. He has no idea what he's done. Dear Jesus, please help me not get mad at him! Help me control my temper!*

Minutes later, Kirk made a suggestion to Dad. "I'll let Ryan work with me and help fix the walls. Then he'll understand what he did. And it would make him feel like he was helping."

WWJ

'When you are angry, do not sin.'...Say only what will help to build others up....Then what you say will help those who listen." Ephesians 4:26, 29

When have you felt angry at what someone else did?
What helps you control your temper?
Also read Ephesians 4:26–32.

HONOR, DISHONOR

"My parents are the meanest in the whole world," Sabina told a group of her friends at the bus stop. Surprised, Marie stared at Sabina and wondered, *Why is Sabina saying that about her folks?*

All the other girls nodded sympathetically. One of them said, "My parents act as if they were born in the Middle Ages."

"Mine are kind of stupid about music and stuff," said another.

Everyone laughed…except for Marie.

The bus arrived, Sabina and Marie boarded and sat together. "Your mom and dad are always so friendly," said Marie. "I like them. I thought you got along fine with them."

Sabina glanced around to see who was sitting nearby. "Of course I like my parents. But I wouldn't tell that to my friends. They'd think I was a baby. They all laugh about their parents."

"But it's not right to bad-mouth your mom and dad."

"What they don't hear won't hurt them." Sabina frowned. "Besides, you aren't perfect. Neither are your parents. And if you keep acting so goody-goody, you won't have any friends." She turned from Marie and talked to the girl in the seat behind them.

Marie started to turn and join in, then stopped. *If I bad-mouth my parents, God will know.* Marie faced forward. *Thank You, God, for my mom and dad. Help me to honor them, even if it means losing friends.*

Jesus told the Jewish leaders, "God said, 'Honor your father and your mother.'" Matthew 15:4

What does it mean to honor your parents?
What could you do or say today to honor your father or mother?
Also read Mark 7:9–13.

CRUMBS IN THE CORNERS

"Don't forget the kitchen corners," Mom said.

"I'm finished," said Jessie. "I'm putting away the vacuum."

"But honey, look! See the crumbs in the corners? It won't take but a second to clean them."

"Mom, you've never complained about my work before. This is the way I always vacuum."

"Jessie, I'm surprised to hear you talk like that. Don't you want to do your best? God sees everything you do. Don't you want to please Him, even when no one else sees you?"

Jessie didn't answer. She plugged in the vacuum cleaner and banged it in the corners of the room.

"Work, work, work! That's all I ever do. I work while Mom gets to do whatever she wants."

That evening, Jessie read aloud with Mom from their book, *What Would Jesus Do?* In the story, several children worked together to retrieve a blind man's cane from a thicket of blackberries. At the end of the story were two questions:

> *When have you worked hard for someone?*
> *Did you complain or did you work cheerfully?*

Jessie rolled her eyes, then grinned sheepishly.

"I know what you're thinking, Mom," she said. "No, I did *not* work cheerfully today."

Mom smiled and said, "Look at the memory verse, honey."

Jessie read, *"Do your work willingly, as though you were serving the Lord himself."* She gave her mother a hug. "Okay, Mom. The next time I vacuum or do my chores, I won't grumble."

WWJ

"Work at everything you do with all your heart. Work as if you were working for the Lord, not for human masters." Colossians 3:23

Which chores are hardest for you to do cheerfully?
What do you think it means to work for the Lord?
Also read Ephesians 6:7–8.

THE RIPPED BIBLE

"Matthew! Why did you bring your Bible?" whispered Katie, his older sister. "Nobody else in this public school is carrying one. You're going to get laughed at," she warned.

Matthew smiled. "I took it to Faith Christian School. Why shouldn't I take it here? It won't bother anyone."

The third grade teacher assigned Matthew a desk. He laid down his Bible while he took pencils and paper from his backpack. He couldn't help hearing the other students whisper and giggle.

At recess, Matthew carried his Bible outside with him. All the basketball courts were filled. "Let me know when there's room for me to play," he told a tall boy who was the game leader.

Matthew sat down on a bench and read a chapter from Genesis while he waited. Finally the tall boy called to him, "It's your turn."

Leaving his Bible on the bench, Matthew joined the game.

During the game Matthew looked back at the bench and noticed two boys kicking something on the ground.

That's my Bible! He ran over to stop them, but it was too late. The Bible's cover was ripped. Its pages were torn and dirty. The boys ran off, laughing.

After school, when Matthew showed the Bible to his mother, he cried. "They didn't understand," he said. "They didn't know how important my Bible is to me. I forgive them. And I'll pray for them."

NOTE: Matthew taped up his Bible cover. He continued taking it to school. His loving and forgiving attitude won him many friends. The students voted to make him class president at the end of that school year.

WWJ

"Suppose you suffer for being a Christian. Then don't be ashamed. Instead, praise God because you are known by that name." 1 Peter 4:16

Why can you still rejoice when others make fun of your faith?
How does God want you to treat those who hurt you?
Also read Matthew 5:7–12.

ALEX'S PARTY

"What? Alex didn't invite you to his birthday party?" Julia stopped brushing her teeth. Toothpaste foamed at the corners of her mouth. She stared at Cody, her older brother, in disbelief.

"It's no big deal," Cody said.

"Alex is supposed to be your friend. *You* invite him to *your* parties." Julia rinsed her mouth. "I won't go to his party if you aren't invited."

"He invited you and I *want* you to go," Cody said. "Then you can tell me all about the party when you get home."

Julia went to the party. Later that night, she told her brother about the starship cake, the soccer match, and all the games and fun.

"I'm sorry you weren't at the party." She paused. "I guess that means you and Alex aren't friends anymore."

"Oh no. I'm still *his* friend," said Cody.

Julia frowned. "If Alex left *me* out of his party, I'd dump him."

"I was hurt and got mad at first," Cody said. "But I know that Jesus doesn't want me to hold a grudge. So I asked Him to help me change my attitude. It took a couple of days, but He did."

Julia thought for a moment. "Pray for me," she said. "I need Jesus to help change my attitude, too."

Paul said, "Follow my example, just as I follow the example of Christ."
1 Corinthians 11:1

How do you react when someone isn't kind or thoughtful to you? How can you be like Jesus to others?
Also read 1 Corinthians 10:23–24.

PRAYERS OF FAITH

Pray and Fast

What You Need:

A Bible

What To Do:

1. Read Matthew 9:15.

2. Jesus told His critics that His followers would fast
    when He no longer walked on earth. Since we are His
    followers, we know He wants us to fast.
    Decide *how long* you plan to fast. Will you fast for one
    meal? One week? One day?

3. Decide *what* you will give up for the fast. Will you give
    up your favorite television show? How about doing
    without candy or talking on the phone for one
    evening? Give up something that's important to you—
    you're doing it for Jesus.

4. Spend some time praying while you fast. Write down
    your requests for some specific things.

5. At the end of the fast, gather to discuss how you felt
    about it and what it accomplished. Maybe you saw
    some definite answers to prayers. Maybe you felt closer
    to God.

NORTHERN LIGHTS

The gas gauge read "empty." Peter looked from the lighted dashboard into the blackness of the Alaskan night, searching for a pinprick of light. "Are we close to any town, Dad?"

Dad shook his head. "No. The next station is at Toad River, forty miles away. We don't have enough gas to make it."

"There hasn't been another car on the road for five hours," said Mom as she handed a blanket to Peter. "It's forty degrees below zero outside. If the car stops, we could freeze to death waiting for someone to come along."

Peter bowed his head and prayed silently, *Dear Jesus, I'm scared. Please help us. Please give us a sign to show us that You'll take care of us.*

When Peter lifted his head, he saw the northern lights shimmer yellow and green in the night sky. "Mom, Dad, look! It's like God leading the Israelites with a pillar of fire! God took care of them in the wilderness. God will take care of us!"

Peter's family drove for another half an hour with the gas gauge needle on empty. The entire time, the northern lights swirled and flickered above them.

Finally. Peter saw town lights up ahead. He cheered, "We made it to Toad River!" The family filled up the car with gas and ate a warm meal at the Toad River Cafe.

When they drove out to the highway for the last two hours of their trip back home, Peter noticed that the sky was black again.

"Mom! Dad! The northern lights are gone. God brought them out just when we needed them, then they disappeared. Thank You, God, for taking good care of us tonight!"

"The Lord guided them by a pillar of cloud during the day and a pillar of fire at night." Exodus 13:21 (NLT)

What do you do when you are lost or afraid?
How does God show you that He is with you?
Also read Psalm 91:14–16.

TWO MIRACLE BABIES

"Mom, I'm the only one in my Sunday School class who doesn't have a sister or a brother." Ethan looked up at his mom. "Why don't you have another baby?"

Mom smiled. "You can't always have a baby when you want one. Babies are gifts from God. Before you were born, the doctors said I would never have a baby. But your father and I prayed for many years, and God answered our prayers. You are His very special gift to us. Our miracle baby."

"Oh! Like Hannah in the Bible. She prayed a long time, too. God answered her prayers and gave her Samuel." Ethan smiled. "I'm going to pray for a baby brother named Samuel."

Dad smiled. "Sometimes God says yes to our prayers. Sometimes God says no. And sometimes God asks us to wait. No matter how He answers, we can trust Him to do what's best."

That night Ethan knelt by his bed. "Dear Jesus, please give me a baby brother named Samuel."

Night after night, Ethan prayed the same prayer. After many months, his parents told him that God was going to bless them with a baby! Ethan helped fix up a room for the baby and shop for baby clothes. Finally, Mom went to the hospital and came home with Samuel.

Ethan held his tiny, red-faced brother in his arms and smiled at his parents.

"God answered yes. This is *my* miracle baby!"

Hannah said, "I prayed for this child. The Lord has given me what I asked him for. So now I'm giving him to the Lord." 1 Samuel 1:27

When has God answered yes to one of your prayers? When has God answered no? Are you waiting for any answers? Also read 1 Samuel 1:1–27.

PRAYER WITH FASTING

"I feel so bad for the people of Honduras. I'm going to pray and fast for them." Tina sat with her mom on the sofa, watching hurricane victims on the evening news.

"I'm glad you want to pray for them," said Mom. "But I don't think children should fast. It's not healthy."

"Mom, I pray for my friend Lacy. I've tried to tell her about Jesus, but she won't listen. I think I need to fast for her, too."

"Just keep praying, Tina. You can't stop *eating*. Making yourself sick won't help anybody."

"Mom, I have an idea. I can eat and fast at the same time."

Mom raised her eyebrows.

Tina explained, "In the Bible, Daniel gave up meat and other rich food. He fasted by eating vegetables and drinking water for ten days. I can do that, too. Prayer with fasting is really powerful. Jesus told the disciples they couldn't cast out certain kinds of demons unless they fasted."

"Okay, honey. So…what do you plan to give up?"

"I'll give up meats and sweets."

"Even if I serve steak or apple pie for the rest of the family?"

"Yes."

"For how long?"

Tina thought for a moment. "Ten days," she said firmly.

On the eighth day of her fast, Tina charged into the house after school.

"Mom! At recess today Lacy asked me to tell her about Jesus! I have a feeling that when I get to Heaven I'll see more answers to my prayers. Like all the ways Jesus helped the hurricane victims!"

"So I turned to the Lord God and pleaded with him in prayer and fasting."
Daniel 9:3 (NLT)

What could you give up as a *fast* to the Lord?
Why won't you always know how God answers your prayers?
Also read Daniel 1:3–21 and 10:2–13.

WWJ

HOME SEARCH

"How will we find the right home to buy?" Robby asked.

His dad stopped the car in front of the sign that said, *Leyland Village Mobile Home Park.* "Let's pray once more for God to provide us with a good home that we can afford." The family bowed their heads and prayed. Then they drove slowly through the mobile home park, looking for homes for sale.

Kari pointed to a blue mobile home. "I like that color."

Robby shook his head. "No. That yard looks too small. I asked God for a big yard." He pointed to a For Sale sign on a corner lot. "That's our house! See all the grass? And it has a swing set in back!"

Dad parked in front of the house. "Let's take a look."

The owner invited them in. "This living room is large enough for our Bible study group," said Mom.

When they had seen the entire house, Robby followed Dad and Mom out the back door. "Is this it or what?" he whispered.

Dad and Mom smiled and nodded.

Robby hopped up and down the back steps while the rest of the family walked around the yard.

Two words that were printed on the bottom step caught Robby's eye. He bent down to read them.

Then he called out, "Hey, everybody! Come see this!"

Dad, Mom, and Kari bent down to read the message in the cement. It said: GOD PROVIDES.

Jesus said, "Ask, and it will be given to you. Search, and you will find.... Everyone who asks will receive. He who searches will find." Luke 11:9–10

When did God provide something you needed?
What will you trust Jesus for today?
Also read Luke 11:1–13.

PRAYING FOR GRANDMA

"Mrs. Price, can we pray for my grandma again?" Penny asked her Sunday School teacher.

"Not again!" groaned the boy sitting beside Penny. "We pray for your grandma every week."

Tears sprang to Penny's eyes. "But my grandma isn't saved yet. I love her, and I want her to go to Heaven."

Every Sunday that year, Penny asked her Sunday School class to pray for her grandmother.

One Sunday, Penny told the students, "My grandma is in the hospital. Please pray that she'll ask Jesus into her life before she dies."

That week Penny asked her father, "Daddy, can we please go visit Grandma on Saturday? I have to talk to her about Jesus one more time. I just know God will answer my prayers."

At the hospital, Penny held her grandma's hand. "I love you, Grandma. I want to see you someday in Heaven."

Grandma hugged Penny and smiled. "You will, dear child. All week I've thought about the things you've told me about God's love and forgiveness. Last night I prayed and accepted Jesus as my Savior."

The next week in Sunday School, Penny raised her hand at the prayer request time.

A girl next to Penny sighed. "We know what you want. More prayer for your grandma again."

Penny smiled. "No. I want us to thank God for answering all of our prayers! Grandma became a Christian last week. She died yesterday. And now she's in Heaven with Jesus!"

WWJ

"The prayer of a godly person is powerful. It makes things happen."
James 5:16

Have you ever quit praying when God didn't answer right away? What are you praying about today?
Also read 2 Corinthians 6:1–2.

LOVING WORDS AND DEEDS

A Blessing Box

What You Need:

A Bible, a shoe box or cereal box, paper, tape, and markers

What To Do:

1. Read Matthew 7:12.

2. Write the words "Blessing Box" on the paper and tape or glue on the box.

3. Take time to think of any way someone blessed you this past week. Write it down and put it in the Blessing Box. During the next week, notice every time someone does something nice for you. Write it down on a strip of paper. Put it in the Blessing Box. Try not to miss any thoughtful acts. (For instance, write down when Mom drives you to soccer practice or fixes dinner. Mom could write that you hugged her or did your homework without being told.)

4. At the end of the week, take out all the papers and read them together. Talk about how it felt to bless each other. Pray for Jesus to show you more ways to bless your family.

Variation: Every time you observe a kind act, write it on a piece   of paper and tape to the refrigerator.

ART OF ENCOURAGEMENT

I wish I could hide somewhere until art class is over! thought Ellie. She clenched her fists under the table as she waited for the class to begin.

I wonder what this new art teacher will say about my work. I'll never forget when the last teacher embarrassed me by saying, "Oh, well, not everyone is an artist!"

"Good morning, class!" Ellie stared at the art teacher.

"Today we're going to make pinch pots. Each of you will take home a real piece of pottery to show your parents!"

Ellie frowned. *Not me. I'll just take home a real piece of junk.*

The teacher demonstrated. She pushed her thumbs into the center of a lump of clay. Then she pinched the sides up and out. When she finished, she held up the little pot for all to see.

The class copied her, all except for Ellie. She sat with her hands clasped on her lap.

Tom leaned over and said, "Go ahead, Ellie. Try it. I know you can do it. You'll have fun!"

"But I'm no good at art," whispered Ellie.

"My uncle says everyone has artistic ability. He ought to know. He's a professional artist."

"Really?" Ellie felt a spark of hope. She picked up her clay. It felt good to push in the middle and pinch the sides.

At the end of class, the art teacher stopped by Ellie's desk. "What a graceful little pinch pot! You're quite an artist!"

Ellie smiled. When the teacher moved on, Ellie leaned over and whispered to Tom, "Thanks for telling me what your uncle said. Art *is* fun. I can hardly wait for next week's art class!"

WWJ

"So cheer each other up with the hope you have. Build each other up. In fact, that's what you are doing." 1 Thessalonians 5:11

What discourages you? Who has encouraged you the most? Is there someone you could encourage today?
Also read Proverbs 15:23.

AMY'S NEW FRIEND

How can that blind girl find her way around the cafeteria? wondered Amy. The blind student swung her white cane ahead of her, looking for a table. She balanced a full tray of food in her left hand as she searched for a place to sit. She stopped beside Amy's table, where one chair was empty.

"Hi. I'm Colleen. Is anyone sitting here?" the girl asked.

"Terribly sorry. We're full," another girl at the table replied in a phony sweet voice. Her friends covered their mouths and snickered.

Amy stared at her Jell-O. *Why do they laugh? The girl's not deaf. I wish I had the courage to say something nice to her. But if I do, the girls will probably make fun of me, too.*

Colleen turned away from the table. As she did, a boy backed into her, knocking the tray out of her hand. It crashed to the floor, spilling her food everywhere.

The boy laughed and walked away. Kids all over the cafeteria rolled their eyes and giggled. Colleen stood where her tray had dropped. Tears rolled down her cheeks.

Amy stood up. *I don't care what anyone says. I'm going to help her.*

"I see an empty table," she said to Colleen. "Let me get you another tray and we'll eat over there together."

Amy helped clean up the spilled food. Then she paid for a new lunch and carried it to Colleen, who sat waiting at a far table. The two girls ate lunch together as new friends.

Jesus said, "In everything, do to others what you would want them to do to you." Matthew 7:12

Think about a time when you took a courageous stand. Why was it hard to do? What happened? Also read 1 Corinthians 13:1–7.

WWJ

CHANGE OF HEART

Come on, Michael and Mindy. Beg me to give you part of my candy bar.
Then when I say no, you can throw fits. I'd love to get you in trouble with Mom.

Kyle lay on his stomach on the family room sofa. With one
hand he wrote in his spelling workbook. With the other hand he
held a chocolate bar. He had peeled the wrapper just enough to
expose the creamy dark candy. His younger brother and sister sat
on the floor watching him.

"Aren't you going to open it?" asked Michael.

"Hmm? Open what?" *I'll tease them until it drives them crazy.*

"The candy bar," said Mindy. "It'll melt if you don't eat it."

Kyle peeled the wrapper down about two inches. It made the
room smell of sweet chocolate. With his eyes on his workbook,
he bit off a nugget of creamy candy. "Mmmm…"

Mom walked in. "Kyle, are you sharing that candy?"

"No. But it's mine. I bought it with my allowance."

"It doesn't matter," Mom said. "It's not polite to eat in front
of the twins. Plus, it's against the rules. You know that."

"It's okay," Michael said. "I don't want any."

"I don't either," said Mindy.

After Mom left, Kyle asked them, "Why didn't you two fuss
and complain about me? Why didn't you get *me* in trouble?"

Michael smiled at him. "I just did what Jesus would do."

"Me too," echoed Mindy.

I can't believe it. My younger brother and sister are better at following
Jesus than I am. Kyle broke off part of the candy bar and gave them
each a big piece. He kept the smallest piece for himself.

Michael smiled. "Thanks, brother. That's what Jesus would do."

WWJ

"God made us. He created us to belong to Christ Jesus. Now we can do
good things. Long ago God prepared them for us to do." Ephesians 2:10

When have you done something kind to a younger child?
Who has influenced you to do what Jesus would do?
Also read Matthew 18:1–6.

HELPER BEE

"We are down to two finalists," announced the master of ceremonies. "As you know, the champion of the Orland County Spelling Bee will win a new computer for his or her school."

Megan, one of the finalists, waited at her microphone.

"She looks nervous," Jill whispered to her brother, Bobby.

The master of ceremonies turned to the other finalist and said, "Spell *syzygy*."

Bobby leaned toward Jill and whispered, "Is that a word?"

Jill nodded. "It's a word used when the sun, earth, and moon are all in a straight line. I remember drilling Megan on that one."

"You know the words as well as she does. If you hadn't spent all your time helping her, *you'd* be up on stage right now."

"We agreed to work as a team. It doesn't matter which of us is up there. We just want to win that computer for our classroom."

Jill looked up as the master of ceremonies told the other

finalist, "I'm sorry, that is not the correct spelling." He turned to Megan.

"Young lady, this is your chance to win! Spell *syzygy*."

Jill held her breath as Megan leaned close to the mike.

"Syzygy. S-y-z-y-g-y. Syzygy."

"That's correct!" said the master of ceremonies.

"Yes!" Jill flung her arms around her brother and shouted, "Megan Jones! You're the new champion!"

"None of you should look out for just your own good. You should also look out for the good of others." Philippians 2:4

In what situations have you put others first instead of yourself? How do you show other people that you are interested in them? Also read Philippians 2:1–11.

HELPING HERSHEY

"Get the ball, Hershey!" Tyler's chocolate-colored miniature dachshund raced through the living room, then whipped his little body around the corner into the hallway.

Tyler heard a yelp and he ran into the hall. Hershey whined as he pulled himself toward Tyler, dragging his hindquarters.

"Mom, something's wrong with Hershey! His back legs won't move. He can't even wag his tail."

At the animal hospital, the vet shook her head. "He must have slipped a disc when he made that sharp turn. There's not much we can do. You should consider putting him to sleep."

"No!" cried Tyler. "Please, is there anything you can do?"

"I don't think your dog will ever recover the use of his legs," said the vet. She gave Tyler some medicine and a sheet of paper. "You can try these exercises. Work with him every day."

Tyler moved Hershey's bed into his room. He fed him his medicine and made sure he had fresh water and food.

Tyler arranged his schedule to exercise Hershey twice a day. Every day he put on his swimsuit, ran warm water in the bathtub, and climbed into the tub with Hershey. He pulled the dog's hind legs back and forth for half an hour.

In the summer, he exercised Hershey in a kiddy pool. He pushed a ball just in front of his nose, so he would move his legs to try and catch it.

One day, a year later, Tyler hollered with delight. "Mom! Hershey wagged his tail!" A few weeks after that, Hershey limped across the kitchen floor on all four legs. Tyler hugged his dog. "God helped us, Hershey! You didn't give up and neither did I!"

WWJ

"Many will say they are loyal friends, but who can find one who is really faithful?" Proverbs 20:6 (NLT)

When have you done something hard without giving up? When have you been a faithful friend?…a faithful Christian? Also read Lamentations 3:23–25.

NEEDING FORGIVENESS

Gone Forever

What You Need:

A Bible, pencil, paper

What to Do:

1.   Read 1 John 1:7–9 and Psalm 51:1–12.

2.   Discuss what happens to our fellowship to God and other people when we lie, cheat, hate, and become angry. What happens to our relationship with each other when we admit and confess our sins?

3.   What does God do when we confess our sins? Is it hard to believe that God wipes the record clean of the sins we've confessed? Why or why not?

4.   Give each family member a small piece of paper on which to list any unconfessed sin (children may draw pictures). Have each pray silently, naming the individual sins, asking God for forgiveness, and thanking Him for remembering them no more.

5.   Fold papers. Rip into tiny pieces and throw away. Sing a song of praise together.

STOP THE TEASING!

Oh no! Shawn and Richy are heading this way. Brianna walked faster toward her classroom.

"Hey, Freckle-face! You look sick!" The boys laughed loudly. "When will you ever get rid of your spots?"

Brianna choked back her tears. "Leave me alone. And stop making fun of my freckles!"

They followed her to the classroom, joking about the hundreds of brown spots that dotted her cheeks and nose.

"Miss Martin, could you please make Shawn and Richy stop teasing me?" she asked.

The boys chuckled as they hurried to their seats.

Outside during lunch recess, the boys continued to tease her. "Stay away from Brianna! She's contagious!"

Finally, Brianna decided on a way to get even.

I'll make fun of Richy's ears, she thought. *And Shawn's big feet. I'll call them names and hurt their feelings.*

Then she realized: *I don't want to hurt them like they're hurting me. Dear Jesus, show me what to do. Forgive me for wanting to get even.*

After school Shawn hollered at her, "I'll bring some soap to school tomorrow so you can scrub your face!"

Brianna just smiled as she climbed the school bus steps.

From then on, every time the boys teased her, Brianna just smiled. She said a silent prayer for them whenever they made fun of her.

And the boys stopped teasing Brianna in less than a week.

Jesus said, "Love your enemies. Pray for those who hurt you. Then you will be sons of your Father who is in heaven." Matthew 5:44–45

When have you needed forgiveness for teasing others? When have you been teased? How did you respond? Also read Matthew 5:38–48.

WWJ

CONFESSION (Part One)

"No other moms make their kids work all the time!" Christina's face burned with anger. "All my friends went swimming."

"You can go as soon as we finish," said Mom. "Please rub the dark stain on the garage door smoothly so it doesn't streak."

Christina plunged her cloth into the can again and let the stain drip across the floor between the can and the door.

"I've had about enough of your sloppy work and poor attitude," Mom said. "Do you want me to leave and let you do this *alone?*"

"No." Christina cleaned the floor spills with a fresh rag.

"Do you really think it's unfair that I ask you to help out for just an hour?" asked Mom.

Christina didn't answer.

Mom shook her head. "Why didn't you put on rubber gloves when I told you to? Now your hands are all stained."

"You made me hurry out here. And I couldn't find any gloves!" Christina hoped her stained hands made Mom feel guilty.

"You are being disobedient about everything I ask."

"I am not!"

"Put the rags in the garbage can and put the lid on it so they won't catch fire," said Mom as she walked into the house.

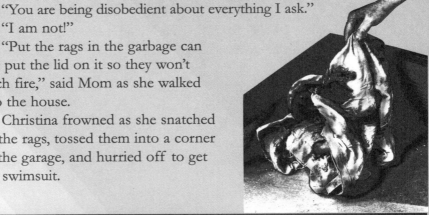

Christina frowned as she snatched up the rags, tossed them into a corner of the garage, and hurried off to get her swimsuit.

"Children, obey your parents...because it's the right thing to do....Then things will go well with you." Ephesians 6:1, 3

Why should you be careful to obey your parents?
What problems have happened when you've disobeyed?
Also read Romans 13:1–5.

CONFESSION (Part Two)

Christina sat straight up in bed. She sniffed the air. *Was that smoke?* She threw off her quilt and followed the smell out of her bedroom and down the hallway.

Smoke billowed out of the kitchen. "Fire!" Christina screamed. An alarm by the bedrooms went off. Her mother and brother rushed from their rooms. Mom hurried the children outside after she made a quick call to 911.

In the driveway, Christina and her brother held their mother's hands and watched flames engulf the garage.

Mom asked, "Christina, what did you do with those oily rags I told you to throw away yesterday?"

Suddenly Christina remembered. "I put them in the trash." She'd been in such a hurry to swim that she had tossed the rags in a corner. They must have caught fire—just as her mother had said they could. Christina realized that the fire had been caused by her carelessness!

Two hours later, the fire trucks pulled away. Firefighters had saved the house but not the garage. Christina stared at the black hole where the garage used to be.

Sobbing, Christina flung herself in her mother's arms. "This is all my fault," she wailed. "I disobeyed. I threw the rags in a corner instead of in the garbage can. They caught fire. Can you ever forgive me?"

Mom put her arms around Christina. "This is a painful lesson," she said. "Because Jesus forgives you, I can, too."

"I didn't know disobeying could cause so much trouble," said Christina. "I pray that I've learned my lesson."

"God is faithful and fair. If we admit that we have sinned, he will forgive us our sins....He will make us pure." 1 John 1:9

When have you learned a painful lesson?
Are you always quick to ask your parents' forgiveness?
Also read 1 John 1:5–10.

NO FREE LUNCH

Principal Carter leaned across his desk. "I think you made a mistake today, Justin. You took Sam's lunch from the shelf above the coat rack."

Justin hung his head. "I didn't make a mistake. I forgot my lunch, so I took Sam's."

"Do you have enough food at home, Justin?"

"Yes. I just can't remember to bring my lunch box."

Principal Carter raised his eyebrows. "What about the frosted cupcake missing from Sally's lunch yesterday? And the cheese and crackers Frank couldn't find?"

Justin sighed. "I took them, too."

"What would Jesus want you to do about taking the other children's lunches?" asked the principal.

"Give them back," said Justin.

"But how can you do that? You already ate their food."

"Oh." Justin thought a minute. "Maybe I could buy Sally a new cupcake. And bring Frank some cheese and crackers from home." He paused. "Mr. Carter, I want to tell them I'm sorry. Do you think they'll forgive me?"

His principal smiled. "I think they will."

"I want Jesus to forgive me, too. Can we pray about it?"

They bowed their heads. "Dear Jesus, please forgive me for taking the lunches. Help Sam and Sally and Frank to forgive me. And please help me remember to bring my lunch."

Justin looked up. "I'll write a note to remind me to bring my lunch. And I'll tape it on the front of my notebook. And now that I've asked Jesus to forgive me, I'm ready to ask Sam to forgive me, too."

"God, create a pure heart in me. Give me a new spirit that is faithful to you. Don't send me away from you." Psalm 51:10–11

When have you taken something that wasn't yours?
Are you always careful to do what is right?
Also read Psalm 103:8–13.

CARELESS CATSUP CAPER

"Hey! Your lip is bleeding!" said Katie.

Beth licked her lips and grinned. "It's catsup!" She took another french fry, dipped it in catsup, and popped it in her mouth.

Katie laughed. "It sure looked like blood…like somebody beat you up. Hey—that's an idea! Let's smear catsup on your face and arm and see who you can fool."

Beth laughed. "Great idea! Make my face look like I've been punched. And give me a bloody nose."

Katie streaked Beth's face and arms with catsup. Then she messed up her hair and dripped catsup on her shirt.

Beth giggled. "This will be fun." She ran outside, waving her arms. "Daddy!" she yelled. "Help me! He beat me up!"

Dad stopped working on the car. "Who hurt you?"

"That boy!" Beth pointed down the street. Just then a boy rode his bike around the corner. Beth's dad dropped his wrench and raced after the boy.

"Stop!" Beth ran after her dad. "It's a joke—it's only catsup!"

Dad stopped. But he didn't laugh. Eyes filled with tears, he walked slowly back to his daughter. He knelt, put his arms around her, and held her without saying a word.

Beth's heart ached. "Forgive me, Daddy. I didn't think you would believe me. I didn't mean to make you sad."

WWJ

"A wise son [or daughter] makes his [or her] father glad."
Proverbs 15:20

When have you played a joke that backfired?
Do you always speak the truth? Are you a joy to your parents?
Also read Psalm 119:41–48.

DON'T BE SELFISH

"I" Problems

What You Need:

> A Bible, heavy gift wrapping paper or several sheets of newspaper, string, a stick, individually wrapped candies

What To Do:

1. Read Genesis 13:5–11.

2. Talk about each person's natural (sinful) inclination to be selfish: to choose or keep the best, the most, the biggest; the desire to be first or to have his or her own way. Discuss ways to practice unselfishness. Emphasize the joy it can bring.

3. Make a simple piñata by placing candies in a large sheet of wrapping paper. Tie all edges together with string and hang it in a doorway. Let children take turns whacking the paper with a stick until the piñata breaks and the candy falls out.

4. Later discuss how the children felt as they scrambled to get the most candy. Talk about selfish attitudes and the attitudes of a giving heart.

RIIKA'S PARTY

"You don't have to come inside Riika's house, Mom. I'll call you in the morning when I'm ready to come home," said Molly.

I don't want Mom spoiling this overnight party. I finally get to hang out with Riika, the most popular girl in fifth grade.

Mom parked the car in front of Riika's house and turned off the motor. "Honey, I'd like to come in and meet Riika's mom."

"She's probably busy," said Molly. "Wait here a minute. I'll take my present in and then come get my sleeping bag and overnight bag."

Mom is so strict! She probably wouldn't approve of Riika and her heavy makeup and dangling earrings...or her eighth grade boyfriend.

Molly rang the doorbell. *It's a good thing Mom didn't ask what movies we'd see tonight. Then she wouldn't let me come for sure!*

Riika's mom answered the door. Behind her, in the living room, Molly could see girls bouncing on the furniture. Other girls watched MTV and danced. Riika was dancing with her boyfriend.

Suddenly Molly saw the party through her mom's eyes.

No way, she thought. *This is not where I should be.*

"Here," said Molly as she handed over her gift. "I can't stay for the party, but please give Riika her birthday present."

Molly climbed back in the car. "I'm going home with you, Mom. I didn't want you to come in because I didn't want you to meet Riika. But when I looked in at the party, I didn't *want* to stay. It's more important to be like Jesus than to be popular."

WWJ

"*So we will all have to explain to God the things we have done.*"
Romans 14:12

Do your friends help you grow *closer* to Jesus?
Is there anyone who is a bad influence in your life?
Also read Psalm 101:1–4.

UNSELFISH PRAYER

What if my mom and I were starving and homeless? What if we had to cross a mountain in the winter? Darin watched the television pictures of hundreds of starving refugees, mostly women and children, crossing the border into Albania.

The TV picture focused on a mother holding a child in her lap. The reporter explained, "This twelve-year-old boy was shot during army crossfire this morning. His mother wrapped her shawl around his neck and face to stop the bleeding. But no medical help is available at this mountain border crossing."

It hurt Darin to see the pain in the boy's eyes. He turned back to his sketch pad, but he couldn't work on his drawing anymore.

"Oh, Jesus, that boy is my age. I wish I could help him. But I can't go to Albania. And I don't even know his name."

Then Darin realized, *I can pray for him!* Setting aside his pens and sketch pad, he got down on his knees.

"Dear Jesus, I'm not praying for myself today. I'm praying for that boy I just saw on TV. You know who he is. I know that You love him.

"Please help him know You. Touch him and bless him. Remind him that You are with him. And keep reminding me to pray for him. Amen."

Jesus said, "If you remain joined to me and my words remain in you, ask for anything you wish. And it will be given to you." John 15:7

Do you pray more for yourself...or for others?
Will you pray for those who are suffering in this world? Do it now.
Also read James 5:13–18.

FATHER'S DAY DINNER

Making this dinner was my idea. Why is she saying it was hers? Jenny poured a cup of raisins into the cookie dough. She stopped and looked at her sister, Karen. "Why did you say this was *your* idea?"

"Because it was. I mean, we both thought of making Dad a special Father's Day dinner."

"No, Karen. It was *my* idea. I'm the one who planned the special dinner for Dad. I asked you to help me."

"Whatever," said Karen. "I'll set the table."

An hour later, Jenny set a platter of roasted chicken on the decorated table. Karen carried in green beans and baked potatoes.

When Dad walked in the door, supper was ready and waiting.

"What a feast!" said Dad as he took his seat at the table.

"It was *my* idea," said Karen.

"Yours?" asked Dad. Karen just smiled and said nothing.

Jenny glanced at her sister. *What about me?* she thought. *Dear Jesus, help me not be mad at Karen for taking all the credit. Help me love her.*

Dad gave thanks and they passed the food around the table. Jenny nibbled her drumstick and poked her potato.

"Why aren't you eating, Jenny?" asked Dad. Jenny said nothing.

Karen set her fork down. Tears filled her eyes. "I'm sorry, Daddy. I wanted you to think this dinner was my idea. I lied. It was Jenny's idea. I just helped her. I'm really sorry, Daddy."

She turned to Jenny and asked, "Will you forgive me?"

"I forgive you. I couldn't have made the dinner alone."

Dad smiled at his girls. "Very good. So…what's for dessert?"

"Burnt cookies," said Jenny, jumping up from the table. "Unless I get them out of the oven *right now!*"

WWJ

"It isn't proper…to brag. And it certainly isn't proper…to tell lies!…Those who erase a sin by forgiving it show love." Proverbs 17:7, 9

When have you loved someone in spite of his or her faults? Has someone ever lied about what *you* did? What did you do? Also read Proverbs 15:1–3, 23, 26, 31–32.

WWJ

SELFISH PRAYER

I'm next. This had better work. Sweat broke out on Calvin's forehead. His teacher was collecting everyone's report cards.

Calvin kept his report card hidden inside his desk. He had not shown it to his parents. His F in math was bad news.

If Mom and Dad saw it, they would ground me forever. No computer games. No friends over. No TV. No life!

"Calvin Taylor," said Mrs. Schurr, reading his name off a list.

Calvin stood up. He pulled his report card out of his desk and glanced at the signature. It was supposed to be his dad's. But Calvin had asked Jarred, one of his classmates, to forge his dad's name. Because Jarred was a poor speller, he had to ask Calvin how to spell his dad's first name, Raymond.

Calvin handed the report card to his teacher. *Please, Lord,* he prayed, *don't let Mrs. Schurr find out that it's not my dad's signature.*

She glanced at it and laid it with the others on her desk.

Whew. Thanks, Lord. The lunch bell rang and Calvin headed out the door. Suddenly he heard Mrs. Schurr call his name. He stopped and turned. She waved his report card.

Calvin's heart flip-flopped.

"Your *dad* needs help with his spelling," said Mrs. Schurr. She showed him the card. Calvin saw that Jarred had misspelled his dad's last name. He had written it as Teller instead of Taylor!

"When you do ask for something, you don't receive it. Why? Because you ask for the wrong reason." James 4:3

When have you prayed a selfish prayer?
Why won't God answer selfish prayers?
Also read James 4:1–9.

LAVENDER AND LACE

"Oh, Mom! I love it!" squealed Kate as she ripped open her Christmas present and found a frilly red dress Mom had made. Dad's camera flashed. Sunni just watched quietly.

Erica and Sunni opened their gifts and found new dresses. "I love mine, too," said Erica, hugging a ruffled blue dress. "It's the most beautiful dress I've ever had!"

Sunni held up her lavender dress trimmed in white lace, then dropped it on the floor. *I didn't want a dress! I wanted a doll.*

"Okay, girls, run to your rooms and put your dresses on. We want to get a picture of you wearing them," Mom said.

Sunni picked up her dress and dragged it across the floor to the room she shared with her sisters.

"What's wrong with you, Sunni?" Kate whispered.

"I…wanted a doll," Sunni grumbled.

When they returned to the living room, Dad told the three girls to sit side by side on the couch. Kate and Erica flounced down in their fancy dresses. Sunni plopped between them in her old jeans. Mom looked disappointed. Sunni didn't care.

"Okay. Close your eyes, girls. Mom has another *surprise*."

Sunni closed her eyes and waited. She felt something soft in her arms. She looked up to find a doll dressed in lavender with white lace. Kate held a doll with a red dress that matched hers. Erica cuddled a blue one.

Sunni felt ashamed. "I'm sorry. I only cared about myself. I didn't even care if I hurt your feelings. Forgive me for being unthankful, Mom."

"I forgive you," Mom said, hugging her.

WW.I

"Don't do anything only to get ahead. Don't do it because you are proud.... Think of others as better than yourselves." Philippians 2:3

When have you behaved selfishly?...behaved unselfishly?
Who is the most unselfish person you know?
Also read Philippians 2:1–11.

BE HONEST

Say or Pay

What You Need:

A Bible, a list of true and false statements about Bible stories, and a list of silly consequences for incorrect answers, both prepared earlier by a parent

What To Do:

1. Read Acts 5:1–11.

2. Talk about being honest in words and actions. Impress upon the family the consequences of honesty and dishonesty. Sometimes rewards and punishments are immediate and visible, sometimes not. Our character and our relationship with God are always affected.

3. Play "Say or Pay." Read a statement about a Bible story. (Example: "Noah married Eve, True or False.") A correct answer earns the player a point or a treat. An incorrect guess earns a consequence (quack like a duck, or shine my shoes, etc.).

WWJ

HIDDEN BY A FENCE

"I don't like Mrs. Warner!" Beau told Travis. He tossed a rock over the fence and into her backyard to prove it.

The sound of something breaking, then a patio door sliding open, started his heart pounding.

"Oh no!" Mrs. Warner exclaimed from her yard.

"I'm in trouble," Beau groaned. "I *broke* something."

"Don't worry about it. She can't see you, so she can't prove you did it," Travis said. "Besides, you don't like her."

Beau agreed. "You're right. She can't prove anything." But a bad feeling tugged at his chest. Beau remembered the time Mrs. Warner baked a batch of chocolate chip cookies for him. They were good, too.

"What are you boys doing?" Mrs. Warner asked.

Beau whirled to look at the fence. Mrs. Warner's head stuck up over the top. Travis laughed. "Why didn't you tell me she owned a ladder?" he asked Beau.

Beau's face felt hot. Mrs. Warner looked real sad.

"Someone broke the flower pot that my husband bought for my birthday. It…means a lot to me."

Beau felt guilty. He prayed a quick prayer asking Jesus what he should do next.

"I'm the one who broke it," Beau admitted. "I'm sorry. I'll save up my allowance and buy another one for you."

"Thanks. You know, just because there's a tall fence between us, doesn't mean I don't know what you're doing."

That's true of God, too, thought Beau. *Forgive me, Lord.*

WWJ

"*Stay away from every kind of evil….May [God] make you holy through and through.*" 1 Thessalonians 5:22–23

When have you told the truth about what you did?
Why does God want you to stop lying?
Also read 1 Peter 3:8–12.

FRAMED

"What big eyes you have!" Jocelyn told her little sister.

Four-year-old Suzanna posed in front of the bedroom mirror. A flowered canvas bag hung over her arm. A huge pair of framed glasses perched on her tiny nose. "My glasses—like yours."

Just then, Mom walked by with a load of laundry. "Suzanna, where did you get those frames?"

"I got lots, Mama." Suzanna opened her bag and showed her mother a stash of frames.

Mom's eyes widened. "That's at least $600 worth of frames! Where did you get these?"

"I'm not sure," said Jocelyn. "I took her along when I bought my new glasses yesterday at Macy's. She probably picked up these frames while I was trying on some different styles."

"We'll have to take them back, Suzanna," said Mother.

"They're mine!" cried Suzanna. "I picked them out."

"We can't just take things from a store. When we take something without paying, that's stealing. God doesn't want us to steal."

Suzanna's faced puckered. Tears overflowed down her cheeks.

Jocelyn knelt and hugged her. "You didn't know it was wrong, Suzanna. You saw me picking out frames and trying them on. But I paid for the one I got. Learn to do what's right while you're young. Then you'll do what pleases God the rest of your life."

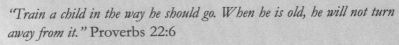

"Train a child in the way he should go. When he is old, he will not turn away from it." Proverbs 22:6

Have you ever done something you didn't know was wrong? What do you think would happen if you were never corrected? Also read Exodus 20:15.

PENNY HONESTY

"Look, Mom, look! I found some money!" said Brian.

His mother smiled and looked in his hand at the two quarters. "Where did you find them?" she asked.

"Out front. Could we go to the store and spend them?"

"Why don't you save them, sweetie. Then you can add to them and buy your dad a birthday present?"

"How? This is the only time I ever found any money."

"You can earn it. Do some extra jobs around the house. For example, I'll give you ten cents to dust the family room, ten cents to sweep the porch, and ten cents to dry the dishes. You'll have enough money for a nice present in no time."

After Brian matched all the socks in the laundry room, Mom handed him a dime and he dropped it into his piggy bank. Then he looked through a catalog and found the perfect necktie.

Soon Brian had earned almost enough to place the order for Dad's necktie. All he needed was one more dime.

"Why don't you hang up Dad's tools?" Mom suggested.

Brian hurried out to the garage, but found only three tools lying on the bench. He hung them up. When Mom came out and checked his work, she counted ten pennies into his hand.

"Good job," she said.

"No, Mom. I can't take these," said Brian.

"But ten pennies are the same as one dime."

"I know that," said Brian. "But I didn't do very much work here in the garage. It wouldn't be honest to take *ten* cents." He handed five pennies back to her. "I'll earn the rest tomorrow

"Dear friend, don't be like those who do evil. Be like those who do good. Anyone who does what is good belongs to God." 3 John verse 11

When have you done something good or honest?
How can other people tell that you belong to God?
Also read 2 Corinthians 8:21.

SOUR GUMBALL

I'm going to steal a gumball right in front of my Sunday School teacher. Randy smirked as he strolled into the convenience store and stepped up to the gumball machine.

"Hi, Mrs. Walters." She looked at him from behind the counter and gave him a big smile. *I'm her favorite student. This will be a piece of cake. One of my friends showed me how to do this.*

Randy made his quarter sound as if he pushed it into the slot. Then he turned the handle. "Mrs. Walters, the gumball machine is broken. It took my quarter, but it didn't give me a gumball."

"I'm sorry," she said and brought a quarter from the cash register. She slipped the coin into the slot and turned the handle. Out rolled a speckled gumball. Randy popped it into his mouth.

"Thanks!" He gave her a big smile. *I knew she'd fall for it. To Mrs. Walters, I can do no wrong.*

All the way home, Randy sucked on the gumball, but the sweetness made him feel sick. *I stole it. I can't enjoy it. Forgive me, Jesus.* He turned around and ran back to the store.

"Mrs. Walters, I have a confession to make. There's nothing wrong with the gumball machine. I tricked you. I'm really sorry."

Her face turned pale with shock and disappointment.

I not only stole, but now I've ruined my relationship with my teacher, who trusted me. Dear Lord, please help me never to do anything like this again.

WWJ

"Anyone who does wrong will be paid back for what he does. God treats everyone the same." Colossians 3:25

Have you ever tried to get something without paying for it? When have you deceived someone who trusted you? Also read Colossians 3:20–25.

TOOTHPASTE LIES

I know I'm not supposed to use my folks' bathroom, thought Launa. *But Tara's hogging our bathroom sink, and I've got to get ready for school.*

Launa squeezed the toothpaste onto her brush. In her hurry, a blob of toothpaste fell on the rug. As she moved closer to the sink, she stepped in it. When she looked down to see what had squished under her shoe, foamy toothpaste dribbled out of her mouth onto the carpet.

What a mess! But I've got to catch the bus. I hope Mom won't notice this. I didn't mean to make a mess on her new carpet.

After school, Mother called the two girls into the bathroom. "How did blobs of toothpaste get all over this new carpet?"

"No idea," said Tara.

"I wasn't around," said Launa, trying not to look at her mom. "Maybe it was Dad."

"Well, I suppose I might have dropped some, too," said Mom.

Whew. I got away with that, thought Launa. But later that day, and the day after that, she grew more and more uneasy. Every time she walked by her parents' bedroom, she felt guilty.

Finally, Launa couldn't stand it any longer. After praying in her room, she found her mother. "Mom, I'm the one who dropped toothpaste on your carpet. I'm sorry for lying. Will you forgive me?"

"Of course I forgive you. Did you already talk to God about it?"

"Yes. Just a few minutes ago. That's how I knew I needed to ask you for forgiveness, too." She gave her mom a hug and hurried into her bedroom to prepare for school.

Sure feels good to know that Jesus and Mom forgave me. There's nothing like confessing...except being honest in the first place!

WW_

"When I kept silent about my sin, my body became weak....Then I admitted my sin to you....And you forgave the guilt of my sin." Psalm 32:3, 5

When have you felt guilty about what you've done?
Have you ever found it hard to ask your parents' forgiveness?
Also read Colossians 3:7–10.

GOD'S CREATURES

Guess Who?

What You Need:

A Bible, your imagination

What to Do:

1. Read Genesis 1:20–26.

2. Talk about the wonderful animals God created and our role in respecting, enjoying, and caring for them. Let everyone share what is their favorite animal and why they enjoy it.

3. Play animal charades. Each player takes turns choosing an animal to imitate with actions and gestures, but no sounds. Have other people guess, asking "Are you a… (name of animal)?"

4. The actor answers by nodding his head yes or no. If no one guesses the animal being imitated, a player can add the sound made by the animal or give other additional hints.

BIRD NEST DISASTER

No one will miss me if I leave now, thought Colleen as she dropped out of the line of campers headed for the archery range. She turned down another path in the quiet forest.

Suddenly she stopped. *A bird's nest!* Climbing the tree, Colleen stretched full-length along the branch. She reached into the nest and gently picked up three bird's eggs. Holding them in her palm, she gazed at the blue spotted robin eggs.

They're so tiny and perfect! She felt the warmth of the smooth, delicate shells. *There's life in these eggs!* Suddenly Colleen felt as if she were trespassing. *I'm stealing the Mama bird's eggs. I'd better put them back.*

When she reached out to put the eggs back in their nest, Colleen lost her balance. She accidentally tightened her hand that held the eggs. Colleen felt warm liquid ooze in her palm.

Opening her fingers, she stared at three broken eggs. *I didn't want to hurt them!* Colleen felt sick inside as she put the shattered eggs back in nest. She didn't know what else to do.

She spent the rest of the week in silent misery. At the final campfire award ceremony, Colleen's counselor presented her with the Best Camper Award. Colleen burst into tears.

"I'm *not* the best camper. I killed three baby birds before they had a chance to live! I hate myself, and I know God hates me. They were His creatures."

Colleen felt her counselor's arms around her. "Jesus knows what you did. He still loves you. Just ask Him to forgive you."

Closing her eyes, Colleen whispered, "I'm sorry for killing the birds. Please forgive me, Jesus. Thank You for still loving me. I love You, too. Amen."

"The Lord is close to those whose hearts have been broken. He saves those whose spirits have been crushed." Psalm 34:18

Have you ever felt like God wouldn't forgive you?
Do you need to ask Jesus to forgive you right now? He will!
Also read Psalm 51:1–8.

HEIDI'S HOME!

"Heidi's not coming back," Brian told his mom. Then he whistled through the screen door for his pet golden labrador one last time. "She's been gone for three days."

Shutting the door, he slumped onto a chair, his face in his hands. "She's probably dead. No use looking anymore." Just then a faint scratching sounded at the back door.

Brian sat up and listened. *Heidi? Could that be you?* Another scratch. Then another. He ran to the door and threw it wide.

There she stood, her fur spotted with dry mud, her tail swinging in a slow circle. Suddenly angry, Brian said, "Bad dog!"

Heidi whimpered and licked his pant leg. Then she collapsed.

"Mom, call the vet!" Brian knelt and stared at the long red gash on his dog's belly. "I'm sorry, girl," he said.

He stroked her neck all the way to the vet's office.

"From the looks of this wound," said the vet, "I'd say she was hit by a car. Two, maybe three days ago."

"And I…" Brian sniffled. "I yelled at her because I thought she ran away."

"Dogs are loyal," said the vet. "She'll always love you."

"Will she ever be okay?" asked Brian.

"After surgery, yes. Then you can show her how much you love her."

"A friend is always loyal."
Proverbs 17:17 (NLT)

Why do you think God made animals, especially dogs?
How are you *loyal* to God? Do you trust Him and serve Him?
Also read Matthew 6:24–25.

KITTY'S IN TROUBLE

"Where's the fluffy calico kitten with the white face?" asked Marty. His mother cat licked another baby and didn't seem to miss the baby calico.

Marty checked under the mother cat. No kitty. He searched around the basket. Nothing. He heard a faint meow come from the garage—from behind a tall metal cabinet.

"Mom!" he called. "I need help. The calico kitty is stuck behind the garage cabinet."

Mom hurried out to help.

"Help me get on top of the cabinet. Maybe I can reach the kitten," Marty said. "It sounds so scared."

Mom hoisted Marty onto the cabinet. Marty stretched across the top and squinted into the darkness behind it.

"The kitty is way down there, but it's too far to reach. We'll have to pull the cabinet away from the wall to get it out."

Marty climbed back down. But, no matter how hard he and his mom tried, they couldn't budge the cabinet. The kitty cried louder.

"Let's pray for God to show us what to do," said Marty.

He joined hands with Mom and they prayed together. When they opened their eyes, Marty noticed a roll of carpet scrap in the rafters. Holding onto one end of the carpet, he unrolled it down behind the cabinet. The carpet reached all the way to the kitty. And the kitty crawled right up the carpet into Marty's waiting arms.

Marty snuggled and comforted it. "Sometimes it surprises me how quickly God answers my prayers. Thank You, Lord."

WWJ

"Let us boldly approach the throne of grace. Then we will receive mercy. We will find grace to help us when we need it." Hebrews 4:16

When have you ever prayed for an animal in trouble?
Do you think God cares about your pets?
Also read Psalm 31:1–2.

UNDERCOVER DUCKS

"Help, Mrs. Schiller!" Lance sprinted into his neighbor's yard. "Some baby ducks are trapped in the sewer!"

Mrs. Schiller looked up from weeding her flowerbed.

Lance stopped to take a breath. "On my way home from school, I found a duck in the street. It quacked and quacked as it walked around and around a sewer cover. I could hear little peeps underneath. Can I borrow your hot tub skimmer? I think I can get them out with a long handle and a net."

Lance followed Mrs. Schiller around to her back porch.

"Here. And take this pail of water, too," said Mrs. Schiller. "You'll need something to help clean off the ducklings."

"Thanks," called Lance, as he hurried back to the sewer outlet.

He tugged at the metal cover while the mother duck paced the pavement. Lance finally slid the cover off the opening. He lowered the hot tub skimmer into the dark, smelly hole.

Feeling the skimmer bump against a little body, he scooped it up and pulled a bedraggled duckling to the surface.

The mother duck waddled over, quacking excitedly.

After placing the baby in the bucket, Lance continued fishing until he found three more ducklings.

"It took a while, but your babies are safe," he told the mama duck. "I would have felt terrible if I had lost even one!"

"[The Lord] is being patient for your sake. He does not want anyone to perish."
2 Peter 3:9 (NLT)

Why is Jesus concerned about people who are lost without Him?
How can you help Jesus rescue *people* who are lost?
Also read Luke 15:3–7.

SUNDANCE

"Somebody help!" screamed Lindsay. She knelt beside Sundance, stroking the horse's neck. "Help!"

The trainer pushed into the stall, and Lindsay moved over to give him room to examine Sundance. "What happened?"

"I don't know!" said Lindsay. "Sundance was fine ten minutes ago. Then she just went down! She can't breathe!"

"She's choking," said the trainer. "But I don't know how to help her. I'll go and call the vet right away."

Lindsay patted the horse's neck and tried to calm down. "Sundance, don't die." She wiped her eyes on her T-shirt. "Lord, I don't understand. I always wanted a horse. You gave us Sundance. And You gave us a stable where we could afford to keep her. Please, Lord, don't let her die."

After what seemed like hours, the vet arrived. He took Sundance to his hospital for surgery.

When he finished an operation on Sundance, the vet talked to Lindsay and her parents. "You have two choices—put Sundance on a watered grain diet, or send her to a farm where she can graze in a pasture. If you keep her in the stable, she could choke again. Next time she might die."

Her parents turned to Lindsay. "It's up to you."

Tears ran down Lindsay's face. "I know what God wants me to do. It would be selfish to keep Sundance in the stable."

Lindsay wiped her tears. "It really hurts to lose her, but I'm glad she's alive. It was wonderful to have her for a while. I know I can always go visit her at the farm."

WWJ

"Who is the man who has respect for the Lord? God will teach him the way he has chosen for him." Psalm 25:12

How can *you* know what God wants you to do?
When has God shown you the right choice? What did you do?
Also read Psalm 25:4–9.

GOD CARES FOR YOU

All I Need

What You Need:

A Bible, a blindfold, a simple obstacle course

What To Do:

1. Read Exodus 14:19–25; 15:22–25; 16:13–17.

2. List the different ways God cares for us (providing for our basic needs of sunshine, water, oxygen; giving us health to work for food, clothing, shelter; giving us the Bible as a guide to wise living; providing salvation and a heavenly home).

3. Discuss how this inspires our trust in God.

4. Experience another's care. The leader blindfolds one player while the others create an obstacle course. The leader then holds the player's hand and leads him or her through the course or gives verbal directions. The other players either remain silent or call out warnings. Take turns going through the obstacle course.

COMFORTING ANGER

"I'm sorry, Jillian. Dad and I don't want you to hang out at the mall with your friends," said Mom.

"You never let me do *anything*. You don't care!" Jillian turned to her sister, Pam. "Mom never lets *me* do anything."

Pam smacked the table with the flat of her hand. "How dare you act like such a brat! She isn't even your real mom."

"N-not my...mom? What?"

"Mom and Dad went through a lot to adopt you. Why do you argue so much with them?" Pam slammed out the door.

Jillian froze with her mouth open. Her face felt hot and she couldn't breathe. *Adopted? Was it true?*

Mom walked over to Jillian and put an arm around her.

"I'm sorry we never told you," she whispered. Tears streamed down her face.

"Is Pam your real daughter?" asked Jillian. "Do you love her more...than you love me?"

Mom's voice rose. "Don't ever say that!" Her sudden anger shocked Jillian. "Don't ever—EVER—say you're not my real child. You *are* my child. I chose you."

For some reason that Jillian didn't understand, Mom's anger...*comforted* her. She hugged Mom while they both cried.

"For the first time in my life I'm almost glad you're strict. When you discipline me, I know that it shows you love me." Jillian's eyes twinkled. "Even though I'd rather have my own way."

Mom pulled Jillian close. "I do love you, my daughter."

"And I love you, my mom."

WWJ

"The Lord trains those he loves. He is like a father who trains the son he is pleased with." Proverbs 3:12

How do you react when your parents discipline you?
How does your parents' discipline show their love for you?
Also read Ephesians 1:1–6.

RATTLER!

"I'm going to catch grasshoppers!" Carla clutched her bucket and climbed out of the van. Jerry grabbed his fishing pole and another bucket and raced after her.

Grasshoppers flew in all directions when Carla ran through the tall grass by the river. "Don't hop so fast!" she called to them.

It wasn't long before Jerry held up his bucket. "I've captured five 'hoppers. Now watch me catch the first fish for supper."

Carla followed the grasshoppers farther along the grassy riverbank. Hearing a rattling sound, she crouched down. *That must be a big grasshopper,* she thought. *It sounds like a baby's rattle.*

Peering through the grass, Carla gasped. A large snake slithered toward her. Its tail shook a pearly white rattle.

Carla froze. The snake stopped. It flicked its forked tongue. Its eyes never left hers. She tried to scream, but no sound came out. She tried to run, but her legs wouldn't move.

I'm going to die, she thought. *Jesus, please help me!*

Finally the snake turned and crawled away. As soon as Carla couldn't see it, her legs worked again. She ran back to the car and told her father what happened.

"Thank God you were paralyzed with fear!" said Dad. "If you had moved, the snake probably would have struck you."

Carla hugged her dad. "I prayed," she whispered, "and Jesus heard me... *Thank You, Jesus!*"

WWJ

"So do not be afraid. I am with you. Do not be terrified. I am your God. I will make you strong and help you." Isaiah 41:10

What is the first thing you do in times of fear or danger?
In what ways do you need Jesus' help today?
Also read Isaiah 43:1–3, 10.

DAD, DON'T LEAVE

Angry voices from the kitchen made Sue tiptoe to her bedroom door. She opened it just wide enough to listen.

"All we ever do is fight!" said Dad. "This time I'm leaving."

"Then leave," said Mom. "You never want to talk about our problems. So go on. Just leave!"

Sue cried as she closed her door. "Oh, dear God, no! Don't let Dad leave. Why did Mom tell him to leave?" Sue stuffed tissues into her backpack. *Why do they have to fight all the time? Why?*

Tossing her jacket over her shoulder, she stepped into the hall-way. "Bye!" she called. "I'm going to school now!" She hurried out without waiting for a response.

Why can't Mom and Dad love each other like Jessie's parents? Where will Dad go? How will Mom get a job? What will happen to me? Oh, dear Jesus, I'm so scared!

At school, Sue's teacher described a project the students could make for Christmas. Sue bit the inside of her lip to keep from crying. *What a miserable Christmas this is going to be without Dad!*

Feeling sick and fighting tears, she raised her hand to be excused to go to the restroom.

She closed herself in one of the stalls, glad to be alone. "Dear Jesus, please don't let Dad leave us," she prayed. "Help my parents stop fighting and start loving each other. And help me not be so scared and upset."

Walking back to class, Sue felt different. She was no longer afraid. She knew—she just *knew*—that Jesus was with her.

NOTE: Although Sue's dad moved out that afternoon, he returned after Christmas to stay with his family.

WWJ

"I have learned the secret of being content no matter what happens....I can do everything by the power of Christ. He gives me strength." Philippians 4:11, 13

What discourages and upsets you the most?
Talk to Jesus about what you need. Thank Him for His strength.
Also read Isaiah 40:28–31.

JOURNEY TO THE EDGE

"I can't see the road! The rain is coming down too hard!"

Even in the backseat of the car, Casey heard the tension in his father's voice. Casey gripped the door handle as they drove through sheets of rain down the winding mountain road.

"Let's pull off to the side of the road until the rain lets up," Casey urged.

"We can't," said Mother. "There's no shoulder where we could park." She peered out of her window. "There aren't even any guard rails on this side of the road. It's a straight drop down to the river."

Casey thought of the river hundreds of yards below. It made him shiver. "Jesus, please keep us safe," he whispered.

Suddenly their front tire blew out! The car swerved. It veered back and forth across the two-lane road and then slid toward the unguarded side of the road.

"Lord, save us!" cried Casey's mother.

Dad pumped the brakes. The car came to a stop at the edge of the steep cliff. One wheel hung off the road, spinning in space. Casey held his breath. He didn't move until his father slowly drove forward and eased the back wheel onto the road.

"Thank You, Jesus, for saving us!" prayed Casey.

"'Lord, help!' they cried in their trouble, and he rescued them from their distress." Psalm 107:6 (NLT)

When have you prayed to God in a time of danger?
Who is in trouble and needs your prayers? Take time to pray.
Also read Psalm 91:14–16.

KIP'S HOMECOMING

"He's here!" Vanessa ran to her dad, grabbed his hand, and pulled him toward the gate. "Kip's home!"

Since her parents' divorce, Vanessa loved her brother Kip more than anyone. She wrote him every day, even though his busy army schedule kept him from answering her letters.

"Settle down," Dad said, grinning.

Vanessa let go of her dad's hand and paced at the entrance to the passenger tunnel.

"There he is!" Jumping up and down, Vanessa waved at a young man in army fatigues. Kip grinned and waved back. Within moments they hugged and laughed.

Voices from the walkway behind them called, "Kip!"

Vanessa whirled around to see three of her brother's friends from high school. Kip hurried to greet them. Vanessa and her dad stood alone while he chatted with his friends. Vanessa felt like she did the day Mom moved out.

At baggage pick up, Kip gave Vanessa another hug. "You don't mind if I go to a movie with my friends, do you?" he asked. "I'll see you in the morning."

"It's...okay," Vanessa said, blinking back tears.

She drove home with Dad. Vanessa saw the same hurt on Dad's face that she felt in her heart. She moved to the center of the front seat and buckled herself in. She laid her head on Dad's shoulder and snuggled against him. "I'm glad God won't ever abandon us," she said softly.

Dad sighed and smiled. He put his arm around her. "Me, too. How'd you get so smart?"

WWJ

"Jesus Christ is the same yesterday and today and forever."
Hebrews 13:8

Has someone let you down? How did you feel? What did you do? Which promises of Jesus encourage you the most?
Also read Deuteronomy 31:6–8.

FACING TEMPTATION

Does It Matter, Just This Once?

What You Need:

A Bible, an aluminum foil halo, two aluminum foil "horns"

What To Do:

1. Read James 1:13–17; 1 Corinthians 10:13.

2. Talk about the difference between temptation (the thought, urge, or encouragement to do wrong) and sin (actually doing evil). Discuss ways to resist temptation (withdraw from the person, place, or situation; pray and ask God's help; quote or read Scripture; enlist an older Christian's help).

3. Help children learn how to respond to temptations.
   Set up role-play situations:
   a. The leader describes a situation (cheating on a test, stealing a coveted toy, bad-mouthing a friend, lying about breaking another's possession, etc.).
   b. Each person must decide how to respond to the situation while the "angel" player with the halo gives good advice and the "devil" player with the horns offers reasons to give in to the temptation.

WWJ

MOVIE BLUES

"I'm glad your parents let you stay at my house while they're gone," said Monica. She and Samantha set up a board game in the front room. Monica's father was watching a movie.

Samantha glanced at the TV. *The music sounds scary. It looks like a murder mystery. I shouldn't be watching this.*

When the girls finished their game, Monica climbed on the davenport to watch the movie. Samantha sat down beside her.

Why is Mr. Pentman letting us watch this show? she wondered. *My parents wouldn't like this.* She knew she should leave the room, but she stayed to watch the rest of the movie.

When her parents returned, Samantha couldn't tell them about the movie. Five months passed. *I wish I'd never watched that movie. These nightmares won't go away!*

Finally Samantha told her mother about the nightmares.

"When did you see a thriller?" asked Mother.

"Five months ago, when you and Dad were out of town."

"Why did you wait so long to tell me?"

"I was afraid I'd get in trouble," said Samantha.

"I am disappointed in you," said Mother. "And I'm disappointed in Monica's father. But I want you to tell me when things like this happen. You've allowed harmful pictures into your mind. Only Jesus can erase them. Just ask Him."

Samantha knelt by the bed and prayed, "Dear Jesus. I'm sorry I watched that movie. And I'm sorry I didn't tell Mom right away. Please forgive me. Take away the awful nightmares. Wash my mind clean. Help me do what is right. Amen."

WWJ

"Always think about what is true. Think about what is noble, right and pure. Think about what is lovely and worthy of respect." Philippians 4:8

What have you been thinking about today?
Is there anything you need to tell your parents…or tell God?
Also read Psalm 119:9–16.

JUST SAY NO! (Part One)

"I landed the lead role in the Winter Festival skit!" Caroline danced up the school auditorium aisle, waving her script in the air.

"Way to go!" Caroline's friend Mattie gave her a hug. "I know how much you wanted that part in the play!"

The girls sat down in the auditorium seats to read through the whole script. When they reached page three, Caroline closed the script abruptly. "I can't say these lines, Mattie! They make fun of Jesus and the real meaning of Christmas!"

"What will you do?"

Caroline swallowed hard. "I think I'll have to give up the part." She prayed out loud, "Dear Jesus, show me what You want me to do."

"But you've wanted to be in the Christmas skit for two years!" said Mattie. "Would you give it up for a few bad lines?"

Caroline thought about it. *What is most important—the play or my faith?* After a few moments, Caroline went to find her teacher.

"Mr. Hewitt," Caroline forced out the words. "I can't accept the lead part in the skit. I'm a Christian. Parts of this script make fun of Jesus. I can't say those lines."

Mr. Hewitt raised his eyebrows. "Since you feel that way, we'll find someone else for the lead. Thank you for telling me."

Caroline turned away, blinking back tears. *I know I did the right thing, Lord,* she prayed. *But it sure hurts.*

"Your troubles have come in order to prove that your faith is real. It is worth more than gold." 1 Peter 1:7

Have you ever given up something you wanted to do because of your faith in Jesus? How did you feel afterwards?
Also read James 1:2–8.

JUST SAY NO! (Part Two)

"Caroline, we can't find anyone else for the lead role in our play," said Mr. Hewitt. "But we can change any lines that trouble you."

"Really?" Caroline smiled. "Thank you, Mr. Hewitt."

Every day after school, Caroline studied her part. Wherever a line troubled her, she struck it out and wrote in a new one. Posters across campus announced the Winter Festival play. Students took home invitations to their parents.

Then, three days before the festival, Mr. Hewitt told Caroline that he had not contacted the play's author.

"Without the author's permission," he said, "we will have to perform the play the way it's written."

"I can't do it," said Caroline.

"You can't quit, either," said Mr. Hewitt. "Everything's all set. The posters, the invitations, the actors."

"But I need time to come up with something," Caroline told him. She found Mattie and shared her problem. "Either I let the school down or I let Jesus down. Let's ask Jesus to show me what to do." The girls prayed together and Caroline got an idea.

Caroline approached Mr. Hewitt. "Why not do something different? Dress a student in the bear suit. He can act out the play while another person behind the curtain reads the script."

"Perfect solution," said Mr. Hewitt.

At the end of the performance, the audience applauded wildly. Mattie nudged Caroline. "God sure came through, didn't He?"

Caroline nodded. Although she regretted losing the part, she felt God's approval. And that was worth the sacrifice.

WWJ

"God is faithful. He will not let you be tempted any more than you can take....God will give you a way out so that you can stand up under it." 1 Corinthians 10:13

How can God help you do what is right, even when it's hard? Why does God let us face disappointments and troubles? Also read 1 Corinthians 10:12–13.

CLOSET SMOKER

"Litterbug!" Jana stooped to pick up a half-empty pack of cigarettes. As she walked toward the trash can to throw the pack away, she stopped. *Why do people smoke? I wonder what it's like.*

Glancing around to be sure no one was watching, Jana stuffed the pack in her jeans pocket.

Back at home, Jana took a box of matches out of a kitchen drawer and ran up to her bedroom. Hiding in the closet, she pulled the crumpled pack from her pocket and drew out a bent cigarette. She held it between two fingers like a movie star, struck a match, and lit the end. When she put the cigarette to her lips, she sucked in a deep breath. She coughed and coughed, choking on the smoke.

Yuck! It's awful! Jana looked at the cigarette in her hand. *I never want to smoke one of these again. But what do I do with it now?*

Ashes from the end of the cigarette dropped on the carpet. Jana hoped that the ash wouldn't stain the rug. Now she understood how cigarettes caused fires.

Oh, how will I explain everything to Mom? She told me never to mess with cigarettes. And what about the smoke smell in my closet? Now my clothes stink!

Jana sighed. "Smoking sure isn't as glamorous as I thought. I wish I'd obeyed Mom in the first place."

"Avoid evil. That will show you have understanding."
Job 28:28

How can being sneaky and dishonest cause you trouble?
When have you been tempted to try something that was wrong?
Also read 1 Corinthians 10:12–13.

DIAL-A-JOKE

"Call the 900 number on your screen and hear a new joke every hour," urged the voice in the TV commercial. Alex wrote the 900 number on notepad paper and slipped it into his pocket.

Mom walked by with an armload of folded towels. "I hope you're not planning to call that joke line. It costs money."

Couldn't be that much money. At least not for one call.

Alex waited a few minutes, then picked up the cordless phone and punched in the 900 number. The voice he had heard on TV now asked, "After the plane crash, where were the survivors buried?" Pause. "Nowhere. You don't bury survivors."

Alex chuckled.

Every hour they have a new joke. I'll call one more time. That'll only be a little extra on the phone bill. Dad will never notice. He phoned again and chuckled again.

During the next few weeks, Alex phoned again and again and again. He phoned so many times that the joke line phone bill was no joke. It totaled over $250.

"Did you think Dad and I wouldn't find out?" asked Mom.

"I only planned to phone in a couple of times," said Alex. "Then I couldn't stop."

"And you didn't tell us about it, either. You'll have to pay for those calls, you know."

"I will?"

"You don't expect us to pay for them, do you?"

"I guess not. I'll have to find work on Saturdays and after school. I guess I'll have to work all summer, too. I won't ever call that joke line again. It's not so funny after all."

WWJ

"You can be sure that your sin will be discovered. It will be brought out into the open." Numbers 32:23

Which sins have you tried to hide?
Why is there no such thing as a *secret* sin?
Also read 2 Peter 3:10–14, 17.

JESUS' EXAMPLE

Cross Collage

What You Need:

A Bible, large paper or poster board, marking pens, scissors, and glue

What To Do:

1. Read 1 Corinthians 1:18.

2. Use a variety of colored markers to write down kind things your parents or brothers and sisters have done. Think of a time you asked yourself, "What would Jesus do?" and then did it. Write as many of these as you can remember on separate pieces of paper. Make the writing colorful. Decorate it if you wish.

3. Cut or tear out each WWJD (What Would Jesus Do) deed you write down and glue them into the shape of a cross on a large piece of paper. Tape it to your door or give it to your mom or dad as a gift.

4. Pray and thank Jesus for all the times He helped you do what He wanted you to.

DIRTY TRICKS

Just one more race! If I win this one, it's on to the BMX national finals!
Lance gripped the handlebars and leaned forward. His bike's front
tire strained against the starting gate.

The gate dropped. Six riders shot down the first ramp, handlebar to handlebar. Lance focused his mind on the dirt course. He
remembered his coach's instructions: ride hard, but ride clean. The
riders jostled for position on the corner. Lance leaned into it. So
did the boy in the orange uniform next to him.

Lance yanked his handlebars. He sailed over a tabletop jump,
easily clearing the wide bump. When the dust cleared, he and the
boy in orange led the pack. Lance leaned into position for a reverse
tilted corner. It was the last obstacle of the race. The boy beside
him did the same, taking the lower lane. At the highest point of the
curve, the boy reached out his arm and shoved Lance's handlebars.
Lance flew over the top of the hill. He landed with a thud on the
other side.

Lance looked up to find his dad standing over him. Just then,
Lance heard the loudspeaker blare: "The winner of the two-mile
race is Chuck Tripper."

Lance jumped up and stamped the dirt. "He cheated!"

"I know, Lance," said Dad. "I saw it, but the ref didn't."

"It's not fair!"

"You're right. But you were competing in two races out here.
Don't lose both."

"I know. This race is only one heat in the race of life. God is
the final judge." Lance picked up his bike. "At the end of *that* race,
I'll be glad I rode hard and finished clean."

WWJ

"Don't be upset because of sinful people.... Trust in the Lord and do good."
Psalm 37:1, 3

How do you respond when people don't play fair with you?
How does God want you to respond to those who cheat?
Also read Psalm 37:1–9.

LOOKING GUILTY

"I didn't do it," Zach said.

"I didn't do it either," said seven-year-old Ellie. Her blue eyes looked so innocent. Zach almost believed his sister—except he knew the truth. He *had seen* Ellie spill her juice.

Mom stood with her hands on her hips. She frowned. "I know one of you spilled grape juice on the rug. Who did it?"

Zach sighed. *There's no point in telling Mom that Ellie did it. She wouldn't believe me. She can't tell when Ellie lies.*

"I'll scrub the rug," Zach offered, even though he knew it made him look guilty. Ellie climbed on the couch to watch cartoons while Zach got a sponge and hot soapy water.

"Ellie," he said as he scrubbed the spot. "Mom can't tell when you lie. But there is someone who can. He sees *everything* you do."

"Who?" Ellie eyed him suspiciously. "You?"

"Nope. God sees you. God hears *every* lie."

She turned her back to him and refused to listen. Zach carried the sponge and soapy water to the kitchen.

When he walked back into the living room, he found Ellie with her palms pressed together and her eyes squeezed shut. Her lips moved in prayer.

She opened her eyes and told him, "I asked Jesus to forgive me. Now I'll go tell Mom the truth. That's what Jesus wants me to do."

"May [God] make you strong in every good thing you do and say."
2 Thessalonians 2:17

Have you ever warned someone not to sin?
Why does God want you to help others do what's right?
Also read 1 Thessalonians 5:14–22.

STINKY WATER

"Look at all this water in our basement," said Mary. "There must be at least an inch down here."

"It smells stinky," said Jessica, her younger sister.

The rain had finally stopped. Mom and Dad were outside digging a ditch to help drain the water away from the house.

Mary sopped an old towel into the basement water and wrung it into a bucket. Jessica marched around, stomping and splashing.

"Hey, quit playing," said Mary. "I need your help."

"There's too much water." Jessica kicked and sloshed. "It'll take forever."

"That's why I need your help. Now, come on!"

"I can't squeeze a towel like you can. My hands are too small."

"Here's a *small* towel." Mary tossed her an old hand towel. Jessica dropped it into the water and lifted it out dripping wet.

She wrinkled her nose. "It smells too yucky. I can't do this!"

"Jessica, don't you want to be like Jesus?"

Jessica widened her eyes. "Yes. But what does that have to do with our flooded basement?"

"The Bible tells us to do everything for the glory of God."

"Even mopping up smelly water?"

"Yes. So even though *I'm* asking you to help me mop up, you really should be helping me to make *God* happy."

Jessica nodded. Then she sopped her towel full of water and squeezed it into the bucket.

"Thanks, sis," said Mary, "With your help, this floor will be dry in no time."

"Work as if you were working for the Lord....You are serving the Lord Christ." Colossians 3:23

How often do you do your best when you work?
What work will you do today for the Lord?
Also read 2 Thessalonians 3:6–13.

MUSLIM IDENTITY

"Why do I have to go to the Muslim school?" Fahid asked his dad. "I am afraid they will hurt me because I'm a Christian."

Father laid his hands gently on his son's shoulders. "Unless we can get the government to change the word 'Muslim' to 'Christian' on your identity card, you must go. But don't worry. I do not think they will hurt you at the school."

"But didn't the police beat *you* because you're a Christian?"

"Yes," said Father. "When we love Jesus, we know we will be persecuted. You must expect it, too, my son. At school, even though they won't hurt you, they will probably make you an outcast. You will long for friends. But Jesus may be your only friend."

Fahid hugged his father. "I will try to be brave. You were brave when the police hung you upside down for three days."

"God gave me strength," said his father.

"You did not deny Jesus. I will not, either. Not even if someone tortures me." Fahid sighed.

"In some countries, Christians can worship without fear. I am praying for freedom of worship for us someday," said Father.

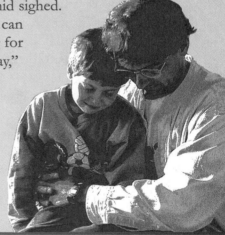

"Perhaps God will use other Christians around the world to help us," said Fahid. "We suffer so much for our faith in Jesus. I pray that God will remind people to pray for all Muslim Christians."

WWJ

"Don't be surprised by the painful suffering you are going through....Be joyful that you are taking part in Christ's sufferings." 1 Peter 4:12–13

When have you experienced persecution because you loved Jesus? How could you help Muslim Christians in places like Iraq and Iran? Also read I Peter 4:12–19.

FUNNIEST SHOW

"You're missing this!" said Tony's dad, sitting on the couch. He howled with laughter at the show on TV.

I'd like to watch that show with Dad, Tony thought. *But Mom said I shouldn't because of what the characters say to each other.*

"Come sit down, son." Dad howled with laughter again. "I can't stand it," he said, laughing and gulping for air.

Dad wants me to watch. Mom says I shouldn't. What do I do? Tony knew he should ask the Lord, but he didn't.

He sat down beside Dad.

"It's funny, huh, son? It's the funniest show on TV."

Soon the characters were using words Tony didn't want to use. And joking about subjects that Tony didn't want to hear.

Tony realized, *Now I know why Mom doesn't want me to watch this.*

He knew he shouldn't laugh at the jokes, but after a while Tony couldn't help laughing along with Dad.

Then one of the show's characters said something dirty. And he used Jesus' name as a cuss word. That startled Tony. He felt like someone splashed ice water in his face. His laughter died.

Tony stood up. "It's wrong when they use Jesus' name to swear," he told his dad. "I'm going to study in my room."

Dad looked at Tony and thought for a moment. Then he turned back to the TV to finish watching the show.

Tony walked to his room and knelt by his bed.

Dear Lord, please forgive me for watching that show. Help me be careful of what I watch on television. And please help my dad, too.

WWJ

"I won't look at anything that is evil....I don't want to have anything to do with evil." Psalm 101:3–4

When have you been tempted to watch something on television that you knew you shouldn't? What happened?
Also read Psalm 101:1–4.

SHOW KINDNESS

Family Tree

What You Need:

A Bible, a tree branch secured in a bucket of cement or dirt, scissors, construction paper, string
Optional: pictures of extended family, note cards

What To Do:

1. Read Jesus' family tree in Matthew 1:1–17.
    Talk about His heritage.

2. Cut leaf shapes from the construction paper. Write the names of family members on the paper leaves or glue pictures of family to leaves.

3. Pray for each person, attaching his or her leaf with string to the tree afterward. Use the tree as a reminder to pray for the family all week.

Variation #1: Write encouragement notes to the family members, telling them you are praying for them.

Variation #2: Find pictures of previous generations.
    Tell any family stories that inspire your family in its Christian faith.

WWJ

UNEXPECTED STORM

"Keep paddling!" Morgan shouted to her sister. Rain pelted her face. She leaned forward and paddled against the lake waves. Panic tightened her chest as wind drove their canoe sideways.

At the other end of the canoe, Kara balanced a paddle across her bare knees while she hugged her arms. Wet braids clung to her thin, rain-soaked T-shirt. "I-I-I'm fr-fr-freezing," she whimpered.

"Paddle! If you don't help, we'll never make it to shore!"

Kara picked up her paddle and jabbed helplessly at the waves. Her arms shook with cold. Her lips looked bluer than the lake.

I told her to wear a jacket, thought Morgan. *She wouldn't listen to me. Dear Jesus, help me not get mad at her.*

Kara dabbed her paddle in the water and cried. Her T-shirt clung to her shaking body.

"I'm cold, too," Morgan said. "Don't give up!"

Her sister cried harder.

Morgan sighed and laid down her paddle. She pulled off her sweatshirt and tossed it to Kara.

"Here. You put it on," Morgan said. Icy rain pelted her bare arms as she began paddling again. She shivered.

Kara pulled the sweatshirt over her head. "Thanks, Morgan."

Finally the bottom of the canoe ground onto shore.

"We made it!" shouted Morgan. The girls jumped out and hugged each other.

"It was my fault that I didn't wear warm clothes," said Kara. "You didn't have to give your sweatshirt to me, but you did. And that kept me warm enough so I could help paddle."

WWJ

Jesus said, "Blessed are those who show mercy. They will be shown mercy."
Matthew 5:7

When and how have you shown mercy to your brother or sister?
When has someone shown mercy (steadfast love) to you?
Also read Psalm 136:1–9, 26.

BROKEN DOWN

"They look like they might need help," said Barry.

On the shoulder of the freeway stood a station wagon with a flat tire. "Let's stop. Okay?" he said.

Mom shook her head. "They could be dangerous."

"I don't think so. It's a family with three kids."

"All right, son." Mom pulled the van onto the shoulder of the freeway. "Lord, protect us, please."

The driver of the station wagon came running. "I could use a jack and some drinking water." Barry handed the man their picnic thermos. Mom took the jack out of her trunk.

The man passed the thermos among his family. After he changed his tire, he returned the jack and the thermos.

"Thanks," he said and walked back to his station wagon.

Barry's mom turned the key in her ignition. The starter whined, but the motor was dead.

Barry jumped out. "Wait! Sir! We can't get our car started!"

The man slammed his door and glanced in his rearview mirror. Barry waved his arms frantically. The station wagon suddenly gunned away into freeway traffic.

"I can't believe he wouldn't help us after we helped him!"

"It doesn't matter how he treated us," said Mom. "Just keep treating others the way Jesus would—He'll take care of us somehow." She turned the key in the ignition. The motor started.

Mom smiled. Barry couldn't help but smile, too.

"Don't be upset because of evil people."
Proverbs 24:19

How do you feel when people treat you unfairly?
When have you been kind even though other people weren't?
Also read Psalm 37:1–8.

SLOW AS MOLASSES

"Whatever you do, don't kick the ball to Jason," said one of the soccer players. Taylor felt sorry for Jason. *The poor guy's brain is as slow as molasses. But that shouldn't mean he can't play soccer with us.*

Jason stood alone on the sidelines. His eyes followed the ball back and forth, zigzagging across the field.

Taylor kicked the ball. A teammate trapped it and tried to sidekick it toward the goal. His shoe grazed the ball and sent it skittering off the field. It rolled to a standstill at Jason's feet.

He scooped it into his arms. "It's mine!" he yelled.

"Kick it back!" shouted Taylor from the outfield.

Jason held it tightly with both arms.

All the team players swarmed around him and demanded, "Give us the ball!"

Clutching the ball to his chest, Jason ran to the teacher. His classmates ran after him. "It's mine!" said Jason.

"Where was the ball before you got it?" asked the teacher.

Jason shrugged and looked down at his shoes.

"Let me help you," said the teacher. She spoke slowly and softly. "These other boys were playing with the ball. So it belongs to them. Let's give it back. Okay?"

With tears in his eyes, Jason handed Taylor the ball.

Taylor thanked him. *It's not fair to keep Jason out of the game just because he's slow to understand. Dear Jesus, how can I help him out?*

"What if I take Jason on my team? He can play beside me," said Taylor. "Is everybody all right with that?" *I'd rather lose a game,* he decided, *than mistreat Jason.*

WWJ

"A child is known by his actions. He is know by whether his conduct is pure and right." Proverbs 20:11

What have you done lately that was "pure and right"?
How do you treat others who are slow to learn?
Also read James 3:13–18.

OUT OF THE HEART

"I have a huge crush on Josh," Liz confided as she and her friend Stephanie lounged on the dock by the lake cabin.

Liz dangled her feet in the lake and leaned back on her elbows. Closing her eyes against the bright sun, she sighed softly, "Ohh, Josh. What a guy."

"Well, I'm certainly not surprised to hear about your crush on Josh," Stephanie replied. "You gab about him nonstop."

Liz laughed. "Why not? Is there anything better to talk about?"

Stephanie was silent. Liz opened one eye to see if her friend was listening. "Steph? Did you hear what I said?"

"Sorry!" Stephanie smiled. "I was just thinking that you would have made a good example for Pastor Ron's sermon last Sunday."

"Why?" Liz asked, clasping her hands and pretending to be love-struck. "Did Pastor talk about true love?"

"Sort of," Stephanie replied. "He said that what we talk about shows people what's in our hearts." She raised her eyebrows and smiled. "Your talk tells me what's on your heart—it's Josh!"

Liz felt a sudden sadness.

"You're a true friend, Steph. You've helped me see what I'm doing. I prattle on and on about Josh, but I hardly ever talk about Jesus. I love Him most of all."

Forgive me, dear Lord, she prayed. *I give You first place in my heart.*

"Your mouths say everything that is in your hearts."
Matthew 12:34

What do you care most about? What do you talk about?
How can you help your family and friends grow closer to Jesus?
Also read Deuteronomy 6:6–9.

FATSY PATSY

How can the teacher just stand there and let everyone make fun of Patsy? She gets teased all the time.

Dylan watched Patsy out of the corner of his eye. She sat at her desk, looking down and turning the pages of a book, pretending to read. Her cheeks looked hot.

Mrs. Trombatore stood with her hands on her hips. She looked around the room as she assigned boy-girl partners for a Thanksgiving poster project.

"Okay," she said, pointing at a girl named Susie, "you be partners with Thomas."

Thomas called out, "I'm not going to be partners with *Fatsy Patsy!*"

Mrs. Trombatore sighed. "I didn't ask you to be partners with Patsy. I assigned you to work with Susie."

Mrs. Trombatore looked at Seth. "You be partners with—"

"Pleeease," Seth begged her. "Not *Fatsy Patsy!*"

The whole class burst out laughing.

Mrs. Trombatore rolled her eyes and continued, "Take Michelle for your partner since you sit right beside her."

Dylan couldn't stand the way they were treating Patsy. He raised his hand and spoke out, "Let me be partners with Patsy. She's the best artist in the class!"

When the class broke into partners to work, Patsy smiled at Dylan. "Thank you. But why did you ask to work with me? Are you a Christian?"

Dylan smiled and nodded. "Yeah. And you *are* the best artist in the class. We'll make a great Thanksgiving poster."

WWJ

Jesus said, "Anyone who has faith in me will do what I have been doing." John 14:12

How do you treat someone others make fun of?
Can others tell that you are a Christian by the way *you* act?
Also read John 14:9–14.

GOD'S MERCY

Have Mercy! Unfreeze Me!

What You Need:

A Bible

What To Do:

1. Read James 2:10–12.

2. Talk about mercy in terms of not receiving the punishment you deserve because of another's compassionate or forgiving spirit.

3. Explain that Jesus shows mercy when He forgives our (confessed) sins instead of punishing us for them.

4. Play "freeze tag." When the person who is designated It tags another player, that player must "freeze" in position for one minute, counting slowly from one to sixty.

5. Encourage the person who is It to show mercy by touching the player again before the sixty seconds is up and "unfreezing" him or her.

IN A RUSSIAN PRISON

Eleven-year-old Laurel looked around at the girls in the Russian prison. *Some of these girls have robbed...or murdered. And not one looks much different from me,* she thought. *There must be at least 250 girls here. They all look so young.* Laurel's heart went out to them.

The warden had said that many of the girls were orphans or children of alcoholics. Laurel's gaze rested on one particular girl, with large, sad eyes. *Oh Jesus, what crime did she commit?*

"It doesn't matter," said a voice in Laurel's heart. *"I love her and I will forgive her. But she has never heard about Me. That is why I brought you all the way to Russia with this mission group."*

"Would anyone like to share with the group?" the worship leader asked the mission team.

I'm the youngest one in our group, thought Laurel. *But I feel that I'm supposed to speak up, even if I'm scared.*

Lauren climbed up on the stage. Holding her gospel bracelet high for all to see, she pointed to the black bead. Her gaze met the sad-eyed girl's in the fifth row.

"Everyone's heart is black with sin," Laurel said, as if talking only to that one girl.

Then she used the red, white, green, and yellow beads to explain God's loving plan of salvation.

Tears trickled down the sad-eyed girl's cheeks while she listened to the translation of Laurel's words in Russian.

"Would anyone like to receive Jesus?" asked the worship leader.

Laurel's heart leaped for joy to see the girl raise her hand—along with more than fifty of her fellow prisoners.

"Pray that the Lord's message will spread quickly. Pray that others will honor it just as you did." 2 Thessalonians 3:1

Are you willing to pray for those in prison?
How would you explain to someone God's plan of salvation?
Also read Psalm 68:6.

GUILTY FEELINGS

"My tooth!" cried Shakia. She touched her mouth and looked at the blood on her fingers…and the tooth in her hand.

"Did I knock your tooth out?" asked Keegan.

"It's okay," said Shakia. "We ran for the ball at the same time. You didn't mean to collide with me."

Keegan felt terrible. *She's my best friend. And I just knocked out one of her front teeth!* Keegan burst into tears.

Shakia's parents ran onto the soccer field. They looked at their daughter's mouth and reassured Keegan, "The dentist can fix this for Shakia. She will be okay."

Despite the good news, Keegan couldn't stop crying. She walked to the sidelines. Her mom asked, "Did you get hurt, too?"

"No. I—I just feel so guilty about what I did."

"Honey, it was an accident. God wants you to feel guilty when you sin, not when you have accidents." She slipped her arm around Keegan's waist. "Even when you sin, do you think Jesus wants you to feel bad and carry a load of guilt?"

Keegan shook her head. "No. He wants me to ask His forgiveness so He can take the guilt away."

She smiled at her mother. "Thanks, Mom. That makes me feel a lot better.

"And I know what might help Shakia feel better—I'd like to take her some flowers."

Mom smiled. "We'll go to the store right after the game."

"The free gift of God's grace makes all of us right with him."
Romans 3:24

Are you carrying guilt instead of asking God's forgiveness? Ask Him now to forgive you. Then trust His forgiveness. Also read Romans 3:20–26.

SHOW MERCY

Lawrence slammed his pencil on the table. "Jeff, you forgot to bring the tile for our rocket's launch pad. Dewey, you didn't buy the right chemicals for the rocket fuel."

Frowning, he paced the kitchen. "I want to win first prize at the science fair this year. We're two days behind schedule!"

"This isn't a real space shuttle launch, Lawrence."

"No, but it is forty percent of our science grade."

Over the next two weeks, Lawrence, Jeff, and Dewey built a model of the Kennedy Space Center on a large piece of plywood. Lawrence built the rocket and experimented with different fuels. Jeff constructed balsa wood buildings. And Dewey created the landscape and geographical features.

Lawrence frowned as the boys set up their project on the day of the science fair. "Dewey, you put those cars too close to the launch pad." As Lawrence leaned over to move Dewey's cars, he lost his balance and fell over, smashing onto the science project. When he got up off the table, their Kennedy Space Center looked as if it had been hit by a hurricane.

Lawrence buried his head in his hands. *I've wrecked this whole project! We'll all fail science!* He waited for Jeff and Dewey to rip him apart. After a few moments, he looked up. "Why aren't you guys ragging me? Aren't you mad?"

Dewey said quietly, "Maybe it's because we're Christians. We've messed up lots of times. God always lets us start over."

Lawrence took a deep breath. "So, does anybody know about *hurricanes?* We have five minutes to find a fan and a jug of water. This will end up being one awesome science project!"

"The Lord is tender and kind. He is gracious....He is full of love. He doesn't punish us...as much as we should be punished." Psalm 103:8, 10

Can you think of a time when someone showed you mercy?
How good are you at showing mercy to others?
Also read Ephesians 2:8–10.

A WEEK OF MERCY

"Nina, you didn't answer my question," said Miss Heartland.

Nina jerked awake. *Uh-oh. It's only my second week in this school and I blew it again. I just can't keep my eyes open. If this keeps up, I'm not only going to fail this class but all my others, too. Dear Jesus, I need Your help.*

"Class, read the last chapter and we'll discuss it," said Miss Heartland.

While the students studied, she came over to Nina's desk. "Are you sleeping at night, my dear?"

Nina lowered her eyes and shook her head.

"Adjusting to a new school can be difficult," said Miss Heartland, her voice soft enough so others wouldn't hear.

"I can't sleep at night," said Nina. "I worry about school. I don't understand the assignments. I'm afraid I will flunk my classes."

"I'll tell you a secret—just between you and me. Okay?"

Nina nodded and smiled.

Miss Heartland leaned a little closer and spoke a little softer. "I have a special assignment, just for you. For the next week, you are going to sleep in every morning and come to school late. Okay?"

"Really? Oh, thank you, Miss Heartland." *And thank You, Jesus, for a teacher who had mercy on me.*

That night, Nina slept soundly. And she went to school an hour late every morning all week. Soon she stayed awake in all her classes and she enjoyed her new school.

"God loves us deeply. He is full of mercy. So he gave us new life because of what Christ has done." Ephesians 2:4-5

Mercy means we don't get the punishment we deserve.
When has someone shown mercy to you?
Also read Ephesians 2:4–9.

SIZZLE! POP! FLASH

Randy darted across the garage, aimed his water gun at Jay, then lowered it. "I wish your dad would let us squirt each other in the garage. We can't play outside when it's raining like this."

He sighed as he looked up at the glowing light bulb with its attached ceiling fan. "What would happen if I sprayed that fan?"

"Duh! The water would drip off."

"But if we turned the fan *on,* water would fly everywhere!" Randy aimed for a fan blade. "Turn on the fan!"

Jay flipped the switch. Randy shot a stream of water high into the air. He heard a sizzle and a loud pop. With a flash, the bulb exploded! The garage plunged into darkness.

"Uh-oh," said Jay. "Wait until my dad finds out!"

Randy pedaled home in the driving rain as fast as he could. He whizzed into his driveway, parked his bike in the garage, and took the stairs to his room two at a time. Before he could change out of his wet clothes, he heard the doorbell ring.

"Randy!" his dad called, "Jay's father is here to see you!"

Randy's heart sank as he slowly went down the stairs.

Mr. Hesse looked at Randy. "Tell me what happened."

"I didn't mean to break it. We were just messing around."

"Randy, when you squirted cold water at the hot light bulb, it exploded. That's dangerous. Water guns are outdoor toys."

"I'm sorry, Mr. Hesse. I'll pay for the light bulb."

"I'd appreciate that. I hope you've learned a lesson."

"I sure have. After this, I'll obey the rules and think twice about what I use for target practice."

"Anyone who accepts being corrected shows understanding."
Proverbs 15:5

What would you say to a friend who breaks a rule?
How do you respond when someone corrects you?
Also read Job 5:17–20.

RIGHT ATTITUDES

Grudge Fudge

What You Need:

A Bible, plus a recipe and ingredients for a batch of fudge
(or another treat such as cookies, scones, or popcorn balls)

What To Do:

1. Read Matthew 5:21–26, 18–48. Ask family members to
   share about a time when they had a conflict with someone.
   What happens to our attitude when our feelings are hurt?

2. Talk about holding grudges. How do you feel inside when
   you hold a grudge? How does it feel when someone won't
   forget something you did wrong? What happens when
   grudges are held?

4. When has someone held a grudge against you, even after
   you said that you were sorry? Has someone ever held a
   grudge against you for something you didn't do?

5. What does Jesus want us to do when someone else is angry
   with us or holds a grudge against us?

6. Plan a way to show friendship and love to someone who is
   unfriendly towards you or who holds a grudge against you.
   Bake a batch of goodies. Pray for the person(s) to whom
   you will give it. Then deliver it.

WWJ

WATERFALL

"My feet hurt," said Nick. "You said it wasn't very far."

"It won't be much farther," said Nick's dad.

"When are we going to eat? I'm hungry."

Nick's little sister, Crystal, frowned. "Quit whining," she said. "You need to grow up."

"I'm thirsty," fussed Nick. "Is it too much to ask for water?"

"Here, son," said Dad, handing him a sport bottle. The trail suddenly bent and rose more steeply.

"Oh no!" said Nick. "Do we have to go up there?"

"It's the only way," replied Dad. Up they climbed, sometimes on their feet, sometimes on their hands and knees.

"I should have stayed home and gone swimming at Jeff's house with my friends. This family stuff stinks," said Nick.

Dad smiled. "You'll be glad you're with us. Be patient. We're almost there."

On their feet again, they rounded a bend. And suddenly they gazed at a rocky bluff in front of them. High on its crown a waterfall sprayed downward. The misty waters fell with a roar, foaming into a fern-shaded pool below.

Nick was the first to take off his shoes and jump into the water. After he swam, he tried catching fish with his hands. Then he explored the caves behind the falls. He had just dived off a boulder into the pool when Dad announced it was time to head back home.

"Do we have to go?" cried Nick. While he dried off with a towel, he told his dad, "I'm sorry I complained in the beginning. I almost let my bad attitude ruin the most fun I've ever had."

WWJ

"Do everything without finding fault or arguing."
Philippians 2:14

What's your attitude been in difficult situations?
How do you keep from fussing and complaining?
Also read Numbers 11:1–10, 33.

LITTLE RICH BOY

"Can I have a candy bar for my cousin? He's shy," said Jamal, a youngster in a torn T-shirt. "And can I have one for myself?"

Tirza stood outside the run-down apartment complex where her church was holding Vacation Bible School. All the grubby little kids wanted candy. *Not one of them knows to say "may I" instead of "can I,"* she thought.

She smiled politely at Jamal. "I remember that I already gave you two candy bars," she said. "Did you eat them?"

"They were for my sisters." Jamal grinned. "They're shy, too."

"Yeah, right. I'll give you *one* more, and that's it." She handed him a chocolate bar and watched him run across the parking lot to a group of kids who stood in the shade of a tree. Tirza could barely hear what they said.

Jamal handed the candy to a younger boy on crutches.

"Where's *your* candy bar?" the little boy asked Jamal.

"I don't need any candy," Jamal replied.

Tirza looked into her bag. She only had one large chocolate bar left. *Jamal really did give away all his candy. He may not have many possessions, but he's rich in love and generosity.*

Tirza closed her eyes. *Jesus, please forgive me for judging him.* She crossed the parking lot.

"I'm sorry I misjudged you, Jamal," Tirza said, holding out the big chocolate bar. "Here, take it. This one is just for you."

"Rich people picture themselves as wise, but their real poverty is evident to the poor." Proverbs 28:11 (NLT)

How can someone who has no money still be considered rich? How are you *rich* in the ways that really count? Also read 1 Timothy 6:17–18.

WEIRD WALLACE

"I lost that thumb when a train run over it," the neighbor told Cameron. The old man stood on the porch, towering over Cameron and his little brother, Andrew. His gray-streaked beard hung nearly to his waist. And whenever he smiled, which was often, they could see his crooked yellow teeth.

Cameron jumped to his feet and dashed inside the house. "Mom! Weird Wallace is out there. He's scaring me again!"

"I've known him for years," said Mom. She kissed the top of Cameron's head. "He loves people. He just doesn't quite know how to act around them. Jesus wants you to judge what's on the inside of people, not what's on the outside."

Later that day, Cameron and his brother pedaled their bikes down the street. Weird Wallace watched them from his front porch. When he waved, Cameron waved back.

But when Andrew waved at the old man, he lost his balance. The bike swerved. Andrew pitched over his handlebars. He landed on his face in the gravel. Andrew shrieked and cried.

Weird Wallace jumped over his porch railing and scooped Andrew gently into his arms. Then he carried the boy up the driveway, calling to Cameron to get his mom.

Hearing the wails, Mom rushed out of the front door. "Oh, thank you, Mr. Wallace. You're a *good* man. Thanks for helping Andrew."

Cameron looked up at his bearded and yellow-toothed neighbor and saw tears in his eyes. "Thank you, Mr. Wallace. You're a very nice man. I'm glad you're our neighbor."

WWJ

The Lord said, "Man looks at how someone appears on the outside. But I look at what is in the heart." 1 Samuel 16:7

How does God judge people?
How do you judge people? By their appearance or their actions?
Also read James 2:1–9.

TOO MUCH WATER

"I know what I'm doing, Mother!" Tom poured another glass of water from the pitcher in the refrigerator and put it to his mouth. He didn't stop until he had drained every drop.

"My coach says to drink lots of water," he said.

"The coach wants you to drink a lot when you're playing in hot weather," Mom agreed, "but I'm afraid drinking four glasses of water after a big meal could make you sick."

Tom poured another glass of water and drank it all.

An hour later Mom and Tom sat on the couch together. Tom groaned, "My stomach hurts." Mom stroked Tom's pale face.

The doorbell rang. "Uncle Jordan is here to take you to the zoo," said Mom. "Maybe you should stay home."

Uncle Jordan shook his head when he saw Tom. "You look awful. Do you really feel like going to the zoo?"

"I'm okay," insisted Tom. "I've been looking forward to this for a week. I'm not going to stay home!" He got into Uncle Jordan's car and they drove off.

Half an hour later, Tom ran into the house and flung himself into his mom's arms.

"Mom! I threw up all over Uncle Jordan's car," said Tom. "Uncle Jordan said it was okay, but I feel terrible. I'm sorry I didn't listen to what you said."

WWJ

"Scripture says, 'Honor your father and mother.' That is the first commandment that has a promise. Then things will go well with you." Ephesians 6:2

Why does God want children to obey and listen to their parents? How much do you pay attention to what your parents tell you? Also read Psalm 27:11–12.

PEA-GREEN UGLY

"Everybody in town has a minivan except us," complained Mandie. She sat sprawled in the window seat, counting all the minivans driving past their house.

Her sister Shauna said, "Dad says we can't afford to buy one."

"Can't afford what?" Mom and Dad walked in the front door. Mom shook the rain off her umbrella and leaned it in the corner.

"Mandie wants a van like everyone else," said Shauna.

Dad smiled broadly. "Mom and I have a surprise. We just finished car shopping for...a van!"

Mandie jumped up. "What? Where is it? I want to see it!"

"Parked in the driveway. Want to go for a spin?"

Mandie yanked on her coat and flung open the garage door. Then she saw it—the ugliest, beat-up pea-green van in the entire universe. She felt like a popped balloon. "That's not a *minivan!*"

"Of course not," said Dad. "It's a full-sized van. We bought something practical that we could afford."

The two sisters crawled into the backseat. Mandie covered her face with her hands as Dad pulled out of the driveway. She slouched low in the seat so none of her neighborhood friends could see her.

"Stop it, Mandie!" Shauna whispered. "You're going to hurt Mom and Dad's feelings."

Mandie glanced at her parents. They looked so happy. "You're right." She sighed. "I know God wants us to be content with what we have." She ran her fingers over the vinyl seats. "I'll try to get used to it," she said. "Hey, maybe we can go camping in this hulk. You can't *camp* in a minivan."

"Don't be controlled by love for money. Be happy with what you have."
Hebrews 13:5

Are you unhappy or dissatisfied with what you have?
How could you be a more happy and contented person?
Also read Hebrews 13:5–6, 15–16.

DECIDE TO DO RIGHT

Proverb Hunt

What You Need:

A Bible, pencil, paper, box, tape, wrapping paper

What To Do:

1. Each morning this week, read one proverb out of the book of Proverbs in the Bible. Have the family discuss its meaning. Tell everyone to look for something during the day that illustrates that proverb.

2. In the evening, gather together and share experiences that illustrated the proverb of the day.

Note: Keep your own "Book of Proverbs" during this week by writing out a proverb from the Bible each day, plus writing down the illustrations you find in your everyday life.

Variation: Cover a small box with wrapping paper. This is your "treasure box." Write out single verses from Proverbs on notecards. Place in the box. Children may open the box and take out a "treasure" from God's Word. Proceed with activity as described above.

CLOSED EYES IN A HUT

Naw Mima listened to the night sounds floating from the jungle into her thatched hut. "I am glad to be a 'Closed Eyes One,'" she told her parents.

Rebel soldiers often raided the Christian part of the refugee camp where Naw Mima lived. The soldiers called refugee Christians "Closed Eyes Ones," because they closed their eyes when praying.

Rat-a-tat-tat! Guns sounded in the distance. Pressing her hands together, Naw Mima prayed, "Give us courage, Jesus."

RAT-A-TAT-TAT!

"The guns come near," Father whispered. The family sat holding hands in the middle of their hut. They prayed quietly.

The voices of soldiers sounded closer. Naw Mima heard them at the hut of nearby Christian friends. "Are you Closed Eyes or Buddhist?" the soldiers called out.

"Buddhist," replied the Christian family.

"Dear Jesus," Naw Mima prayed, "give me and my family courage not to deny you."

The soldiers moved on to the hut of a Christian family next door. "Are you Closed Eyes or Buddhist?"

"Buddhist," declared the Christian family.

Naw Mima lifted her head and sang, "Jesus loves me, this I know." The rest of the family joined her.

Finally the soldiers stood outside Naw Mima's hut. They called out, "Closed Eyes or Buddhist?"

Tears poured down Naw Mima's face as she whispered, "I will see you tonight, Jesus. I love you." She stood up with her family and they stepped outside their hut saying, "We are Christians."

"The Lord will save me from every evil attack. He will bring me safely to his heavenly kingdom." 2 Timothy 4:18

When have you let other people know that you are a Christian? When have you been tempted to deny Jesus by what you say or do? Also read Revelation 3:20–21.

ADAM BOMB

"Adam! What are you doing? Are you eating grass?" Chelise watched her little three-year-old brother play on the front lawn.

Adam grinned. "You know dose mushwooms Mommy said not to eat?" he asked. "I like 'em. Dey taste good."

"What?!" Chelise shrieked. "Those are poisonous!"

She jumped up and ran to Adam. "Open your mouth!" On his back teeth were specks of brown mushrooms. She grabbed him and dashed into the house, screaming.

Chelise prayed while Mom phoned poison control. Then her mom mixed syrup of Ipecac with grape juice and had Adam drink it.

When Adam finished drinking the juice, Mom drove him to the hospital. Chelise sat in the back with her brother. "Here, Adam. I'll hold the bucket for you to throw up into." But he never vomited.

When Adam arrived at the hospital, he still hadn't vomited. So the nurse gave Adam more medicine mixed with juice.

"More juice. I like juice," he said. His tummy started to swell. It grew until it looked like he had swallowed a basketball.

Finally, Adam vomited the mushrooms. Then he sank into a deep sleep called a coma for two days.

When Adam opened his eyes, he smiled and said. "I'm hungwey. I want more mushwooms."

Chelise looked at Mother in disbelief. "I finally understand why God tells you to discipline us," she said. "It helps us stop doing wrong and getting hurt."

"A child is going to do foolish things. But correcting him will drive his foolishness far away from him." Proverbs 22:15

When have your parents showed their love by disciplining you? When is it hardest for you to obey your parents and teachers? Also read Proverbs 16:20–21.

NO PIECE FOR THE WICKED

"What are comic books doing in Sunday School?" Micah whispered to his friend, Kurt. Micah sat down on the chair next to the comic books in the back row of seats of his Sunday School class.

"I brought them from home," whispered Kurt. "I'm selling them for a quarter each. Want to buy one?"

"Maybe," said Micah, feeling a twinge of guilt. Dad had a strict rule against comic books, and Micah didn't want to disobey.

During the rest of the class, Micah couldn't concentrate on the teacher's lesson. All he could think about was how much he wanted one of Kurt's comic books.

When the offering plate was passed around, Micah looked at the four quarters Dad had given him. He dropped three into the plate and kept one in his hand. When class ended, Micah tossed the quarter to Kurt and slipped a comic book into his jacket.

Later on that day, Micah's family gathered around their table for dinner. Dad blessed the food. Everyone joked and chatted while they ate—except Micah. Guilt hung over him like a fog. When he tried to swallow Mom's pot roast, it stuck in his throat.

I feel terrible, he thought. *I finally understand the Bible verse that says, "There is no peace for the wicked."*

"Would you like a *piece* of chocolate pie?" Mom asked.

Micah burst into tears and rushed from the room. He grabbed his comic book, ran back into the kitchen, and thrust it at Dad.

"I'm really sorry," he said. "I disobeyed you, Dad. I need your forgiveness."

First Dad grounded Micah for two weeks, then he hugged him. And Mom brought Micah a *piece* of pie.

"'There is no peace for those who are evil,' says my God."
Isaiah 57:21

When have you felt miserable because you did something wrong? Why is it important to confess and ask forgiveness?
Also read Proverbs 6:20–23.

GARAGE SALE THIEF

"Keep your hands off!" said the old woman. She yanked her wicker basket away from Erika.

"I…I was only trying to help you," stammered Erika. "My mother asked me to add up the prices of what people bought at our garage sale. You have quite a few things in your basket."

Erika stood quietly beside the table in her driveway. She noticed the old woman's shabby clothes and messy hair.

The woman tucked the basket under her arm. "How much do I owe?" she said, looking away from Erika.

"I need to see what's in your basket," said Erika. A cup, a small scissors, a hammer, and a pair of eyeglasses poked out beneath several cloth napkins. Erika reached over and lifted a napkin.

The woman scowled and slapped Erika's hand. "Here's one dollar." Flinging a dollar bill on the table, the woman stomped over to an old car and drove away.

Erika stood with her mouth open. "Mom…that woman just took a lot of things and only paid one dollar."

"Why didn't you stop her?"

"She looked so poor," said Erika. "We would have given it all to her if she'd just said she couldn't afford it…right?"

Mom nodded. "Yes. All she had to do was ask."

"She's wrong to think she has to steal because she's poor," Erika said. "God would supply all her needs—if she'd ask."

"*Those who have been stealing must never steal again. Instead, they must work.*" Ephesians 4:28

Do God's children ever need to steal? Why or why not?
What would you say to someone who stole from you?
Also read Exodus 20:1–17.

PONY EXPRESS PROMISE

Billy could hardly stand still as he placed his left hand on the manila envelope Miss Grooter held.

"I know the Pony Express Promise by heart," Billy told his teacher. He raised his right hand and said proudly,

> "Sure and fast; from first to last;
> I will not fail to deliver the mail."

I'm the class messenger for a whole week! Carrying his important package, Billy walked down the main hallway leading to the office.

If I take the long way to the office, I could miss most of math class.

He turned into a side hall, stopped by the drinking fountain, then headed for the boys' bathroom. He took time to look at the student artwork displayed outside each classroom. Finally, he delivered the envelope to the office.

When Billy returned to his classroom twenty minutes later, Miss Grooter frowned. "Where have you been?"

"To the office."

His teacher looked him in the eye. "Billy, did you go straight to the office when you delivered the mail?"

"Well…I stopped for a drink."

"There is no fountain in the hallway between here and the office."

Billy shuffled his feet. "I…I went the long way around."

"The Pony Express Promise says 'sure and fast.'"

Billy hung his head.

"I need a Pony Express Rider who delivers my mail quickly. I will have to choose someone to take your place this week."

Billy returned to his seat, sick at heart. He understood now. *Knowing* the Pony Express Promise wasn't enough. He had to keep it.

WWJ

"You are so proud of knowing the law, but you dishonor God by breaking it."
Romans 2:23 (NLT)

Why is it so important to keep God's laws?
Which of God's laws do you know, but sometimes disobey?
Also read Ecclesiastes 5:4–6.

SHOW THAT YOU CARE

Lights in the World

What You Need:

A Bible, a pumpkin, knife, large spoon, newspapers, candle in a candleholder, matches, a pen or a marker

What To Do:

1. Read Matthew 4:16–17 and Matthew 5:14–16. How can we be lights in the world? How do we show God's love to each other? To our neighbors? If we are God's lights in a dark (sinful) world, what kind of faces will we show?

2. Draw a face on the pumpkin. Cut the top of the pumpkin to make a lid. As you scoop the pulp from inside the pumpkin, discuss how the pumpkin, its pulp, and its seeds relate to spiritual truths about sin and our lives.

3. How is the pulp inside the pumpkin like sin that prevents the light from shining? How difficult is it to remove the pulp? How difficult is it to overcome lying, cheating, and anger in our lives? How is slippery pulp like slippery sin? How are the seeds like seeds of God's love inside of us?

4. When the pumpkin is cleaned out, cut out the face, insert a candle and light it. Discuss ways Christians can be lights in a dark world. How can we show that God cares and that we care?

Note: Additional Scriptures on being lights: John 1:1–9; 3:18–21; Ephesians 5:6–9; Philippians 2:14–15; 1 John 1:5–7; 2:9–11.

A FRIEND INDEED

"Mom, can I go over and play with the new kid?" Nick asked.

"Sure," said Mom. "You've had no one to play with since your friends left on summer vacation. Let's go introduce ourselves."

When the two families sat down, the new boy's mom said, "I begin my job tomorrow, and Marcus will have to stay home alone. I don't like him to play outside without adult supervision."

"He's welcome to play with Nick. I'll be glad to watch them," said Nick's mom.

"That's okay. I play games on my computer," said Marcus.

After they returned to their apartment, Nick said, "If Marcus doesn't want to play with me, I don't want to play with him."

"Maybe he's afraid to make friends," Mom said. "You used to be so shy you had no friends at all. Remember that?"

"Yes. And I was lonely, too." Nick knew that Marcus was probably feeling alone in a new town. *Jesus, please help me make friends with him.*

The next morning, Nick rang the new boy's doorbell. "I'm going swimming with my mom. You can come if you want."

Marcus shook his head.

Each day that week, Nick invited Marcus to go somewhere with him and his mom. And each time, Marcus shook his head.

I'm not giving up, Nick promised himself.

On the eighth day, Nick invited Marcus to go skateboarding.

"Okay," said Marcus, and off they went on their skateboards. For a week after that, the two boys played together. Then Nick's friends returned from their vacations and joined in the fun.

Nick realized, *Marcus has taught me and my other friends a lot about skateboarding. I like him. Thanks Jesus, for helping me not give up on him.*

"Let us not become tired of doing good. At the right time we will gather a crop if we don't give up." Galatians 6:9

Is there someone who hasn't responded to your efforts of friendship or your prayers? How could you show love to them?
Also read Galatians 6:9–10.

KINDNESS TO STRANGERS
(Part One)

"The last box of Grandpa's things is in the truck. All that's left now is the furniture," Danny told his mom. He wiped the sweat from his face with his shirtsleeve. He stood and looked around the apartment where his grandpa had lived until a week ago.

Danny's mom sat down on a chair and sighed. "I guess we'll have to hold a garage sale. I hate to sell Dad's furniture, but we have no place for it at our house."

Danny ran his hand over the table on which his grandpa had repaired toys to give to needy children at Christmas. He touched one of the arms of the leather chair where Grandpa used to sit, sipping coffee and reading his worn, black Bible.

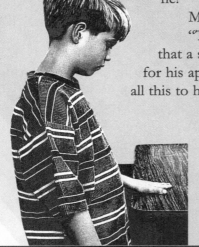

"Wait a minute," said Danny. "Grandpa once supported a Korean orphan, didn't he?"

Mom wiped her tears and nodded. "The Sunday bulletin at church said that a student from Korea needs furniture for his apartment. Why don't we give all this to him? Wouldn't Grandpa be happy if we shared his furniture?"

Mom's face brightened. "What a wonderful idea!"

"Imagine," said Danny, "even though Grandpa's in Heaven, he'll still be giving down here on earth!"

WWJ

"Your gifts meet the needs of God's people. And that's not all. Your gifts also cause many people to thank God." 2 Corinthians 9:12

Does your family have extra clothing or furniture to share? To whom could you show your generosity?
Also read 2 Corinthians 9:6–13.

KINDNESS TO STRANGERS
(Part Two)

"We brought furniture for you," said Danny. He stood in the doorway of the Korean college student's apartment.

"Yes. Somebody call and tell me. My name is Mun-Hee."

"Downstairs. In our pickup truck," said Danny. He helped his dad and Mun-Hee carry a bed frame, mattresses, a desk, a table, four chairs, and two lamps up the narrow flight of steps.

Mun-Hee's wife and young daughter stared with curiosity as each item came through the door of their small unfurnished apartment.

Their curiosity soon turned to astonishment when Danny's mom walked in the door. She brought a box of dishes and a freshly baked meatloaf and an apple pie.

"You helping us. Why? We are strangers to you."

"Before my grandpa died, he gave money every month to a little boy in Korea. I'm sure Gramps would like to give his things to someone like you. We're happy you can use them."

"Your grandfather, he was Christian?"

"Oh yes. We're all Christians."

"I would like to know about your God. You can tell me?"

"Better than that. There's a Korean church just a few blocks from here. If you like, we'll take you there this Sunday."

"We come," said Mun-Hee.

"All right!" Danny smiled and pumped Mun-Hee's hand.

Gramps would be so glad! Giving away his furniture helped this family want to hear the good news of Jesus.

WWJ

"*[God] shows love to the foreigners living among you....You, too, must show love to foreigners.*" Deuteronomy 10:18–19 (NLT)

How could you and your family show love to the foreigners in your neighborhood or city? What could you give them? Also read Leviticus 19:33–34.

OLD BLUE FINGER

"Why does your finger look so black and blue, Grandpa? Did you slam it in the car door?" asked Talisa.

"Goodness, no," he said. "I cut it on the hoe. And I think it got a little infected from the fertilizer I shoveled around my rose bushes."

"Maybe you ought to go to a doctor."

"Oh, honey, I'll be okay. Now remember, you came here to ride your pony. Go outside and ride. Don't worry about me."

Talisa climbed onto Golden Tail's saddle. *No. I can't ride now. Gramps needs to go to the doctor. Dear Jesus, help him not be stubborn.*

"My finger's not black," insisted Grandpa as he sprinkled fertilizer around another rose bush. "It's just a dark shade of blue. It'll be fine."

"You once had a cut on your arm, Gramps. Remember that? It took forever to get better. Your finger looks worse."

"Will you stop worrying, honey, and just go riding?"

"No," said Talisa. "I'm not going riding until you see a doctor."

They climbed in the car, and Talisa prayed all the way to the hospital. *Dear Jesus, please take care of my Grandpa.*

The emergency room doctor told Grandpa, "You have a dangerous staph infection. If you'd waited to come until tomorrow, we couldn't have treated you except by taking off your hand. Thank God the infection didn't kill you."

"I thank my honey, too, for looking out for Old Blue Finger."

Jesus said, "I give you a new command. Love one another. You must love one another, just as I have loved you." John 13:34

How do you love and care for your grandparents?
When has someone loved you like Jesus loves you?
Also read John 13:34–35.

MAN OVERBOARD

"That guy doesn't know what he's doing." Duncan stopped rowing and pointed toward a stout, middle-aged man in a canoe, stabbing the water with his paddle.

Dale laughed. "He'll be going for a swim if he's not careful. At least he has enough sense to wear a life vest and stay close to shore."

The boys watched the canoe tilt right, then left as the paddler tried to gain control of his craft.

A wind blew up, whipping the water into small whitecaps.

Dale peered at the clouds scudding across the sky. "I think bad weather's coming. We'd better head for shore."

At that moment, the man's canoe tipped over and dumped its owner into the river. "Help!" he cried as the current carried his paddle and canoe down the river.

The boys maneuvered their raft across the swift waters toward the floundering man. When the raft passed near the man, Duncan grabbed him by his life vest and pulled him onto the raft.

"Thanks!" The shivering man huddled on the boys' raft.

Dale covered the man with his jacket. "Our campground is just around the next bend. We can call for help from there."

While the three waited at the campground, the man said, "I'm glad you floated by! Thank you for rescuing me."

Duncan shook his head. "We had just decided to head for shore. If we'd turned back a minute or two sooner, we wouldn't have seen you. It wasn't luck. It was God. *He's* the one you can thank."

WWJ

"Who knows? It's possible that you became queen for a time just like this."
Esther 4:14

Why do you think God put you in your family?...in your city? Watch for ways God wants to use you to bless others this week. Also read Acts 8:26–29.

THE BLESSINGS OF OBEDIENCE

Games Without Rules

What You Need:

A Bible, a new card game or board game with rules printed on the box lid or on an accompanying flier

What To Do:

1. Try to play the new game without rules.
   Talk about why rules are needed in the family, school, workplace, or government.

2. Read the Ten Commandments in Exodus 20:3–17.
   God gave these rules to the people of Israel.
   Explain how the Ten Commandments offer a good set of rules for the "game of life."
   The Ten Commandments do *not* lead to salvation.
   Read Matthew 5:17–20.

3. Now read the rules for the game.
   Play the game again, this time *with* the rules.
   Have fun!

Variation #1: Read the "Golden Rule" in the New Testament—Matthew 7:12.

GUILT TRIP

"Harmonee, this is the third time I've asked you to do the dishes," said her mother.

"I'll do them, as soon as my show is over." But forty-five minutes later, Harmonee sat at the dining room table working math problems with Christian, her twin brother. Mother walked past, carrying an armload of laundry.

"Harmonee, please do the dishes."

"I will—as soon as I finish my math." Then the phone rang. Harmonee talked to her best friend for half an hour.

Again, Mom walked past. She looked upset, so Harmonee hung up the phone. "When you promise to do the dishes," Mom said, "I expect you to keep your word."

"Thanks for the guilt trip," Harmonee muttered under her breath. She stomped into the kitchen. Silverware clattered and pans banged as she washed them in the sink.

Christian leaned against the refrigerator and ate his dish of yogurt. "I think Mom named you wrong. She should have called you Dis-Harmonee."

"But I don't have time to do dishes."

"Who does?" said Christian. "Do you want Scruffy to do them?"

Harmonee glared at him. "Mom always makes me feel guilty."

"No. You're wrong. She's only reminding you what to do. You're the one who's treating Mom *badly*. Ask God's forgiveness. Change your attitude, sis. Then you won't feel guilty anymore."

Later, as Harmonee loaded plates into the dishwasher, she thought about what her brother said. *He's right. I owe Mom an apology.*

WWJ

"You are God's chosen people....So put on tender mercy and kindness as if they were your clothes. Don't be proud. Be gentle and patient." Colossians 3:12

What is your attitude toward helping your parents?
Do you feel guilty? Do you need to ask anyone's forgiveness?
Also read Psalm 32:3–6.

FIRESNAKE

Six-year-old Jay hid his burned hand behind his back as he sat down for lunch. *I hope Dad doesn't notice my hand.*

"Son, why are you eating with your left hand?" Dad asked.

Jay hesitated, then he laid his right hand on the table. His dad gasped at the sight of the puffy, reddened skin above the boy's wrist. "That looks serious. What happened?"

"A...a snake bit me."

"A snake? It might have been poisonous!" Dad jumped up from the table and grabbed his car keys. "Don't move. I'll carry you out to the car. I'm getting you to a doctor right away."

Dad scooped Jay up and hurried out the door.

"Dad, wait!" His father stopped on the front porch.

"It isn't a snake bite," said Jay. "It's a burn. I...I was playing with matches."

"Matches?" asked Dad.

"Yes," admitted Jay. *I feel bad about disobeying. But it feels good to tell the truth.* "Over there." Jay pointed to a black smudge and burned matches on the sidewalk alongside the car.

"But son, look how close you were to the gas tank! You could have blown up the car and gotten killed!"

Jay was quiet. "I didn't think about what I was doing," he said. "I didn't like your 'No matches' rule. But now I know it was for my own good."

"Children, obey your parents in everything. That pleases the Lord."
Colossians 3:20

What rules do your parents have to protect you?
Do you always obey your parents? Will you obey to please God?
Also read Ephesians 6:1–9.

IN HIDING

If this dumb camp won't sign me up for horseback riding, I won't follow their stupid rules! David ripped the activity roster from the wall, stamped out of the camp dining room, and slammed the screen door behind him.

He waited until his fellow campers left for handicrafts, then slipped into his cabin. Grabbing some comic books from his suitcase, he headed for the nearby woods. He propped himself against a log to read

The afternoon wore on and the sunlight began to fade. David ran out of things to do. His empty stomach rumbled. *I wonder what everyone is doing now? Having more fun than I am, that's for sure!*

He picked up his comic books and jogged back to camp.

When he entered the camp, David saw his parents talking with the camp director. His mother was crying.

I never thought the camp staff would be worried enough to call my parents!

The camp director spotted him. "There's David!" he called out. "He's safe!"

David's mother rushed over to hug him. The director followed. "Where were you? People searched all over for you."

"You didn't let me ride the horses, so I hiked to the woods."

"You broke our rule about leaving camp by yourself. Now you'll have to leave. Pack up and go home with your parents."

David hung his head. "Forgive me for what I did. I'm sorry. It wasn't worth it." He raised his eyes and asked the director, "If I promise to obey the rules, may I come back next year?"

WWJ

"The authorities are sent by God to help you. But if you are doing something wrong...you will be punished." Romans 13:4 (NLT)

What do you do when you don't get your way?
When have you broken a rule because you wanted your way?
Also read Romans 13:1–5.

HOW COULD THAT HAPPEN?

"I just found out the twelve-year-old kid who shot that grocery store clerk last week goes to *our* church!" Adria gossiped with her friend in front of the church.

Logan's eyes opened wide, "He's a *Christian?!*"

"I think so. He never misses church," Adria answered. "He even helped with our homeless outreach."

"I can't believe a *Christian* kid would shoot someone!"

"Well, maybe he *isn't* a Christian. He bullies kids at school and makes trouble in class. I know that just going to church doesn't make you a Christian." Adria smiled and lifted her chin. "I'm glad *I'm* not like him," she said proudly.

"Yeah, I know kids who come to church just to see their friends," Logan added.

"Or because their parents make them."

"Then they sit in the back and talk," said Logan.

At Logan's words, Adria's pride faded. *Sometimes I talk to my friends instead of worshiping. And I'm more interested in seeing them at Sunday School than learning about Jesus.*

Adria sighed. "I'll never shoot someone, but I'd better change my attitude. I guess I'm a hypocrite sometimes, too."

"Isn't that why we need to obey God and come to church?" said Logan. "We *all* need forgiveness."

WWJ

Jesus said, "Not everyone who says to me, 'Lord, Lord,' will enter the kingdom of heaven. Only those who do what my Father...wants will enter." Matthew 7:21

In what ways are you a "hypocrite"? Do you do what God wants? Why do *you* attend church or Sunday School?
Also read Matthew 7:21–29.

POPPING WHEELIES

"I need to go home and get my helmet," said Spencer.

"What for? We're riding on grass. Nothing's going to happen." Trent mounted his bike and jumped the curb onto the school lawn.

"Are you coming?" he called back to Spencer.

"Got to get my helmet! That's my dad's rule."

Trent swung around. "What's the big deal? *I'm* not wearing a helmet. Let's go."

"I'll be right back," said Spencer. Soon he returned from home, wearing his helmet. He and Trent zipped over a low hill. They zigged and zagged through the trees. On the flat ground they popped wheelies.

Then Trent's front tire struck a sprinkler in the lawn. He dived headfirst over his handlebars. He landed in the grass and laid there for a minute. Then he stood up and blinked. "What time is it?"

Spencer looked at his watch. "About three o'clock."

Trent took a step away, then turned around. "What time?"

"Three o'clock," repeated Spencer. "Now quit goofing around. Let's ride across the playground."

Trent set his bicycle upright. "Is this three o'clock?"

"Are you okay, man?"

Trent didn't answer. He only stared glassy-eyed into space.

"Come on," said Spencer, "we'd better get you home."

After two days of tests, the doctors finally told Trent's family that he would recover from his head injury.

"My mom appreciates you," Trent told Spencer later. "You've taught me to listen to my parents—and obey safety rules."

"My son, accept my words....Good sense will keep you safe. Understanding will guard you." Proverbs 2:1, 11

How do you respond when your parents give you rules?

Why do you think God gave you parents?

Also read Proverbs 1:8–9 and Proverbs 3:1–2.

DO YOUR BEST

Walk in Job's Shoes

What You Need:

A Bible, the biggest pair of shoes in the house

What To Do:

1.   Read Job 1:13–22.

2.   Set the shoes in the middle of the floor. Tell everyone: "Today we're going to think about how it felt to walk in the shoes of a very godly man—Job. Even though Job lived a righteous life, God allowed Satan to test him. It probably didn't seem fair. I'm going to ask some questions. When you think you know the answer, come to the center of the room and step into *Job's shoes.* Then give your answer."

3.   Ask questions from the reading. For instance: "How do you think Job felt when he had flocks and children and wealth? How do you think Job felt when his children died? How do you think Job felt when he got sick? Do you think Job ever felt angry at God? How would *you* feel if these trials happened to you?" *(Expect thoughtful answers. Don't let anyone rush to the shoes. End by stressing that Job never blamed God, and God restored everything to him.)*

4.   Pray together. Thank God for the examples of faith we find in the Bible. Ask God to help you *walk* each day, full of faith and love.

HOP-ALONG HANK

"Coach had better not put Hop-Along Hank on our team!" said Jake. He and Grayson stared at a player named Hank, limping across the baseball field. "It would take him twenty minutes to get to first base."

The coach hauled the bat bag into the dugout. "Listen up, guys!" he barked. "I want you out on the track. Four laps."

Jake groaned. "That's a whole mile." As he and Grayson sprinted to the track, Jake glanced back at their limping teammate. "Hank will never make it," said Jake.

Around the track they ran, slowing a little and panting more with each lap. As they reached the end of their mile, Hank had just completed his first lap, swinging his arms and dragging his lame leg. He looked exhausted, but on his face beamed a broad smile.

"Hank!" yelled the coach. "That's enough. Come on in."

"Not until I finish!" Hank called back. On he went, around the track four times, smiling the whole while.

Jake thought, *There's nothing wrong with my legs. But I was the one who complained about running four laps.* He felt a twinge of guilt. Then, as he watched Hank start his final lap with a limp and a smile, Jake felt a rush of thankfulness.

"Thank You, Lord, for my legs," Jake said under his breath. "Forgive my bad attitude toward my challenged teammate."

Hank completed his laps and scooped his mitt off the grass. Jake saw him glance around for a warm-up partner.

"Hey, Hank!" Jake lobbed the ball to him. Hank reached high and caught it without taking a step. Jake smiled. He had a lot to learn from this guy with the lame leg.

"Give thanks no matter what happens. God wants you to thank him because you believe in Christ Jesus." 1 Thessalonians 5:18

How is a good attitude contagious?
Do you have a thankful heart today? Take time to praise God.
Also read 1 Thessalonians 5:16–18.

WWJ

FLOWER POWER

Cordelia's skate bumped over some trash, and she pitched forward onto the empty parking lot. "Ow!" She cried as she pulled glass slivers from her bleeding knee.

Laurel skated over. "What happened?"

"I cut my knee." Cordelia looked around the pavement littered with trash. "There's junk everywhere. Let's clean it up—it's a way we can serve Jesus today."

The friends skated home to get large garbage bags, then hurried back to the office parking lot. An hour later they had filled two bags with old cans and rubbish.

"Wow! This place looks great," said Cordelia. "But it still needs something more," she said. "Oh! I know—flowers!"

Hurrying home again, the girls collected three flowering potted plants and arranged them on the front steps of the building. "Now it looks perfect!" said Cordelia.

A voice from behind startled her. "What looks perfect?" Scot and Phil balanced on bikes. "I see!" Scot said before she could answer. "You cleaned up this old parking lot."

"Let's go clean up the empty lot by my house." Phil said. The boys took off on their bikes.

The two girls giggled. "Macho Scot and Phil—of all people!" said Cordelia. "You never know who a good deed might influence."

"Do everything you say or do in the name of the Lord Jesus."
Colossians 3:17

Who needs your help this week? Who can you serve?
Why should you always try do more than you *have* to do?
Also read Hebrews 12:11.

WEIRD HELP

Leila held her breath as she reached out her fingers and carefully picked up the plastic bag holding Dylan's diaper. She hurried outside, yanked open the garbage can, and threw in the bag. Then she leaned over the fence, breathing in fresh air.

Butter, Leila's favorite cow, lumbered up to the fence and licked Leila's hand. Leila wiped off the cow's drool.

"I hate slobber!" she fussed. "And I hate bad smells. I asked God to help me get over it, but He hasn't."

Leila patted Butter's head. "You're hot!" Alarmed, she felt the cow again. Leila dashed into the house to ask her mom, "Can cows have temperatures? Is Butter sick?"

The vet arrived an hour later. "Butter has milk fever. I'm afraid I'll have to put her to sleep. I'm sorry."

"No! Don't kill Butter!" Leila threw her arms around the cow's neck. "Tell me what to do. I'll do anything to save her."

"Do you have a strong stomach? You'll have to deal with some really foul-smelling odors to help her get well."

Leila looked at Mom. "If I pray, I know God will help me."

Over the next three days, Leila shoveled manure and helped the vet give shots to her cow. She picked flies off Butter's back and rubbed stinky sulfur on her.

A week later, Leila and Mom watched Butter graze with the rest of the herd.

"You saved her life," Mom said. "I'm proud of you."

"It's weird," Leila said. "It didn't bother me to do really gross things for Butter, but I still choke at Dylan's diapers. I guess God helps you do whatever you have to do."

WWJ

"I work hard with all of Christ's strength. His strength works powerfully in me."
Colossians 1:29

When has God helped you do something you couldn't do alone? For what difficult task do you need to ask God's help today? Also read Philippians 4:10–19.

OILED HAIR

"I don't want to wash you," said Jeff. "It's too much work."

"Mommy's cooking," said three-year-old Kevin. He sat in the bathtub, slapping the water to make bubbles.

"Yeah. And *I'm* supposed to wash your hair. I don't want to do it. So do it yourself. Here." Jeff handed his little brother a washcloth.

Kevin spread the washcloth across his chest.

"Wash your face and your ears," ordered Jeff.

"Mommy uses soap."

"Well, I'm not Mommy," said Jeff. "Just scrub."

Kevin dragged the washcloth over his face and ears. "Wash my hair," said Kevin. "Dirty hair."

"I don't know where the shampoo is," said Jeff. "And I'm not going all the way downstairs to ask Mom." He uncapped a bottle of baby oil. "Here. Use this." Kevin dumped half the bottle onto his head and ruffled it through his hair.

At lunch, Mom noticed Kevin's hair. "Is your hair still wet? It ought to be dry by now." She felt his hair and then sniffed her fingers. "Jeff, can you tell me what's in Kevin's hair? Baby oil?"

Jeff felt embarrassed. "I couldn't find the shampoo," he said.

His mom gave him a stern look.

"Okay. After lunch I'll find the shampoo...and the soap. Then I'll wash him the way I should have washed him in the first place."

"The lazy person is full of excuses."
Proverbs 22:13 (NLT)

Why should we work hard instead of being lazy?
When have you been lazy about doing your work?
Also read Proverbs 13:1, 4, 18.

WRESTLING BROKEN

"Get a leg on him, Dustin!" screamed Allan. He knew his friend couldn't hold on much longer with his bandaged hand.

The referee made a couple of quick circles with his arm and shot up two fingers.

Hurrah! Two more points for Dustin! But his hand looks swollen. Why does he insist on wrestling with a broken hand? wondered Allan.

The buzzer sounded. The match ended. Dustin collapsed onto the mat, his face contorted with pain.

The two boys made their way to the bleachers. Dustin moaned. His middle finger had swelled three times bigger than normal and his whole hand was purple.

"I'm sure your hand is broken," said Allan. "You can't even move your fingers. You shouldn't wrestle anymore."

"But I have to."

"Why?" asked Allan.

"The Bible says we're supposed to do our best at everything," Dustin said. "That's one way we glorify God."

"Yeah, but the Bible also tells us to be *wise*. It's just common sense not to wrestle with a broken hand."

Dustin sighed. "That's true…what a relief."

"Why don't you ask your mom to take you to the doctor for an x-ray," Allan suggested. "He'll cast it so you can wrestle without pain in a few weeks."

Dustin rolled his eyes. "Have you ever wrestled without pain?"

"Okay," Allan said, smiling. "I guess you can wrestle with *less* pain in a few weeks."

WWJ

"You who are childish, get some good sense. You who are foolish, gain understanding." Proverbs 8:5

How can the Bible give you common sense?
How are you glorifying God in what you do this week?
Also read Proverbs 8:1–9.

TELL THE TRUTH

The "Truth" or a "Lie"

What You Need:

A Bible

What To Do:

1. Read Proverbs 19:9 and Colossians 3:8–9.

2. One person in the group makes three statements.
    Two of them should be true; the other should be a lie.
    (The person might say something like: I ate rice for dinner tonight.
    I am thirsty. I lost a quarter today.)

3. The rest of the group has two chances to guess which
    statement was the lie. After the first person's lie is discov-
    ered, the next person makes three statements. The game
    continues until everyone has had at least one turn trying to
    trick everyone.

4. In the game we just played, we had fun trying to trick each
    other. But this is the only time in your life when you can
    "lie" without consequences. We always receive consequences
    when we lie because God hates lies. God loves the truth.
    Make some false statements like, "Mom, I did my home-
    work." Let the group give possible consequences for the lie.

5. Pray for God to stop you when you are tempted to lie.
    Confess any lies. Pray for courage to tell the truth.

IGNORE IT? OR REPORT IT?

"Hey, come back with my spoon!"

Justin watched Corky duck out of the cafeteria with a spoon in his hand. He sighed. "Corky's teasing some little kid again. I think somebody should turn him in, don't you, Michael?"

At recess, Justin and Michael noticed Corky standing by a trash can. He bent the metal spoon back and forth until the handle broke off. Dropping the handle into the trash, Corky stuffed the rest of the spoon into his pocket. Justin looked at Michael, who just shrugged.

On the bus ride home, Corky sat down behind Justin. He leaned forward and shoved a large ball of foil in Justin's face.

"You couldn't hit the bus driver with this even if you were up there sitting on his lap," taunted Corky.

"Get lost!" said Justin. A minute later something whizzed past Justin's ear and hit the driver on the head. The bus swerved. Corky slid across the aisle as the driver brought the bus to a stop.

Striding down the bus aisle, the driver held up the foil ball and asked, "Who threw this?" Children pointed in Justin's direction.

The driver unrolled the foil to reveal the broken spoon. He stopped in front of Justin. "Get out. Now! Riding the school bus is a privilege. You can walk to school for the next month."

The next day Michael exploded. "Justin, you're not going to walk two miles every day because of something Corky did, are you?"

"But I don't want to squeal," said Justin.

"You're the one who said somebody should turn Corky in. If you don't do something, he'll keep on bullying everybody."

Justin headed for the door. "I'll think about it," he said.

"Remember, it is sin to know what you ought to do and then not do it."
James 4:17 (NLT)

When have you neglected to do what you knew was right?
What do you do when you see someone doing wrong?
Also read Proverbs 21:3 and Micah 6:8.

PIRATE SCARE

Lucas walked into the kitchen and stopped short. His mother stood frowning with her hands on her hips. His little brother's face was wrinkled up. It looked like he was going to cry.

Mom spoke sternly. "Mark, yesterday I told you to put your bike away in the basement. Now it's sitting out in the rain, rusting. Because you didn't take care of it, you can't ride it for two weeks."

"But Mommy, I was afraid of the pirates in the basement!" Mark's voice trembled.

His mother shook her head. "No silly excuses, Mark."

"I saw the pirates!" Mark insisted. "I really did!"

Lucas backed toward the door. *Oh no! Mark actually believed me when I told him that pirates used our basement as a hideout!* Lucas shook his head. *It was just a joke. I didn't mean to get Mark in trouble. But if I admit it to Mom,* I'll *be in trouble....*

Mark turned and saw Lucas just as he slipped out the door. "Lucas! Tell Mom about the pirates. She doesn't believe me!"

Lucas hesitated. He looked from Mom's stern face to Mark's anxious one. "It's true, Mom. I told Mark a story about pirates in the basement. So it's *my* fault that he didn't put his bike away. I'll help clean the rust off."

Lucas put his arm around his brother. "Forgive me, Mark, for not telling you the truth. Come on. I'll show you that there aren't any pirates in the basement."

"My mouth speaks what is true. My lips hate evil. All the words of my mouth are honest." Proverbs 8:7–8

When have you been tempted to tell a lie instead of the truth? Have you lied to someone? Have you asked his or her forgiveness? Also read Proverbs 8:5–14.

SAY WHAT YOU FEEL

"Hasn't Cindi showed up yet?" Mom stuck her head through Madeline's door. "You've been ready for an hour."

"Any time now, Cindi's van will pull up and honk. And, fifteen minutes later, we'll be skating. I'm so excited that she wants to be friends with me!" Madeline said.

Three hours later, Madeline leaned against her mom's shoulder as they sat on the sofa. Her eyes were red and puffy from crying. Cindi never did show up to go skating.

The doorbell rang. When Madeline answered it, Cindi and Nicole stood there giggling. Cindi hugged Madeline and said, "Oh, I am like...so sorry. I asked Nicole to come along at the last minute. Then we just, I don't know how, forgot all about you! I am like...really embarrassed. Can you ever forgive me?"

Madeline forced herself to smile. "Sure. It's okay." *What else can I say?* she wondered.

"Oh, I'm like...so totally relieved. But like I told Nicole, you are just *soo* nice...you'd forgive me."

Cindi gave Madeline another quick hug. "Well, Mom's waiting. We need to hurry." Cindi and Nicole breezed out the door. "Love you!" Cindi called from the car.

Madeline slowly closed the door.

"Well?" Mom asked. "Do you feel better...or worse?"

"I feel kind of sick. It hurts when someone breaks a promise. I need to think about how to say it nicely, but someday I need to tell Cindi how much she hurt me."

WWJ

"If your brother sins against you, go to him. Tell him what he did wrong. Keep it among yourselves." Matthew 18:15

When have you told someone how he or she hurt you?
How do you let others know how you are feeling?
Also read Matthew 18:15–20.

X MARKS THE LIE

"But, Mom," Mason pleaded, "I only watched one little TV program. It wasn't a bad one, either."

"That's not the point." Mason's mother looked him square in the eye. "I told you not to watch any TV at all until *after* all of your homework was finished. You watched anyway, and then—what really upsets me—you lied to me about it."

She marked a large *X* on the monthly calendar hanging in the kitchen. "No TV for two weeks, starting from today."

Each evening, his mother marked off the day with an *X*. At first, Mason played outside after school, hardly missing his favorite cartoon shows. Then it started raining. Day after day, Mason stayed inside. Day after day, the television stayed off.

I can't wait any longer, he decided one afternoon. He added two more *X*s to the calendar. He marked the two days before his TV restriction had started. He smiled. *Now it looks as if my two weeks are almost up.*

That night his mother started to mark another *X* off the calendar. "What are these extra *X*s? Did you put them there?"

Mason hesitated to tell the truth. "Yes," he finally admitted.

"You can't shorten your punishment this way," Mother said. "But I am glad you chose to tell the truth instead of lying. So I'll plan some fun activities we can do together to make the time go faster."

"Do not tell lies."
Leviticus 19:11

Have you ever lied to get out of trouble?
How does it cause more trouble to lie than to tell the truth?
Also read Proverbs 12:19–20.

THROWING ROCKS

"What can we do today that's different?" Kyle asked the neighbor kids who sat with him in the city park. They gave him blank stares. One of the boys tossed a small rock into the air and caught it. Tossed it and caught it. Tossed it and caught it. Bor-ing.

Hey! That's a good idea. Kyle stood up and looked across the wide highway with its heavy traffic flow of cars and big rigs. He gathered a handful of small rocks. "Let's see who can throw these stones the farthest across the highway."

"From here? Are you kidding?" asked Barkley.

"No, Barkley, not from here," said Kyle. "Come on." They all grabbed fistfuls of rocks and jogged to the edge of the highway.

"Here goes," said Kyle. "See if you can tell where it lands."

He wound up like a baseball pitcher and sent a rock high over the cars and the big rigs. Between bumpers the kids could just make out where the rock landed.

"Not bad," said Barkley. "My turn." He threw with all his might. His rock fell short of Kyle's. Then the other boys took turns throwing. Some were poor shots. Their rocks skipped across the roofs of cars or glanced off the sides of big trucks.

Soon, a highway patrol car pulled off the road. "Throwing rocks is dangerous," said the officer. "You might scare someone and cause an accident. Or you might damage a vehicle."

"We didn't think about that," said Kyle. "We were just seeing how far we could throw. We won't do it anymore."

"See that you don't."

When the officer drove away, Kyle said, "We weren't very smart. Thank God that nobody got hurt! I'm going home."

"The Lord is honest and good. He teaches sinners to walk in his ways. He shows those who aren't proud how to do what is right." Psalm 25:8–9

Should you go along with the crowd?
How can you know what Jesus wants you to do?
Also read Psalm 19:9–13.

THANKFUL HEARTS

Joyful Noises

What You Need:

A Bible, a comb, waxed paper, jingle bells, saucepan, spoon, dental floss or string

What To Do:

1.   Make musical instruments:
     Wrap waxed paper around a comb.
     Tie jingle bells around your ankles with dental floss.
     Use the spoon and saucepan like a drum.

2.   Read Psalm 150:1–6.

3.   Make a joyful noise to the Lord! Sing and clap.
     March around and jingle the bells on your feet.
     Praise the Lord as you hum into the comb and bang
     on the pan with your spoon.

Variation: Partially fill a plastic container with dried beans.
            Use a tight lid on it. Shake it while you sing.

BEE STING

Cheryl didn't see the bee on her hand until it was too late. She and her brother, Sam, were picking blackberries. Sam dropped a few into his bucket. He ate most of what he picked.

"If you keep eating your berries," said Cheryl, "you won't have any to take home." Just then, the bee sunk its stinger into the back of her hand. "Ahh! Help!" She waved her hand wildly in the air.

"What's the matter?" asked Sam.

"A bee just stung me!"

Sam and Mom and Aunt Bernice hurried over.

"Look," said Cheryl, "it's already swelling up."

Aunt Bernice frowned. "Cheryl's having an allergic reaction. We need to get her to the hospital right away."

Cheryl's face turned white. Sam forced a smile. "You'll be okay, sis." *Dear Lord, please help her. She doesn't look so great.*

An hour later, Sam and Aunt Bernice sat and prayed in the hospital waiting room.

Mom came out with the news. "The doctor gave Cheryl a shot that stopped the allergic reaction," she said.

"Will she be all okay?" asked Sam.

"Yes, honey. We can take her home."

The door opened and a nurse wheeled Cheryl into the waiting room. "It's a good thing you came here when you did," said the nurse. "By the time the doctor saw Cheryl, she was having trouble breathing. If the bee had stung her head, she might have died."

Sam gave his sister a hug. "I prayed for you, sis. I'm thankful God took good care of you. Now let's go home. I want to help eat *your* blackberries."

WWJ

"The Lord protects those of childlike faith; I was facing death, and then he saved me." Psalm 116:6 (NLT)

Can you be thankful even when God doesn't do what you ask? What are you thankful for today?
Also read Psalm 116:5–9.

THE BEST CHRISTMAS PRESENT

Did any of the girls in Bethlehem get to hold Baby Jesus? wondered eight-year-old Jana as she cuddled her new cousin. *Did Jesus cry? Was He wrinkled and bald?*

Jana sat on the rug and listened to Uncle Nick read the Christmas story to the whole family gathered around the tree. She rocked tiny Justin in her arms. He whimpered softly.

"Are you hungry, little fellow?" Jana whispered, tucking the blanket around him. "Do you want your mother?" She carefully rose up from the floor, holding him tightly.

"Aunt Debbie, I think Justin needs to be…" Suddenly Jana stumbled over someone's foot. She screamed as she pitched forward. All she could think of was Justin.

He'll be crushed if I land on top of him. His head mustn't hit the floor!

She twisted her body sideways and clutched him to her chest as she took the full brunt of the fall.

Justin cried loudly as Aunt Debbie lifted him out of Jana's arms.

"Is he okay?" Jana's voice shook. "Did his head get hurt?"

Aunt Debbie looked Justin over. "Thanks to you, Jana, he's fine. You saved his life by falling on your side."

"Thank God!" said Jana. "It's the best Christmas present I could get."

"Give thanks to the Lord, because he is good. His faithful love continues forever." Psalm 118:29

What are you thankful for today?
Take time to share how God has blessed you this past year.
Also read Psalm 118:24–29.

HALF CUP OF RICE

"Why can't you ever fix something I *like?*" Chloe scowled and pushed away the pot roast and carrots.

"It's yummy," Gage said. "Stop your nagging."

Chloe glared at her brother. "Don't tell *me* to stop nagging. Mom, can I turn the television to another channel?"

"I need to watch the news about the election," Mom said. "If you don't like the carrots, at least eat the meat."

"Look!" said Gage. "What's wrong with all those kids on television?"

Chloe glanced up. On the television screen, a large group of foreign children clustered around an American aid worker. They stretched out their plates toward him. The man handed them each half a cup of rice. Chloe could see every bone and rib in each child's body. They were starving.

"Is that all the food they get?" Chloe asked. "Why am *I* complaining?" She pushed her fork into a carrot. Silently, she thanked God as she chewed it. It tasted pretty good, actually.

"I don't want any dessert," she said when Mom cut the pie. "Could we have one day a week when we eat only a half cup of rice for supper? It would help me remember all the blessings God gives us."

"That's a good idea," Mom said.

"I think so, too," Gage agreed.

"I'd like to pray and thank God for our good dinner again," said Chloe. "I want God to know I really mean it."

"Let the peace that Christ gives rule in your hearts....And be thankful."
Colossians 3:15

What do you complain about the most?
When do you have the most trouble being thankful?
Also read Psalm 146:5–10.

MUDDY SURPRISE

"I still can't believe this river used to be a street!" Three days after the hurricane, Pepe and his sister searched through the ankle-deep muddy water for clothes or pans or anything they could use—anything the hurricane had not destroyed.

Maria grabbed a piece of splintered wood as it floated past. "Maybe this came off our house," she said sadly.

Pepe looked at the jumbled mass of boards and mud. "We can't think about everything we lost, Maria." He watched two men digging up a truck the hurricane had buried. "Remember, God saved us. We could have been buried under the mud."

Encouraged by Pepe's words, Maria added, "We did find enough boards to build a shelter. Lots of people don't have anyplace to live."

"That's right." Pepe bent down to fish something out of the dirty water. "Look!" he exclaimed, "a shirt!" He wrung it out and handed it to his sister.

"It fits me!" cried Maria, laughing and twirling as she held up the shirt.

"God sent you a surprise when you were feeling sad and discouraged." Pepe smiled. "God is reminding us that He will take care of us."

Maria smiled, too. "And we will trust Him."

"And this same God who takes care of me will supply all your needs."
Philippians 4:19 (NLT)

Talk about the ways God has blessed you during hard times. Pray for those who are struggling through natural disasters. Also read Philippians 4:18–20.

THANKFUL (Even When You Hurt)

"Ruthie, why didn't you cry when Dad died?" Kevin scooped moist sand onto the sand castle and patted it down.

"I *couldn't* cry," said ten-year-old Ruthie.

"We all cry when we're sad." Kevin wished the ache in his heart would go away. Every night it made him cry himself to sleep. "Didn't you care that Dad died?"

"Of course I cared!" Ruthie flung a handful of sand at the half-built castle. Her eyes blazed with anger.

"I'm sorry," Kevin said.

His younger sister sat without moving. She stared at the sand castle. After a while, she jabbed her shovel in its wall.

"I got mad," she explained. "We prayed and prayed every night for the past six months that Dad would live. But God didn't answer our prayers."

"Oh yes, He did." Kevin smoothed over the hole her shovel made. "You don't remember when Dad first got cancer, do you?"

Ruthie shook her head.

"You were two years old. The doctors said Dad had only six months to live. So we prayed. Dad's cancer went away for a long time."

"Really?" Ruthie looked at him, the anger gone from her eyes.

"Yes. God answered our prayers and gave Dad to us for eight extra years. If Dad had died when he first got cancer, you wouldn't even remember him."

Tears welled up in Ruthie's eyes. "I'm so glad Dad lived longer," she said. "Thank You, God, for answering prayer!"

WWJ

"Our God is a God who strengthens you and cheers you up....May you have perfect peace as you trust in him." Romans 15:5, 13

What would you tell someone who felt God didn't answer prayer? Have you ever felt mad at God for not answering your prayers? Also read Ephesians 5:19–20.

MAKING CHOICES

Life's Journey Map

What You Need:

A Bible, plain paper, and marking pens

What To Do:

1.   Read Joshua 24:14–17, 19–22.

2.   Have each person make a "map" of his or her life. Draw pictures of major life events, then connect them together with a line.

3.   Share these events with each other. Tell about choices the person or others made at the time of each event.

4.   Discuss whether the choices were good, bad, or neutral. Ask whether the person thought about God or the Bible's instructions when making the choices. Speculate what might have happened if another choice had been made.

Note: This is a great opportunity for parents to pass on their spiritual heritage as they relate stories of God's guidance and provision in their lives.

Variation #1: Make a family map rather than individual "maps."

Variation #2: Use an actual map of your state or country.   Place sticky notes at sites of major life events.

HUNCHBACK

"Hey, you! Hunchback! Can you understand English?"

The stooped man trudging down the sidewalk stopped and turned his droopy, wrinkled face toward the taunting boys.

Jim and Tommy laughed as they rode away on their bikes.

That evening, the boys told their dad about the strange man.

"What makes a person valuable in God's eyes?" asked Dad.

Tommy's grin faded as he thought over Dad's question. *How could a crippled old man be worth much?* Tommy wondered.

Dad made a phone call, then turned to his sons. "Tomorrow I want to take you two on a little field trip."

The next afternoon, Jim and Tommy hopped into the van with Dad. "Where are we going?" they asked. Dad just smiled.

Soon they pulled into the parking lot with a sign: WVRC.

"This is the Willamette Valley Rehabilitation Center," said Dad. "It's a place where handicapped people work."

"Handicapped?" The boys glanced nervously at each other.

After a tour of the center, the director took them into a small room. "Come see the work of our best worker."

"Look at those carvings," said Tommy. "The hawk looks real."

"This is Russell, our best worker," the director said.

When the woodworker turned to face them, both boys gasped. "The hunchback!" Russell smiled, then turned back to his carving.

Dad asked, "Do you boys want to tell him anything?"

Tommy gulped, then said, "I'm sorry that we laughed at you and called you names. We should have respected you."

"Please forgive us," added Jim.

"Scripture says, 'Do you want to love life and see good days? Then keep your tongues from speaking evil.'" 1 Peter 3:10

How does Jesus want you to treat people with handicaps?
When are you tempted to say mean things to others?
Also read Colossians 3:12–15.

EXPERIMENT IN GLASS

Crash! Clunk! The noise of breaking glass woke Nate from his nap on the porch swing. *That racket came from the garage,* he thought.

He jumped up and dashed around the house, stopping at the corner of the garage to listen. *Is it a burglar?*

Crash! More glass shattered. Nate peeked into the garage. His four-year-old brother held a brick in one hand and a quart jar in the other. Broken glass covered the concrete floor.

"Adam! What are you doing?"

Adam grinned. Before Nate could stop him, Adam raised his arm and hurled the jar against the wall. *Crash!* The jar smashed and hundreds of glass slivers shot across the floor.

"Jars break!" Adam said. "See! Watch *this.*"

"Stop!" yelled Nate.

Adam threw the brick anyway. *Clunk!* It hit the wall and fell down. "Bricks *don't* break!" He reached for another jar.

Nate grabbed it away from him. "You broke Mom's canning jars! She'll feel bad when she finds out!"

Tears filled Adam's eyes. Nate put his arm around his brother. "You didn't know it was wrong, Adam. I'll help you clean up. And I'll go with you when you tell Mom you're sorry."

"Thanks," said Adam, wiping his eyes with his sleeve. The boys worked together and swept up the mess.

"A wise son makes his father glad....A person who has no sense enjoys doing foolish things." Proverbs 15:20–21

Have you ever done something wrong without knowing it? When have you helped a younger child learn what was right? Also read Proverbs 17:10, 25, 27.

ROID RAGE

"I can't believe the coach didn't play you even once!" Calvin told Joey. He could see that Joey was ready to cry.

"Coach says I'm too small for football. I don't have enough muscles, yet."

A car squealed to a stop beside them. Calvin's high school brother, Hans, rolled down his window. "Want a lift?" The boys took off their muddy football cleats and climbed in the backseat.

Wanting to cheer Joey up, Calvin said, "My big brother can get you a pill that will make your muscles grow in two weeks!"

Hans slammed on his brakes and hollered at the car in front of him. "Watch out you idiot!" Then Hans let go of the steering wheel so he could pull up his shirt sleeve. "Look at these muscles, kids!"

Hans flexed his biceps and grinned. "I used to be a runt like you," he told Joey. He swerved the car down the street and screeched to a stop in front of Joey's house.

"Why are you acting weird?" asked Calvin. "Will you get Joey some steroid pills or not?" Then Calvin felt guilty.

Dear Lord, he prayed, *is it wrong for me to offer steroids to Joey? I know they are drugs, but they haven't hurt Hans. They've made him a big football star.*

That night, Calvin got the answer to his prayer. The police called his parents and told them that Hans had deliberately rammed a car with another teenager in it. Both boys were badly injured.

The police said the steroids sent Hans into "roid rage." The drugs made his violent temper flare up.

The next day Calvin told Joey about Hans. "Don't take pills to make your muscles bigger. Be happy with the way God made you. And let your body grow naturally."

WWJ

Jesus said, "Everyone who hears my words and puts them into practice is like a wise man. He builds his house on the rock." Matthew 7:24

Why is it more important to obey God than to be a sports hero?
How have you been tempted to break God's laws?
Also read Matthew 7:24–27.

ANYTHING TO WIN

I know I'll win first prize. I'm the best artist in the class. Geena proudly handed her paper Easter egg to the teacher. She stood and watched her teacher staple it to the hall bulletin board.

Geena smiled at her creation—a glittery egg with flaps folded back to reveal a baby chick. Then she stiffened. *Tiffany's egg is almost as good as mine is.* She frowned. *What if the judges think it's better than mine? She'll win first prize and I won't!*

All during reading group Geena worried about Tiffany's egg. Then she had an idea. She slipped a black crayon into her pocket and raised her hand. "May I go to the bathroom?"

The teacher nodded. Geena walked out of the classroom and straight toward the bulletin board. She looked around to be sure the hallway was empty. Then she took out her black crayon and slashed it across Tiffany's egg. *She'll never win now.*

Tiffany and the other students were horrified when they discovered Tiffany's ruined egg. Tiffany cried. But no one knew who did it. And no one ever found out.

The teacher displayed Geena's first place ribbon at the front of the classroom. Each time Geena looked at it, she remembered the ugly black mark across Tiffany's beautiful egg. Geena felt as if she had a black slash across her own heart. *I can't even enjoy my award. And I'll never know whether I won because I'm an artist or because I'm a cheater.*

"Be on guard! Turn back from evil."
Job 36:21 (NLT)

When is it hardest for you to do what's right?
How can your sins harm your relationship to God? To others?
Also read Psalm 37:16–29.

WHOM SHOULD I OBEY?

"I don't want to play soccer on Sunday," Erin told her father. "Do I have to?"

"You do if you want to go to college," said her dad. They sat on a bench beside the soccer field, waiting for the teams to arrive.

"Do you know how much college costs these days?" asked Dad. "You need a scholarship to get through those four years."

"But, Dad, I'm only eleven." *And I'm not worried,* she thought. *I know that God will provide a way for me to go to college.*

"You don't understand, Erin. You've got to get a head start. The only way is to play in Sunday tournaments."

"But Sunday is the Lord's day, Dad."

"Well, that doesn't bother me. I'm not a Christian. But haven't you told me that the Bible says to honor and obey your father? Now will you obey the Bible and do what I say?"

Which is more important, Lord, not playing soccer on Sunday or obeying my Dad? She thought a moment. *The Bible does say to honor my father. So I'll obey him. And I'll trust You, Lord. You love me. You'll take care of this situation. Maybe I can bring one of these girls closer to You.*

Erin grinned at her father. "Okay, Dad. I'm ready to play."

"That's my girl!"

She gave him a kiss and ran out onto the field. "Before we warm up," she said to her teammates, "can we pray? Let's ask the Lord to help us keep good attitudes and not get hurt."

NOTE: Erin prayed before that game…and before every soccer game that year. By the end of the season, one of her teammates accepted the Lord. Years later, Erin did receive a scholarship to college…but it was for her *grades,* not for soccer.

"[The Lord] doesn't take delight in the strong legs of men. The Lord takes delight in those who....put their hope in his faithful love." Psalm 147:10–11

When have you done something you didn't want to do? What was your attitude like? Did you seek to please God? Also read Ephesians 6:1–2.

HONOR OTHERS

Make a Jesus Tree

What You Need:

A Bible, a tree branch and a jar or bottle to hold it, a collection of objects depicting Jesus' life, paper, scissors, and markers

What To Do:

1. Read John 15:1–8.

2. Bring a tree branch inside and set it up in a bottle or secure it in a pot with plaster of paris.

3. Decorate it with objects (or pictures) that remind you of an aspect of Jesus' life. Cut out and color crosses of different sizes as reminders of His greatest gift.

4. Other decorations: cut out pictures of fathers and sons to symbolize Jesus as the Son of God, make sheep from cotton balls to show Jesus as the Lamb of God, draw and cut out butterflies as reminders of Jesus' resurrection, cut out crowns and circles as reminders of Jesus the eternal king.

5. Pray together. Thank Jesus for who He is: savior, shepherd, Son of God, friend, bread of life, prince of peace, sacrifice, the resurrection and the life.

Variation: Decorate a tree in your yard or turn your Christmas tree into a *Jesus tree.*

SUMMER SOFTBALL

"Don't let Matt play or we'll lose for sure," said one of the boys on the baseball team.

"He can't catch and he can't hit," said another boy.

Okay, so I don't play as well as you guys, thought Matt. *I always get stuck in left field, and I can't throw the ball far enough to get anybody out. I need to be closer, like a shortstop.*

The batter socked the ball. Matt ran for it, keeping his eyes on it the whole way. Out of the sky it arched. Down and down. Matt reached up...and missed. The ball thumped the grass just to his left. He scooped it up and threw it with all his strength. His arm hurt instantly. The ball fell short of the pitcher's mitt and the runner scored.

The story of my life. Will nobody listen to me? Put me closer.

"On the bench," said the coach.

Matt groaned. *I didn't mean that close.*

For the rest of the game Matt sat on the bench. *No problem. If I can't play, at least I can do something. I'll cheer for the rest of them.*

"What an eye, Bobbie! You can do it, Peter! Way to go, Darrell!"

Matt jumped to his feet. He waved his arms. He shouted more often and much louder than any parent. He was a one-boy cheering section. *With me out of the game, they have a chance to win,* he thought. *They haven't won for the last five games. But there's always a next time. Maybe that's today.*

It wasn't. Even though Matt stayed on the bench, his team lost. But they didn't lose for lack of support. In that department, Matt won like a champ!

"Don't pay back evil with evil. Be careful to do what everyone thinks is right...live in peace with everyone." Romans 12:17–18

How does Jesus want you to react when you are criticized?
How can you live peaceably and honor others today?
Also read Romans 12:10–18.

ENDURING LOVE

"Grandpa!" Carson called to his ninety-two-year-old grandfather. "Grandma needs you."

Grandmother's Alzheimer's disease mixed her up and made her unhappy. Grandpa cared for her by himself. He maneuvered his wheelchair from the kitchen to her chair. He reached for her hand and asked, "What do you want, dear?"

She frowned. "The bathroom," she said grumpily.

"Follow me," Grandpa said. Grandma shuffled behind Grandpa's wheelchair to the bathroom. Carson remembered when she used to push his tricycle and play with him.

"Get me a drink," she demanded when she came back.

"Okay." Grandpa wearily turned his wheelchair to go back into the kitchen.

"I'll hold your hand, Grandma," Carson told her when she sat down in her chair. He knew Jesus loved Grandma even though she couldn't do much anymore.

"You will?" Grandma held out her hand and Carson took it. As long as he held it, she seemed happy. She didn't ask Grandpa for anything for a long time.

When Carson was getting ready to leave, Grandpa hugged him. "Thanks for giving me a break. You helped...a lot."

"Love...endures through every circumstance."
1 Corinthians 13:7 (NLT)

When have you helped an elderly person? What did you do? When have you showed love, even though it wasn't easy? Also read 1 Corinthians 13:4–7.

MISERABLE BRAT

"I hate this new church," Tiffany muttered to herself. "I don't know anyone here." She fidgeted on a hard metal chair in the front row of her Sunday School class.

A smiling girl sat down next to Tiffany. "Hi," she said with a smile. "I'm Keegan. You're new, aren't you?"

"Yes. My dad is the new pastor. He's in charge of the whole church." Tiffany wanted to impress Keegan. "He practically owns this place."

"Girls," the teacher said, "please pay attention to the lesson."

"I don't have to," Tiffany mumbled. "My dad is your boss."

The teacher put her arm around Tiffany and whispered in her ear. "The pastor's daughter needs to set a good example."

Tiffany's cheeks burned. *The teacher is right,* she thought. *I haven't been acting the way Jesus wants me to.*

After class, Tiffany apologized to the teacher. "I'm sorry I was so disrespectful. Please forgive me. I'm glad you corrected me."

"I forgive you." Her teacher hugged her. "And I'm glad you're in my class."

Tiffany found Keegan. "I'm sorry I acted like a brat."

"It's okay," Keegan said. "I know how it feels to go to a new church and try to make friends. We moved here last year." She smiled. "Do you think you could come to my house to play this afternoon?"

She wants to be my friend! Tiffany thought. *Thank You, Lord. This new church might not be so bad after all.*

"If a child is corrected, he becomes wise. But a child left to himself brings shame to his mother." Proverbs 29:15

When have you been disrespectful? Did you ask for forgiveness? How do you feel when you've been corrected?
Also read Proverbs 28:13–14, 25–26.

NANNA'S WHITE CANE

"Nanna, wait! I'll help you cross the street." *I wish she'd use her white cane,* Angela thought. *Without it, people can't tell that she's blind.*

Instead of waiting, Nanna impatiently stepped off the curb.

A sports car screeched to a stop. The woman in the car looked upset. "I—I almost hit you!" she shouted. "Didn't you see me?"

"We're sorry," Angela answered as she hugged Nanna. "My grandma is legally blind. She only sees shapes and things up close."

"Then she should use a white cane! That way people would know to watch out for her."

Angela knew it embarrassed Nanna to carry a cane. Nanna didn't want people to feel sorry for her.

Dear Lord Jesus, I want to help Nanna, Angela prayed. *Show me how.*

Angela guided her grandmother across the street. Suddenly she had a great idea and decided to surprise Nanna with it.

All afternoon, while her mother and Nanna chatted in the kitchen, Angela worked. She sorted through Mom's fabric scraps and found white eyelet fabric and white sequins. When she finished her sewing, she pulled the fancy covering over a cane Nanna kept at Angela's house. Angela carried the newly decorated walking stick downstairs. She prayed silently as she placed it in Nanna's hands.

"What's this?!" Nanna held it close to her face.

"Can you see it?" asked Angela.

"Yes," Nanna said, with tears in her eyes. "It's…beautiful." Nanna stood up and tried it out. "No one could feel sorry for me when I carry a beautiful cane like this," she said. Then she laughed and hugged her smiling granddaughter.

WWJ

Jesus said, "You may ask me for anything in my name. I will do it."
John 14:14

How has Jesus given you wisdom when you needed it?
What do you need Jesus to help you with today?
Also read James 1:5–8.

COUSIN RONNIE

"What are you doing under Aunt Marie's coffee table?" Mom asked her six-year-old daughter, Kathy.

"Playing with my doll," whispered Kathy. She didn't want anyone to notice her, especially her cousins. She couldn't tell her mom how she felt. She knew that her cousins didn't want to play with her. Mom left her alone and went back to the kitchen to help Aunt Marie.

Later, the other children came into the room. Twelve-year-old cousin Ronnie peeked under the table. "I've missed you, Kathy."

"You did?" She was surprised.

"Sure. I've been looking for you. Come out and play with us."

When Kathy tried to come out, her head banged against the top of the coffee table. She fell back down. All the cousins laughed, except Ronnie. Kathy rubbed the bump on the top of her head. Her eyes filled with tears. It hurt.

Ronnie reached his hands to her. Kathy wanted to play with him, so she got up to walk out again, bumping her head once more.

The cousins howled with laughter. Ronnie glared at them.

"Don't laugh when someone gets hurt!" he said. "Show some kindness." He knelt down and laid his hand on the top of Kathy's head. "Let me help you, little cousin. Now you won't hurt your head. Just crawl out."

She did. And Ronnie spent time playing with her the rest of the afternoon.

WWJ

"Godliness leads to love for other Christians, and finally you will grow to have genuine love for everyone." 2 Peter 1:7 (NLT)

When have you treated a younger child with respect and kindness? How have you treated younger children in your neighborhood? Also read 2 Peter 1:5–11.

CHRISTMAS JOY

The Path to Bethlehem

What You Need:

A Bible, brown construction paper or grocery sacks, tape or thumb tacks, a picture of the nativity from an old Christmas card or draw a nativity picture

What To Do:

1. Read Luke 2:1–6.

2. Count the days remaining until Christmas.
    Cut that number of round "stones" out of brown paper.
    Form a path by tacking the stones to a bulletin board or taping them to a door. Tack or tape the picture of the nativity at the end of the path.

3. Each day before Christmas, cross out one stone to mark off the days.

4. As you mark out each stone, ask God to help you remember the real meaning of Christmas.
    Thank God for sending Jesus.

THE CHRISTMAS CARD

What can I give my teacher for Christmas? I don't have money to buy a present, and there's no time to make something.

Laying in bed, Cherie's thoughts turned to the Christmas story. *That's why He came to this earth…to be born by a regular birth….*

"A poem—I'm writing a poem in my head!"

Cherie jumped out of bed, got a pencil and paper, and wrote down the words. *I can make a card for Miss Korvaar.* Folding a green piece of paper, she drew a manger and a heart, then wrote her poem.

> Jesus was born in a stable;
> To save, He was willing and able.
> To die on the cross for our sins,
> Because we need cleansing within.
> That's why He came to the earth.
> To be born by a natural birth;
> To be born as a man, to live as a man,
> And to suffer as a man on the earth.

At recess Miss Korvaar found Cherie. "I discovered your card on my desk. Thank you so much! Did you write the poem?"

Cherie nodded.

Tears glistened in Miss Korvaar's eyes. "It's beautiful. I'll always treasure this." She held it tenderly.

Later, as Cherie worked at her desk, she thought about her teacher's reaction to her card.

My simple poem touched Miss Korvaar! I don't know what she believes about Jesus, but I pray someday she will love Him like I do.

WWJ

"The word of God is living and active. It is sharper than any sword that has two edges….It judges the thoughts and purposes of the heart." Hebrews 4:12

Why is it powerful to speak or write God's Word?
What are some ways *you* can share God's Word this week?
Also read Isaiah 55:9–11.

KAYLI'S SACRIFICE

How would I feel if I had lost my house and everything we own? Kayli curled up by the Christmas tree and stared at the lights. She blinked back tears as she thought about Shelly.

This morning Kayli's Sunday School teacher had told about a family whose house burned down. They lost everything in the fire—even their clothes. One girl, Shelly, was Kayli's age. The teacher asked everyone to bring a present for her next Sunday.

We don't have any money to buy a gift, thought Kayli. *Dad's been out of work for the past two weeks.*

Kayli leaned forward to read the tags on her two presents under the tree. She ran her fingers over the gift wrapped in green foil. Then she lifted out the wrapped package with the gold and green bow. Carrying it into the kitchen, she set it down on the table and put both arms around her mother.

"Mom," she said, "is it all right if I give one of my presents to the girl whose house burned down?"

"But, sweetheart, all you have is two gifts this Christmas."

"I have everything I really need. We have a house and clothes and food," replied Kayli. "The girl whose house burned down has nothing. I want to give her a present."

"I think God is very pleased with you right now," her mother told her.

"I know I am."

"You know the grace shown by our Lord Jesus Christ. Even though he was rich, he became poor to help you." 2 Corinthians 8:9

When have you given away something that you treasured?
What are you giving to Jesus this Christmas? *How* do we give to Him?
Also read Hebrews 13:15–16.

CHRISTMAS BABY, 1924

Matthew snatched his coat off the hook by the door and plunged through three feet of snow to the barn. *Dear Jesus, all I want for Christmas is my mom. Show the midwife how to help her,* he prayed.

Dad had sent for the midwife early after the doctor warned him, "Joe, your wife's way too old to be havin' babies. She'll need help delivering that child. It's likely she'll die."

Matthew urged his horse down the lane and onto the road. *Don't let her die, Lord,* he prayed. *And…save the baby.*

When he reached Doc's house, Matthew leapt from his horse and pounded on the door. A light came on upstairs and Doc peeked out, his hair tousled.

"Please come quick! My mom's in trouble."

Forty-five minutes later, Matthew pushed open the kitchen door to his house. Doc rushed past him to Mom's bedroom. The clock on the wall said one minute after midnight—it was Christmas morning.

Matthew took off his snowy coat and shoes. He sat in the rocking chair and leaned back his head. When Dad came out of the bedroom, Matthew opened his eyes and asked, "Dad, is Mom…?"

"She's still working hard." Dad's voice sounded hoarse.

Matthew closed his eyes and prayed. Soon he heard a baby cry. He didn't try to hide his tears a few minutes later when he held Mom's hand and bent over to kiss his brother's nose.

"God saved your life, Mom, and gave us a new baby. That's *almost* as good as the first Christmas," he whispered. "Thank You, dear Lord."

"A child will be born to us. A son will be given to us….The Lord's great love will make sure that happens." Isaiah 9:6–7

How does the birth of a baby remind us of God's love?
How did the birth of Jesus prove God's love for us?
Also read Luke 2:6–20.

MORE FUN THAN CHRISTMAS

"Karl, look what I found!" called Judy. "I know Maria will love this." Judy lifted a brown teddy bear out of a box of stuffed animals by the Christmas tree in the church foyer.

Judy's brother hurried over with the wrapped cardboard box they were packing for Maria and Anthony, two needy children from Sunday School. His eyes danced.

"Have you ever seen so many toys?" he asked with a grin.

"I can't believe everyone at church gave so generously!" Judy chose a doll with braids dressed in purple satin for Maria.

"Look!" Karl pointed to a yellow dump truck. "Anthony could load that with dirt and rocks."

Judy and Karl dug through the piles of donated gifts. They crammed toys into Maria's and Anthony's box. They chose picture books, a puzzle, a jump rope, and two balls. Judy found a little stuffed lamb for Maria and an elephant for Anthony.

"This is more fun than opening our own presents," Judy said. "We've never gotten half this many gifts."

Karl stopped and looked at his sister. "Do you wish all of these presents were for you instead of for Maria?"

"No way!" Judy insisted. "I keep imagining the look on Maria's face when she opens these gifts. That makes me as happy as getting a whole room full of presents."

"You are the children that God dearly loves. So be just like him. Lead a life of love, just as Christ did." Ephesians 5:1–2

How do you show that you love other people like Jesus does? What actions will you take today to show God's love to others? Also read 1 John 3:16–23.

WHAT'S WRONG WITH JOSH?

"Why don't you wrap these while I start dinner?" said Mom.

April gathered the bags of presents and bounded up the stairs. On her way to her room, she noticed that Josh's door was shut. *That's unusual,* she thought. She knocked on the door.

After a long while, the door opened just enough for Josh to peer out with one eye. "What do you want?"

April pushed her way into the room. "What are you up to?"

He looked down at the floor. "Nothing," he replied. "Go away!"

April's gaze swept the room. Toys and clothes everywhere. Nothing unusual. She felt uneasy as she returned to her room. *Please Jesus, help Josh. Something's wrong.*

"Dinner!" called Dad.

Starting down the stairs, April noticed that her brother's door was still shut. *Dear Lord, something must be wrong with Josh. He's always the first to the table.* She opened his door a crack and asked, "Josh?"

His face appeared from under the bed. "Go away!"

At dinner, the family made playful guesses about the presents they would find under the tree on Christmas. Josh was silent. He toyed with his food. April kept praying. Finally he burst into tears.

"What's the matter, son?" said Dad.

"I saw a present under the tree with my name on it," said Josh. "I knew it was the game I wanted. So I opened it. I've been playing with it under my bed. I thought it would make me happy. It didn't." Josh sobbed. "I've ruined my Christmas."

April and her dad got up and went over to hug Josh. She tousled his hair. "Hey, we love you, no matter what you've done. And remember, nothing can spoil the *real* gift of Christmas—Jesus!"

WWJ

"Let us give thanks to God for his gift. It is so great that no one can tell how wonderful it really is!" 2 Corinthians 9:15

Which are more important to you: Christmas gifts or the gift of Jesus? Are you hiding any sin in your life? Will you confess it?

Also read 1 John 1:5–10.

GOD'S POWER AND GOODNESS

Lights at Christmas

What You Need:

A large white candle, smaller white candles set in candle-holders, matches

What To Do:

1. Before opening Christmas gifts, light the large white candle, which represents Jesus, the Light of the World and God's best gift to us.

2. Give each person a candle. Take turns lighting your candles from the large one. Have each person tell something God has done for or given to them during the previous year.

3. Pray together. Thank God for Jesus and all His gifts.

Variation #1: Instead of or in addition to the prayer, sing a "thank-you" song to God, such as "Praise God From Whom All Blessings Flow" or "Thank You, Jesus."

Note: For safety, the children's candles may be set in candle "skirts" to protect little hands. Cut a circle 3–4" diameter out of cardboard or heavy paper, snip an "X" in the center, and push the candle through the center slits before lighting.

ASLEEP AT THE WHEEL!

Grandma's eyelids flicked shut and her head sank forward. She was falling asleep at the wheel of the car.

Traveling fifty-five miles per hour, the car drifted across all three lanes of the interstate freeway.

"Grandma! Wake up!" shouted Jaedine. She gripped the dashboard with both hands. "Oh, dear Jesus! Oh, dear Jesus!" she prayed.

Grandma jerked awake. She must have thought she was in a nightmare. She wrenched the steering wheel. The car veered off the highway and bounced across a ditch. It smashed through a fence and kept going.

Grandma stared through the windshield, as if stunned. She did not think to hit the brakes. Jaedine sat frozen with fear.

The car hurtled into a parking lot and skidded between two parked semi trucks. The car finally stopped when it rammed a third semi truck. The car windshield splintered into a hundred cobweb patterns from one side to the other.

Jaedine took a long breath and then whispered, "We're alive."

Grandma turned to her slowly and nodded. "I fell asleep."

The two of them forced the car doors open and climbed out. The front fenders and part of the car roof looked like a giant wad of crumpled paper.

Jaedine and her grandma walked to a nearby gas station and called the police. When the officer arrived, he looked at the damage and shook his head. "You two are lucky to be alive."

Jaedine wrapped her arms around Grandma. "It wasn't luck," she said. "It was God. He was watching over us."

WWJ

"The Lord watches over the faithful....Be strong, all of you who put your hope in the Lord." Psalm 31:23–24

Can you think of a time when God protected you?
What are some ways you can thank God for His protection?
Also read Psalm 91:2–12.

FIRE!

"Master John! Wake up! The cottage is on fire!"

Young John awoke to find old Nurse at his bedside. She held his baby brother in her arms. "Follow me!" she said. "Quickly!"

Still sleepy, John groped under the bed for his shoes. Then he hurried out of his room. He heard crackling. The air felt hot.

He finally realized: *The house is on fire!* John ran to the stairs. Thick smoke rolled up the stairway. It blocked his way and burned his throat and lungs. He ran back to his room and pushed open the window. He leaned out and hollered, "Help!"

With a roar, flames swept in the door of his room. John climbed onto the window ledge, balanced himself, and looked down. *If I jump, I may die. If I don't jump, I'll surely die. God help me.*

Below him, a man lifted a neighbor boy on his shoulders. John grabbed the boy's hands and was lowered to his waiting parents.

John and his family watched the straw roof of their house collapse in a burst of flames. Dropping to their knees, they all thanked God that their family was still alive.

After that, John was known as "a brand, plucked from the burning." He grew up to be John Wesley—a minister, an evangelist, and the leader of a Christian group called Methodists. John often said this fire experience as a boy helped prepare him to serve Jesus.

WWJ

"You were like a burning stick that was pulled out of the fire."
Amos 4:11

What difficult experiences have brought you closer to Jesus?
Will you continue to thank Jesus, even during times of trouble?
Also read 1 Corinthians 3:9–17.

BACKYARD BONFIRE

"Don't get too close to the flames. You might burn yourself or catch your clothes on fire," said Mom.

"I'm being careful." Davy stood beside the burning trash heap, tossing in leaves and twigs and dry weeds.

He soon ran out of fuel for the fire. *What's next?* He looked around. Mom was hoeing a shallow trench in her vegetable garden. *Nothing there I can burn.* The trash barrel stood nearby. He fished out a small cardboard box and a few wads of paper. He tossed them into the fire. *That helps. But I still need more.*

Davy searched the backyard. Finally he saw a green leafy branch growing through the slats in the fence. He broke it off and flicked it onto the fire. At once white smoke rose up where flames had danced moments before. "Whoops! That's putting the fire out. I'd better get rid of it."

He kicked the leafy branch off the bonfire. By accident he also kicked burning coals into the grass. Seeing the glowing embers on his shoe, Davy stomped his feet. When he looked up, he saw the dry smoldering grass burst into flames, spreading the fire.

"Mom! I need your help!" hollered Davy.

Mom looked over, then ran for the garden hose. She turned it on full force and doused the flames in the grass and the trash heap.

Davy thrust his hands into his pockets. "I was just trying to keep the fire going...I didn't think about what might happen."

"Thank God you weren't hurt!"

Davy's eyes sparkled. "Hey! God took care of me even when I forgot to ask Him for help. Thank You, Lord!"

"The Lord is good. His faithful love continues forever. It will last for all time to come." Psalm 100:5

Do you think God will help you even if you don't pray?
Why does God want you to pray? Do you ever forget to thank Him?
Also read Psalm 100:1–5.

DEAR MARIA

"Daddy, you've never accepted Jesus as your Savior," said Maria. "Remember that before Mama died, she accepted Jesus."

"Don't worry about me," said Dad with a smile.

But I do worry, thought Maria. *Especially when he works deep in the mines.* After she packed his soup in his lunch box, she added a gospel booklet her pastor had given to her. Handing the lunch box to her father she urged, "Read the little booklet, Daddy. Please."

He smiled, kissed her cheek, and left to work the night shift.

Late that night, an explosion awoke Maria. "Daddy!" she cried. *He could be trapped. Oh, Jesus, please save him before it's too late!*

Three days later, a man from the mines came to see Maria. "Your father died deep inside a shaft two days after the explosion. He and seven other men ran out of oxygen before we found them. They were seated in a circle. Their faces looked peaceful. Your father was holding this in his hand."

He handed Maria the gospel booklet from Dad's lunch box. On the last page, where it stated God's plan of salvation, Maria found a message that Dad had written:

"Dear Maria, While we waited to be rescued I read this booklet to my friends. We all prayed and asked Jesus into our hearts. When you read this, I will be in Heaven waiting to kiss your pretty cheek. I love you very much."

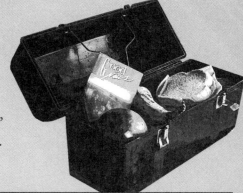

Maria smiled through her tears. *I lost my dad, but I'll see him again.*

Jesus said, "I am the resurrection and the life. Anyone who believes in me will live, even if he dies." John 11:25

Who are you asking God to save?
What would you say about Jesus to a non-Christian friend?
Also read John 11:11–27, 38–44.

SMALL SAMARITAN

"Now I know that Jesus loves me," Ramana told Missionary Howard. They held children's Bible summer camps near ten-year-old Ramana's village in India.

"I used to be a Hindu. But now I am a Christian," Ramana said.

"We're so glad you attended camp this week," said Howard.

"I must leave now. My mother is very sick. I want to see her."

"Be sure to pray for her," said Howard. "We'll be praying with you that Jesus will heal her."

At his home a week later, Ramana woke near midnight to hear his mother's raspy breathing in the next room. For all of Ramana's life, his mother had suffered from asthma. Tonight her breathing sounded worse than ever. It frightened Ramana.

He slipped out of bed and into his mother's room. She clutched her chest. The pain was so great that she couldn't speak. Then she choked. Ramana felt that she was dying. She could barely breathe.

"Mama," he said gently, "Jesus Christ heals people. If you will let me, I will pray that He heals you—right now."

His mother's head moved slightly, nodding yes. At the summer camp Ramana had seen people anointed with oil. He hurried to the kitchen and found the oil. Touching his mother's forehead with his oiled fingertip, he prayed.

"Dear Lord, please heal my mother. I ask this in Jesus' name."

Almost at once his mother sat up. With a look of astonishment, she breathed deeply. Then she smiled. "Ramana, my dear son, you have healed me."

"No, Mama. It was Jesus who healed you. He is my Savior. And He can be yours, too. Let me tell you about Him."

"Are any of you sick? Then send for the elders of the church....Ask them to anoint you with oil in the name of the Lord." James 5:14

What do you do when one of your parents is sick?
Remember: God answers prayer in the way He knows is best.
Also read Psalm 23:1–5.

THANK GOD FOR YOUR HERITAGE

Let Your Light Shine on the Elderly

What You Need:

A Bible, paper, colored pencils, a loving attitude, and a willing spirit

What To Do:

1. Read Matthew 5:16.

2. Fold a piece of paper in half to make a card.
Draw some animals and flowers on the paper.
Write a short greeting and sign your name.
Take to an elderly relative, neighbor, or retirement home resident.

3. Let your light shine on an older person for one hour:
Read to someone with fading eyesight.
Look at their old photos together.
Bring flowers. Bring a homemade card.
Mop the floors, vacuum, and dust.
Listen to an older gentleman's stories.
Fix a simple snack or lunch and share it together.

4. Ask to pray with them before you leave.

BABY REO

"You wrecked my new bike!" Kenneth grabbed the bent-up bicycle frame from his brother Frederick. "I'll get you for this!"

The sound of a car horn stopped the boys' fight and sent the whole family racing to the front yard. There sat Daddy in a brand-new Baby Reo car—the first car in the entire county!

Daddy grinned from ear to ear. "Well, what do you think?"

For Kenneth, it was love at first sight, from the silver side-mirrors to the spoked wheels to the highly polished fenders. He reached out to stroke the shiny black fenders.

"Kenneth, don't touch the paint. You'll leave fingerprints! Get in to dinner, now." Daddy smiled proudly at his car.

As Kenneth turned to follow the family into the house, up flew their rooster, Old Red. He attacked the car door, pecking at his reflection in the shiny paint.

Kenneth yelled, "Shoo! Shoo!" Old Red flapped away, leaving deep scratches in the shiny paint.

"My new car!" Daddy hurried up behind Kenneth. "Who left the chicken coop open?" he asked in a stern voice.

Kenneth's heart sank. He had left the door unlatched. "I did." He cringed, waiting for the tongue-lashing he knew he deserved.

Daddy silently put his arm around Kenneth. "I'm sorry. I can see I've been acting too proud. This car will eventually wear out. But you're more valuable to me than any hunk of metal."

Kenneth sighed in relief and gratitude. Remembering his bent bicycle, he reached out and put his arm around Frederick. "You're more important than a pile of metal, too."

"Do not love the world or anything in it....The world and its evil longings are passing away....those who do what God wants...live forever." 1 John 2:15, 17

When have you found it hard to forgive someone who damaged a possession of yours? What possessions are too important to you? Also read Matthew 6:19–24.

A REASON TO OBEY

"Don't move," Max whispered to his sister as they crouched on the picnic table. Mom stood ten feet away, holding an empty rifle. A rattlesnake coiled around the table's leg.

If Pearl or Mom die, it will be my fault, thought Max.

Ever since they lost their house and moved into the tent beside Dog Creek, Mom had one rule: Always keep the gun and the bullets together.

But Max had disobeyed. When he moved the gun to clean it, he'd left the bullets on the picnic table.

Max's heart banged in his chest as he eased his fingers around a bullet. "Can you catch it, Mom?" he whispered. He remembered times when they played catch. Mom always dropped the ball.

"I'll try," Mom whispered back. She stood very still.

Max threw the bullet. It grazed Mom's fingers, then landed in the grass. The snake slid within striking distance of Mom.

Pearl trembled beside Max and began praying, "O Jesus…"

"Shhh!" Max hissed. "Pray silently."

Max's fingers found another bullet. Carefully, he tossed it to his mother. *Jesus, save us!* he prayed silently.

In one quick movement, Mom caught the bullet, loaded the gun, and shot the snake in the head. Max and Pearl ran crying to her.

"Thank God, we're safe. I'll never disobey you again," Max sobbed.

"I'm in deep trouble. God, save me and keep me safe."
Psalm 69:29

What rules do your parents have for your safety?
Do you obey rules even when you don't understand them?
Also read Psalm 69:13–18, 29–33.

GANGRENE

"Get away, Old Bessie! Leave my sister alone!" Gladys waved the hoe and chased the cow away from her sister.

"Are you all right, Agnes?"

Tears poured down her sister's face. She rocked back and forth in pain, holding her injured foot. "It…hurts!"

Gladys helped her sister limp to the house. Dad hitched up the wagon and rode into town to get the doctor.

"I have to amputate her foot to save her life," the doctor said. "She's unconscious, so she won't feel the pain."

When Agnes woke up and saw what the doctor had done to her, tears slipped down her cheeks. For a week she seemed to feel better, then her fever spiked.

When the doctor returned, he looked at the dark flesh and smelled Agnes's infected stub. His face paled. "It's…gangrene! I'll have to amputate more of her leg."

"Will it hurt her?" Gladys asked.

The doctor stared down at the floor. He didn't have anything to take away Agnes's terrible pain or put her to sleep for the operation. "She'll die if I don't operate," he said softly.

"Go ahead," Agnes said. "God will take care of me."

"Let me pray," said Gladys. "Dear Jesus, please make Agnes unconscious again…so it won't hurt so much." When she prayed, Agnes passed out. And the doctor cut off her leg above the knee.

NOTE: Agnes lived to be one hundred and one years old. She married and had children and grandchildren. She got around fine with only one leg. "Don't feel sorry for me," she told everyone. "I don't need two legs. God saved my life. He helps me stand."

WWJ

"We are full of joy even when we suffer. We know that our suffering gives us the strength to go on." Romans 5:3

How do you think God feels when His children suffer?
Why can you still trust God when bad things happen?
Also read Romans 5:1–5.

IF THE SHOE FITS

"I'm not ever going back to school!" William ran down the dirt path toward home. He brushed away the tears that streamed down his cheeks. His big brother, Ralph, caught up with him and laid a hand on his shoulder.

Shrugging off his brother's hand, William rushed through the open door of the family's sod house. His mother looked up from snapping beans. "What's wrong, William?"

"I'm not going back to school." He pointed at his bare feet. "The kids make fun of me because I don't wear any shoes."

"Son, you know we can't afford shoes for all thirteen of you children. You'll have to wait until Ralph outgrows his pair."

Ralph pulled the shoes from his feet. "Here. William can wear my shoes to school. I'll find work in the fields, Ma."

"Really? Do you mean it?" William's eyes lit up.

Mother sighed. "William, I can't let your brother do this. He waited his turn for the shoes. Now you must wait yours."

Ralph placed the shoes in William's hands. "Ma, I'll give up my shoes so William can go to school. I want him to study and learn so he doesn't have to spend his life picking cotton."

William hugged his big brother tightly. "I'll never forget this, Ralph. I'll study hard and someday I'll buy *you* a pair of brand-new shoes!"

Jesus said, "No one has greater love than the one who gives his life for his friends....Here is my command. Love each other." John 15:13, 17

Who has done the most to help you? Have you thanked him or her? What have you given up for someone lately?
Also read John 15:9–17.

PASTURE PRAYER

Tillie eyed the bull warily as she climbed the pasture fence. *Angie's dad didn't mention any bulls when he said I could read in his pasture. I may be a city girl, but I know enough to watch out for bulls!*

For a few minutes, Tillie watched the other cows. Then she sat down on the grass to read her book.

Tillie didn't look up until her stomach growled. When she reached for her lunch bucket, she noticed the cows all milling around a heifer whose sides were heaving. *Something's wrong! I should find out what it is. Oh, that bull is standing in the way.*

She took a deep breath and edged slowly toward the herd. To her amazement, she saw the nose and forelegs of a calf emerge from the heaving cow. *This cow needs help! I'll never make it to the farmhouse and back in time. What could I do?*

"Dear Lord," Tillie prayed aloud, "please show me what to do. That little calf needs help being born."

Her grandpa's tales of his life on a farm popped into her mind. Remembering how Grandpa chased away a bull, Tillie pulled off her jacket. With heart thumping, she walked up to the bull and snapped her jacket at him. He turned and trotted away.

Tillie heaved a sigh of relief, then gave a shaky little laugh. *Thanks, Lord, for helping me know what to do.*

She moved her way through the herd to the mother cow. Then she wrapped her jacket around her hands and grabbed the calf's slippery forelegs. Each time the mother cow pushed, Tillie pulled on the calf. Soon the little calf slid onto the soft grass. Tillie watched in delight as it struggled to its feet.

Thank You, Lord, for showing me how to help. And thank You for a healthy baby calf!

WWJ

"*The wisdom that comes from heaven is pure....It thinks about others. It obeys. It is full of mercy and good fruit.*" James 3:17

When have you asked God for wisdom in making decisions? How has God helped you?
Also read 1 John 5:14–15.